ST GEORGE'S CHAPEL, WINDSOR
History and Heritage

ST GEORGE'S CHAPEL, WINDSOR

HISTORY AND HERITAGE

Edited by

Nigel Saul and Tim Tatton-Brown

Dedicated to Eileen Scarff

THE DOVECOTE PRESS

First published in 2010 by The Dovecote Press Ltd
Stanbridge, Wimborne Minster, Dorset BH21 4JD

ISBN 978-1-904-34983-9
Text © The Authors 2010

The authors have asserted their rights under the Copyright, Designs
and Patent Act 1988 to be identified as authors of this work

Designed by The Dovecote Press
Printed and bound in Spain by GraphyCems, Navarra

All papers used by The Dovecote Press are natural,
recyclable products made from wood grown in sustainable,
well-managed forests

A CIP catalogue record for this book is available
from the British Library

1 3 5 7 9 8 6 4 2

CONTENTS

THE CONTRIBUTORS

MARTIN ASHLEY is Surveyor of the Fabric to St George's Chapel, Windsor.

NIGEL ASTON is Reader in Early Modern History at the University of Leicester and author of *Christianity in Revolutionary Europe, c. 1760-1830* (Cambridge, 2002).

MARTIN BIDDLE is Emeritus Professor of Archaeology in the University of Oxford and Fellow of Hertford College. He is principal author of *King Arthur's Round Table* (Woodbridge, 2000).

STEVEN BRINDLE is a Senior Properties Historian in English Heritage's Properties Presentation Department and has published extensively on the history of architecture and engineering. In the 1990s, as an Inspector of Ancient Monuments for English Heritage, he was involved in the post-fire restoration of Windsor Castle.

SARAH BROWN is a lecturer in History of Art in the University of York and editor of *History of the Stained Glass of St George's Chapel* (Windsor, 2005).

DAVID CARPENTER is Professor of Medieval History at King's College, London, and has published extensively on the reign of Henry III.

ELEANOR CRACKNELL is Assistant Archivist to the Dean and Canons of Windsor.

JOHN CROOK is a widely published independent architectural historian, archaeological consultant and photographer based in Winchester.

ROBERT DUNNING was editor of the Victoria County History for Somerset until his retirement in 2005. He has written extensively on the medieval bishops of Bath and Wells and their administrations.

JANE GEDDES is Professor of the History of Art at the University of Aberdeen and author of *Medieval Decorative Ironwork in England* (London: Society of Antiquaries, 1999).

RALPH GRIFFITHS is Emeritus Professor of Medieval History at the University of Swansea and formerly Chairman of the Royal Commission for Ancient and

Historical Monuments in Wales. He is author of *The Reign of King Henry VI* (2nd edn., London, 1998).

ROGER JUDD was Assistant Organist at St George's Chapel for twenty-three years until 2009. He is currently working on a history of the St George's Chapel organs.

JULIE KANTNER is a research student at King's College, London, working on a doctorate on the itineraries of England's thirteenth century kings.

PETER KIDSON is Emeritus Professor of Medieval Architecture at the Courtauld Institute, University of London. He is an authority on the use of systems of proportion and measurement in Western architecture.

CHRISTOPHER KITCHING CBE was an Assistant Keeper at the Public Record Office from 1970 to 1982, and then successively Assistant Secretary and Secretary of the Royal Commission for Historical Manuscripts. Since 2009 he has been Vice Chairman of the Trustees of Lambeth Palace Library.

DAVID LEWIS is an independent scholar who lives in Windsor and has completed a University of London PhD on the history of medieval Windsor using the St George's Chapel archives.

JULIAN LITTEN is an authority on English burial vaults and funerary customs. He organised the burial of the Unknown Mariner from the *Mary Rose* at Portsmouth in 1984 and the re-enactment of Prince Arthur's funeral at Worcester in 2002.

DAN MILES is a partner in the Oxford Dendrochronology Laboratory and an Honorary Research Fellow at the University of Oxford. He also advises on historic carpentry and joinery to English Heritage and other bodies.

JULIAN MUNBY, an authority on timberwork construction, is Head of Buildings Archaeology at Oxford Archaeology and was co-author of *Edward III's Round Table at Windsor* (Woodbridge, 2007).

CLARE RIDER has been Archivist and Chapter Librarian to the Dean and Canons of Windsor since 2008.

JANE ROBERTS is Librarian in the Royal Library, Windsor Castle, and author of *Royal Landscape. The Gardens and Parks of Windsor* (New Haven and London, 1997). In 2004 she curated the exhibition *George III and Queen Charlotte. Patronage, Collecting and Royal Taste* at the Queen's Gallery, Buckingham Palace.

NIGEL SAUL is Professor of Medieval History at Royal Holloway, University of London. He was editor of *St George's Chapel, Windsor, in the Fourteenth Century* (Woodbridge, 2005).

ANNE SUTTON is an independent scholar whose work centres on the Mercers' Company of London and the history of Yorkist ceremonial. She is co-author (with L. Visser-Fuchs) of *The Royal Funerals of the House of York at Windsor* (Richard III Society, 2005).

TIM TATTON-BROWN is a freelance archaeologist and architectural historian. He is Consultant Archaeologist to St George's Chapel, Windsor, and Salisbury Cathedral.

STEPHEN TAYLOR is Professor of Early Modern History in the University of Reading. He is currently working (with Kenneth Fincham) on a study of religious conformity in the period of the English Revolution.

HUGO VICKERS, a biographer, lecturer and broadcaster, is author of *St George's Chapel, Windsor Castle* (The Dovecote Press, 2008). He has been a Lay Steward at the Chapel since 1970 and was appointed a Deputy Lieutenant for Berkshire in 2010.

LIVIA VISSER-FUCHS is an independent scholar interested in the cultural history of Yorkist England. Her recent work has centred on Anglo-Burgundian relations and the life of the soldier-author Jean de Wavrin.

BERNARD WORSSAM, a geologist, was employed on the field staff of the British Geological Survey from 1947 until his retirement in 1985. With Robin Sanderson, he is currently studying the stones of St George's Chapel.

PREFACE

The production of this book has been greatly facilitated by many people, but we would particularly like to acknowledge the great help given by John Crook with the illustrations – he took most of the modern pictures for the book and, in effect, has been the picture editor. Jill Atherton has produced a series of very fine new line drawings for the book, and this has been helped by a bursary award from the Society of Architectural Historians of Great Britain. We would also like to record our appreciation of the assistance given by Clare Rider, Archivist to the Deans and Canons of Windsor; Eleanor Cracknell and Enid Davies, Assistant Archivists – all at Windsor, who helped with the provision of illustrations from the rich collections of the Dean and Canons.

The cost of producing this volume has been generously subvented by three of Eileen Scarff's 'volunteers' in the Archives, and their support has been essential. Any profits made from the sale of the book will go to the 'Adopt a Book' scheme at St George's Chapel Library, a scheme that was entirely Eileen Scarff's brainchild.

Finally we must thank David Burnett of the Dovecote Press for undertaking the publication of the book.

NIGEL SAUL AND TIM TATTON-BROWN

October 2010

ABBREVIATED REFERENCES

BL: The British Library

Hope, *Windsor Castle*: W.H. St John Hope, *Windsor Castle: An Architectural History* (2 vols., London, 1913)

SGC: St George's Chapel Archives

TNA: The National Archives (formerly the Public Record Office)

Keen and Scarff: *Windsor: Medieval Archaeology, Art and Architecture of the Thames Valley*, ed. L. Keen and E. Scarff (British Archaeological Association Conference Transactions, 25, 2002)

FOREWORD

THE VERY REVEREND PATRICK MITCHELL

When I became Dean of Windsor in 1989, I soon discovered that the College of St George had recently appointed an outstanding Archivist. Dr Eileen Scarff was already possessed of wide experience and creative vision. For the next twenty years, until her retirement in 2008, she patiently built up a happy and harmonious department; and she saw the great collection of priceless documents and books properly housed and preserved in a worthy setting, complete with humidity-control, safe fire-proof storage and proper facilities for scholars. Her remarkable achievement involved persuading the Chapter and other bodies that one part-time Archivist working in the cramped and uncomfortable atmosphere of the Schorn Tower was quite inadequate. She successfully applied for repeated grants for the adaptation of the medieval Vicars' Hall and Undercroft to re-house the Library and Archives of the College. Constant energy and tact were needed to achieve all these results.

The twenty-five essays in this volume, all written by distinguished scholars, bear witness to Eileen Scarff's skill in building up her department and in training and encouraging staff. The present book, edited by Nigel Saul and Tim Tatton-Brown, will remain a classic account of the Chapel, its history, its unique archives and their rescue from inadequate housing and poor conditions. It is an inspiring story.

As a former Chairman of the Cathedral Libraries and Archives Association, I can witness to the enormous respect in which Dr Scarff is held in the world of scholarship.

Above all, I wish to thank Eileen herself for all that she contributed to the life of the College through her professional skill, her lively sense of humour and her generous team spirit.

PATRICK MITCHELL
Dean of Windsor, 1989-1998

Fig. 1. The Curfew tower and part of Henry III's Lower Ward curtain wall of *c.* 1227, on the west side of Windsor Castle.

ONE

THE BUILDING STONES OF THE LOWER WARD
OF WINDSOR CASTLE

Bernard Worssam

WINDSOR IS SITUATED on an isolated outcrop of Chalk which, relatively resistant to erosion, rises as a low hill above the surrounding clays and sands. The River Thames, cutting sideways, has produced a steep cliff on the north side of the hill. Over the centuries, more than thirty types of building stone have found their way into Windsor Castle. This account deals mainly with the more conspicuous and some of the more unusual types of stone used in the Lower Ward of the castle, in which St George's Chapel and the buildings of the College of St George are situated.

Most immediately obvious to visitors approaching Windsor Castle is the hard grey siliceous sandstone, or sarsen stone, used from the twelfth century onwards for the castle's walls and towers, giving them an appropriately stern and imposing appearance (see Fig. 1). In the Windsor building accounts this stone is called heath stone, being in medieval times obtained from Bagshot Heath, some ten miles (15km) south of Windsor. It had the advantage of being readily enough trimmed into squared blocks and, in use, that of excellent resistance to weathering. In 1951 Sir Owen Morshead, resident in the castle for some twenty-five years, noticed that the stone 'is washed clean by every shower of rain, and does not flake or spall'.

With an unusual geological origin, the stone was simply found as boulders scattered over the ground surface. Bagshot Heath is an area of high ground on the outcrop of the Barton Sand, a thick deposit of fine-grained sand of marine origin of an early Tertiary age, some 40 million years before the present. Much later but still within the Tertiary period, with the Barton Sand elevated to form a land surface, the boulders must have formed as siliceous concretions, either within the subsoil in a semi-tropical arid climate (some contain fossil plant rootlets), or at greater depth by the action of circulating groundwater. Examined under a hand-lens, the original clear quartz grains of the Barton Sand are seen to have been cemented together by crystal overgrowths developed as a result of the solution and redeposition of quartz.

As the land surface became subsequently lowered by river-erosion the concretions, too massive to be moved far, must have accumulated as collections of boulders while their enclosing sands were washed away. The place-name that occurs most frequently in Edward III's accounts as a source of sarsens is Collingley (now Collingwood) between Bagshot and Camberley. In 1365-6, Henry le Smyth and associates were paid £96 'for cleaving 96,000 heath stones from Collingley at 20s per 1000' and 23s 'for splitting 400 great stones from the aforesaid heath at 6s per 100'. Between 1361-2 and 1368 no fewer than 560,000 split heath-stones were supplied to Windsor.

The earliest large-scale use of sarsen stone at Windsor appears to have been by Henry II, who between 1170 and 1185 built a towered curtain wall around the Upper Ward and along the north side of the Lower Ward. He must also have built a stone shell keep (rebuilt in the early thirteenth century) on the early Norman motte around which the whole castle has been erected.[1] The keep was raised to its present height in 1830-31, by Sir Jeffrey Wyatville adding a wall of brickwork faced by sarsens from the High Wycombe area. After heavy rain in 1987-88 it was found that the weight of the heightened tower was too much for the chalk-rubble motte to bear, so its foundations were replaced by a new concrete ring-beam, standing on piles drilled into the Chalk bedrock.[2]

Fig. 1 shows the Curfew Tower and part of the western curtain wall of the Lower Ward of the castle, both the work of Henry III, dating from about 1227. The wall retains its original sarsen stonework, darker grey in the photograph, including bands of a light grey stone, in fact an unusually light-coloured variety of Kentish Ragstone. This is a hard, glauconitic sandy limestone, which would have been transported by barge from a quarry near Maidstone. Kentish Ragstone was the main building stone of the Tower of London, but was rarely employed at Windsor. It may have been used for this curtain wall because of its availability as large blocks, which could act as through-stones to strengthen the wall.

The Curfew Tower has served as the bell tower of St George's Chapel since 1477. Its distinctly French appearance dates from 1862-3, when the architect Anthony Salvin remodelled its top part after the design of a tower on the walls of the French city of Carcassonne, it was said at the suggestion of the emperor Napoleon III, visiting Queen Victoria in 1855. Salvin also refaced the tower and an adjacent part of the curtain wall. Like his predecessor Wyatville he used sarsen stone from the High Wycombe area. Boulders there, originally formed in Reading Beds (early Tertiary) sands, occur in the Clay-with-flints, a residual deposit on the Chalk outcrop. Salvin's sarsens were cut by machine, giving a mechanical

Fig. 2. The early 13th century stone vault in the base of the Curfew tower.

appearance to his stonework that contrasts with the pleasing slight irregularity of the adjacent medieval masonry. His white stone bands are for some reason at different levels from the medieval ones; they are probably of Portland stone.

Internally, the walls of the basement of the Curfew Tower are hollowed out to form a circle of deep alcoves from which rises a high vaulted ceiling (Fig. 2), all faced in ashlar of blocks of Chalk, with dressings and some ashlar courses in Reigate stone. Chalk, apart from certain harder beds such as the Totternhoe Stone, is not usually thought of as a building stone, but these walls are in very good condition. The chalk is soft, white, with occasional wavy grey marl streaks and is quite free of flints. This is just the character of the chalk that would have been obtained for Edward III's proposed Round Table building of 1344, from a quarry at Bisham, beside the Thames half a mile east of Marlow Bridge.[3] The Geological Survey map, Beaconsfield Sheet 255 (2005 edition) shows this quarry to have been on the outcrop of the Seaford Chalk Formation, corresponding to the former *coranguinum* Zone of the Upper Chalk, in which flint nodules occur in regular layers at roughly 2-ft intervals, with soft white unfossiliferous chalk between them.

Reigate stone, the 'firestone' of some building accounts, is a grey, finely glauconitic siliceous stone from the Upper Greensand formation of Surrey.

Fig. 3. The 13th century north wall face of the Albert Memorial Chapel on the south side of the Dean's Cloister.

Unlike any other type of sandstone in the British Isles it is composed essentially of chemically precipitated silica spherules rather than of detrital quartz grains.[4] Under a hand lens, the stone is characterised by closely scattered tiny dark green/black glauconite grains and sparse mica flakes in a finely granular grey matrix. Reigate stone was used extensively in the Thames valley area from Windsor to Canterbury from the eleventh to the sixteenth century, though certainly by the fifteenth century it had proved unsuitable for exterior use.[5]

As well as providing the Lower Ward with a towered curtain wall, Henry III in the 1240s built a new 'great' chapel dedicated to St Edward in this lower part of the castle. Largely rebuilt in the 1490s, his chapel became the Albert Memorial Chapel in 1863, its interior lavishly decorated with coloured marbles. Its north wall (Fig. 3) forms the south side of the present Dean's Cloister and remains as originally designed for Henry III. Faced with Chalk with some Reigate stone blocks like the Curfew Tower basement walls, it is enlivened by a blind arcade, the columns of which have Purbeck Marble shafts, each with flanking attached shafts, with stiff-leaf capitals and moulded pointed arches of Reigate stone. There is a low Reigate stone bench along the foot of the wall. The original great West Doorway of the chapel, with flanking columns like those of the cloister, is now the East Doorway of St George's Chapel's ambulatory.

Fig. 4. The vault and upper part of the north wall of 1353-54 inside the porch beneath the Aerary.

The College of St George, established by Edward III in 1348, took over Henry III's chapel and adjacent former royal apartments in the Lower Ward. As a grand entrance to the College buildings, the Aerary [Treasury] Porch (Fig. 4) was erected in 1353-4. Pevsner described the porch as 'unrestored and . . . a prime example of the Dec – Perp transition'.[6] A building account of 1354 states that a 'vault of Egremont stones' was purchased expressly for the new Aerary. Egremont stone is a medieval name for Totternhoe stone, a hard, rather granular variety of chalk named after a village near Dunstable.[7] The internal walls of the porch, as can still be seen, are of Reigate stone.

Externally, the western wall of the porch, looking on to the courtyard now known as Denton's Commons, is of small-block coursed rubble partly of Totternhoe stone. Some houses on the north side of the courtyard, partly reconstructed from twelfth- and early thirteenth-century domestic royal chambers, include Totternhoe stone ashlar facing.

To the west is the Vicars' Hall of 1415-17, which now houses the College Archives and Chapter Library in its undercroft. Its northern, gable end, rising above the castle's curtain wall, is of sarsens with a grand Bath stone oriel window by Anthony Salvin of 1864. Its eastern wall is faced with evenly-coursed small blocks of a fine-grained yellowish-grey (and in places quite yellow) oolitic limestone. The wall was repaired by Sir George Gilbert Scott in 1871-72. The Chapter Acts for this period provide details of the work. The first building estimate, reported at the Chapter meeting on 4 May 1871, included an amount for repairing the east wall of the Library and putting in new windows and doorways. The second, recorded in the Chapter Acts for 3 July 1872, was for refacing the wall with 'Oxfordshire stone' in accordance with Scott's specification. As it is an oolite, this can only be a variety of Taynton Limestone – the other possibility would be Wheatley (or Headington) stone, which is an only partly oolitic, detrital-shell limestone. Gilbert Scott's stone, with its grey to yellow colour, is most likely to have come from Milton or Little Barrington (see below). Many of the stones in the wall are beginning to flake and spall along their edges. Bath stone was used for new windows, doorways, chimneys and quoins. The northernmost of three tall Tudor windows is in part of original Taynton stone, while two small pointed undercroft windows, one of them originally a doorway in part retain their probably fifteenth-century Reigate stone surrounds.[8]

In 1471, after regaining the throne from Henry VI at the battle of Tewkesbury, Edward IV decided to build a new, more splendid St George's Chapel, west of Henry III's chapel, which would both serve the Order of the Garter and become his own tomb and chantry. Construction was started in 1475, and by Edward's death in 1483 the choir had been carried up to its full height and roofed, and the north wall of the nave had been begun. Work then stopped, until the nave walls were started again in the 1490s. In 1503 a bequest in the will of Henry VII's minister Sir Reginald Bray enabled the chapel to be completed, with the present magnificent stone vaults, but without the proposed crossing tower.

The exterior of the chapel as it now stands comprises four main types of building stone, these being Taynton and Caen stone dating from the original construction, and Bath and Clipsham stone introduced in subsequent repairs. Taynton stone comes from the Taynton Limestone Formation, an outcrop in the valley of the

River Windrush, a tributary of the Thames, above Burford in Oxfordshire. It is an oolitic limestone, or oolite, consisting of small spherical grains (ooliths), mostly of 0.3 to 0.6 mm diameter, in a matrix of calcite (crystalline calcium carbonate). Shell fragments, up to about 5 mm in diameter, tend to be concentrated along lines of cross-bedding, forming layers that, being harder than the rest of the stone, weather out to form ribs that were known to quarrymen as 'bars'.

The building accounts for the chapel for 1475-83 mention (as well as some Caen stone) stone from Taynton itself and from Little Barrington, Windrush, Sherborne and Milton-under-Wychwood.[9] Stone from the last three of these places is pale yellowish-grey, while that from Little Barrington is said to have been a deep yellow-brown; stone from Taynton,[10] where quarries were most extensive, is more shelly and of a brownish-yellow colour.

Bath stone is first mentioned in the St George's archives as used for repairs in 1828. 'Freestone' recorded from 1792 to 1806 may also have been Bath stone, though before the opening of the Kennet and Avon Canal in 1810 the transport of this stone to Windsor is likely to have been expensive. The stone is a pale yellowish grey, variably shelly oolite. Used externally, it tends to weather to a characteristic gingery-brown colour in sheltered locations, as at the heads of arches. A notable feature is that many of its varieties show thin veinlets, 1 to 2 mm in width, cutting across the bedding, and known to quarrymen as 'watermarks'. As with Taynton stone, fresh surfaces under a hand-lens show a honeycomb-like texture, owing to ooliths, which are soft, having fallen out of their enclosing hard calcite matrix.

Caen stone, from Normandy, is a limestone of the same geological age as Bath and Taynton stones but is pale yellow, very fine-grained and composed not of ooliths but of tiny particles or pellets of around 0.1 mm diameter, barely distinguishable under the hand-lens. Recent examination has noted that all the tracery and mullions of the great West Window of the chapel were probably of Caen stone, while major repairs carried out in 1841-42 were also of Caen stone.

Clipsham stone, from the Lincolnshire Limestone Formation of Rutlandshire, has had a reputation for excellent resistance to weathering since its first use for repairs to Oxford colleges in the 1870s.[11] It contains ooliths plus a high proportion of whitish opaque pellets of 1 to 2 mm or more in diameter, together with shell fragments, in a calcite matrix. It is grey in colour, and the pellets give it a speckled appearance. Clipsham stone was used by the architect A. Y. Nutt between 1903 and 1906, but it is most noteworthy for the very extensive use made of it by Sir Harold Brakspear in his restoration of the 1920s. (see Chapter 20)

The four types of stone are illustrated in Fig. 5, part of the north side of the

Fig. 5. Detail of the different types of stone used in the lower part of the great west window of the chapel.

great West Window of the chapel. On the left, two blocks of brown laminated stone are Taynton stone, probably original, and the narrow vertically-set block between them is of Bath stone. The central mullion, most of the window's battlemented transom and the heads of the lights below it are of Caen stone, whitish where rainwashed, brownish-yellow where sheltered beneath the transom. The greyish speckled stone is Clipsham.

In 2004-07, major stonework repairs were undertaken along the south side of the nave from the Bray Chapel westward and on the whole West Front. With scaffolding in place, identification of the types of stone present was undertaken by the writer and Robin Sanderson. It was found that the original Taynton stone is still preserved to the extent of 80 to 90 per cent of the ashlar walling below window-sill level of the nave south aisle and on the West Front. This stonework has survived the lighting of fires, causing red-stained patches along the foot of the walls, it is said by Roundhead soldiers camping out during the Commonwealth. Taynton stone forms quite a high proportion of the stonework at higher levels in the Bray Chantry, but along most of the south elevation, and in nearly all of the Beaufort Chantry, it has largely been replaced by nineteenth-century Bath stone or by Clipsham stone. The statuettes dating from 1882 in alcoves high up on south-aisle buttresses, are of Ancaster stone, a fine-grained Lincolnshire Limestone oolite. Clipsham stone is used for most of the window mullions,

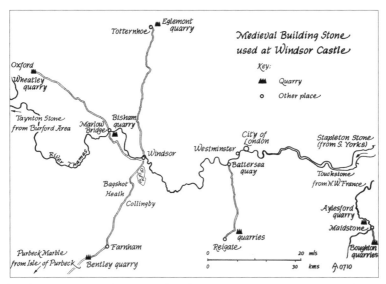

Fig. 6. Plan showing principal sources of building stone used at Windsor Castle.

transoms and tracery, for all parapets and the reinstated King's Beasts, for the undersides of flying buttresses, and for the large buttresses installed by Brakspear to help to support the Bray Chantry, as well as for refacing the south side and the east end of the Albert Memorial Chapel. It is also the building stone of the King George VI Memorial Chapel, completed in 1969.

Inside St George's Chapel the columns of the nave and choir arcades are of a cross-bedded shelly oolite, clearly Taynton stone, but of a yellowish-grey variety such as Windrush or Sherborne stone. The panelled walls of the nave and choir aisles are of Reigate stone, while the west wall of the nave is of Taynton ashlar with some replacement Bath stone blocks. In the ambulatory and choir aisles, the battlemented window-sills with a carved vine-leaf frieze beneath are of newly-cleaned Caen stone, showing up well in contrast to the Reigate of the wall.

The nave was originally paved with foot-square slabs of Purbeck Marble.[12] These still form the floor of the Beaufort Chantry, for instance, where the grand tomb of the Earl and Countess of Worcester, of c.1526, is also of Purbeck Marble. In 1789-90 the nave and aisles were re-paved with Painswick stone, an oolitic limestone from the Cotswolds, and an unusual choice for south-east England. Much of it still survives in the centre of the nave. The choir has been paved with diagonally-set black and white marble squares since the 1680s.

The organ screen at the east end of the nave, designed by the architect Henry Emlyn, was built in 1790-92 of Coade stone. This artificial stone, or more exactly stoneware ceramic, was first produced by Mrs Eleanor Coade in 1769 in her Lambeth factory.[13] Its good resistance to weathering has been shown by the figures, dating from 1799, of Edward the Confessor and St George high up on the western gable of St George's Chapel. A third figure, of the Virgin and Child, had by 1929 suffered fracturing caused probably by the corrosion of an iron armature. During the recent stone-restoration of the West Front a new figure was modelled and cast in new Coade material following the original recipe.[14] The arches along the front and sides of the organ screen were rebuilt in the 1920s by Sir Harold Brakspear, using Bath stone of the Corsham variety. This stone has ooliths of 0.3 to 0.5 mm diameter, with small (2-mm diameter) shell fragments scattered throughout; there are a few calcite veinlets.

The grave of Edward IV at the east end of the north choir aisle is covered by a floor slab of black Tournai Marble, a variety of Carboniferous Limestone from Belgium. Slightly silty and hence mildly abrasive, its alternative name 'touchstone' derives from its use since medieval times in assaying precious metals; thus a sample of gold rubbed on a block of the stone leaves a streak that can be compared with that left by gold of known quality. The standing wall monument of 1789-91 above the grave is to a design by Henry Emlyn. It is set within a Gothic arch lined with Tournai Marble and includes two re-used Tournai Marble colonettes.

The way out from Windsor Castle for visitors to St George's Chapel is through the King Henry VIII Gate. Dating from c.1513, the gateway tower is faced with sarsen stone. Its plinth and its turret quoinstones were probably originally all of Kentish Ragstone, some blocks of which survive, mostly on the inner face of the gateway, the majority having been replaced with Bath stone; and on the evidence of a few remnant blocks the archway surrounds, now largely of Bath, may originally have been of Caen stone.

Between this gate and the next tower to the east, the Mary Tudor Tower, the sarsen-clad castle wall is replaced by a range of Military Knights' Lodgings, faced with brown Taynton stone ashlar. A paler-coloured Bath stone replaces some facing-stones on the inner side and a higher proportion of them on the outer, south-facing side. It has also been used to repair window-surrounds and, apparently, to renew the battlements that crown the block. These Lodgings were erected in 1557-58, in the reign of Queen Mary I. The accounts include payment for Caen stone for the battlements to be brought from Reading Abbey,[15] by then in ruins but which, much though Mary might have preferred it otherwise, had no prospect of reinstatement.

TWO

KING HENRY III AND WINDSOR CASTLE

David Carpenter and Julie Kantner

IN 1263 the *Flores Historiarum* ('The Flowers of History'), a contemporary chronicle of events in England, described Windsor castle as

> *'that most flourishing castle, of which at that time there was not another more splendid within the bounds of Europe'.*[1]

The comment reflected the way in which the castle had been transformed both as a fortress and a palace since the start of Henry III's reign in 1216. That transformation can be seen (at least in part) in the surviving building and can be studied in detail through royal letters commissioning the work. While its main outlines have been clear since William St John Hope's architectural history of the castle, published in 1913, later scholars have added and refined many of the details.[2] Most recently, 'The Time Team royal dig' at the castle in 2006, thanks in good part to the documentary work of Eileen Scarff, established for the first time that the great hall of the castle in the lower ward ran east-west along the curtain wall and measured approximately 28 feet by 100 feet internally, considerably smaller than had been thought, a point to which we will return. In this chapter, using a new analysis of Henry III's itinerary, we will consider the functions of the castle, to which the building works responded. We will also, using new work on the authorship of the above quotation, consider the impact the castle made on contemporaries.

But, first, a word is needed on architectural developments under Henry III. These were, in part, military. Henry, son of King John, had come to the throne at the age of nine in 1216, during a civil war in which Windsor had stood siege and been several damaged. Not surprisingly, therefore, during Henry's minority (he attained full power in 1227), work started on the wall and three great towers which to this day form the west end of the castle, as well as on a new gateway to which a barbican was added in 1249-50 (both of these are now lost.) Also in the minority, work probably started on a wall and flanking towers to protect the southern side of the motte, while the round keep on its top may also have been remodelled. Attention was likewise given to the castle's domestic arrangements, with the great hall in the lower ward, probably damaged during the siege, being rebuilt in 1223-4. It was not till Henry III's marriage to Eleanor of Provence in 1236, however, that work on the domestic side of the castle started in earnest. Then, in the late 1230s, and again twenty years later, Henry built and rebuilt apartments for his queen in the upper ward, together with apartments there for his children. He also commissioned, in 1240, a complete new suite of rooms in the lower ward, consisting of a chapel, and chambers for himself and his queen. All these domestic buildings were magnificently decorated. There was a stone lion on the gable end of the hall and within a royal seat, in the middle of the table, painted in gold with the image of a king holding a sceptre. The queen's apartments in the upper ward had stained glass with the image of the Tree of Jesse, and windows which opened and shut on to a herb garden. Just enough survives in the lower ward to give some physical impression of this display – the window embrasures and superbly carved capitals in the canon's house to the west of the hall, the cloister arcading with its Purbeck marble shafts, stiff leaf foliage, and painted head of a king, and the western wall of the chapel with its extraordinary pair of doors studied with wrought iron stamped spirals and signed proudly by its creator 'GILEBERTUS'.[3]

What then was the purpose of all this building and adornment on which Henry spent more money than on any other palace or castle? That it was partly for hard military reasons there can be no doubt. Few even today, driving along the M4 motorway, can fail to appreciate Windsor's strategic importance, rising up on its chalk cliff within the valley of the Thames, and commanding both the approach to London, and the way out to Reading and beyond. Windsor, moreover, was the only major royal castle in the London area, apart from the Tower itself, which was often less than secure given the doubtful loyalties of the citizens. The palace at Westminster, of course, was completely unprotected. No wonder then, that the defences of Windsor were rebuilt in so formidable a fashion after the 1215-1217 civil war, and no wonder that, in the period of reform and rebellion between 1258 and 1267, control of the castle passed between the king and his opponents at each swing of the political pendulum.[4] When, in September 1261, Henry, struggling to re-assert his authority, ordered three knights from each county to come to him at Windsor, rather than attend a baronial assembly at St Albans, he was summoning them to a place which would give him absolute security, project his power far and wide over the valley of the Thames, and also, he might hope, awe the knights with the might and majesty of his kingship.[5] Two years later, in

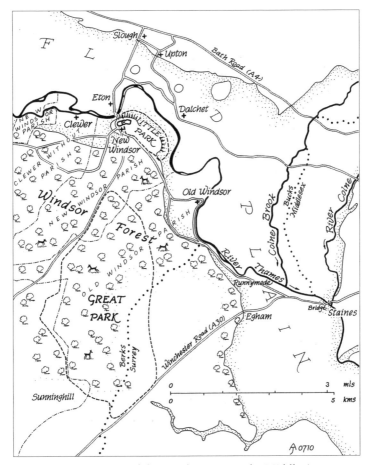

Fig. 7. Map of the Windsor area in the Middle Ages.

1263, it was at Windsor, garrisoned with large numbers of foreign mercenaries, that Henry III's son, the Lord Edward, planned to make his stand against Simon de Montfort, and it was there that his mother, Queen Eleanor of Provence, sought to join him, leaving Henry in the Tower of London tamely to surrender. Later in October 1263, Edward and his father moved from Westminster to Windsor when launching their campaign to overthrow the Montfortian government, summoning earls, barons and knights to join them there with horses and arms. Both the king's castellan, Drogo de Barentin, and his successor, John fitz John, put in by Montfort after his May 1264 victory at Lewes, munitioned the castle by seizing the goods of neighbouring villagers and forcing them to join the garrison.[6] It is scarcely surprising that in this period one London burgess, with land at nearby Horton, left it deserted and uncultivated 'for fear of Windsor castle'.[7]

This menace was equally apparent after Montfort's defeat and death at Evesham in August 1265. Next month, with London itself still recalcitrant, Henry summoned a large body of magnates to Windsor and threatened to advance on the capital. The mere threat was enough. The mayor and forty of the leading citizens came penitent to Windsor, where they were first kept outside the castle, and then, on entering, despite their safe conduct, were imprisoned in a 'tower' for a day and a night until, in the evening of the following day, all but the ringleaders were released into the bailey.[8] One wonders if the citizens had uneasy thoughts about the fate of Matilda de Braose and her son, who had been starved to death by King John in the vaults of Windsor castle.

Windsor's aspect, therefore, was never less than military and minatory, yet there was far more to it than that, which brings us to the whole question of how often the king himself visited the castle. Here the evidence is plentiful because from the start of King John's reign in 1199 it is possible to know where the king was on the great majority of days in each year: with John the percentage is in fact 69% and with (between 1234 and 1258) Henry 92%. This knowledge comes from royal letters, which were issued in great profusion and recorded on rolls which are now kept in The National Archives at Kew, the letters usually ending with the statement that they had been witnessed by the king at a given place on a given date. The itinerary of King Henry III was first established from these sources by Theodore Craib of the Public Record Office, in 1923. It was considered from a Windsor angle by Steven Brindle and Stephen Priestley, as part of their work on the castle for English Heritage, the striking conclusion being that Windsor comes second only to Westminster as the king's most favoured residence: hence of course all the expenditure on its halls, chapels and chambers.[9] What follows explores this conclusion further. It is based on a detailed analysis of the king's itinerary for the period which historians sometimes call Henry III's personal rule, that is the period between 1234 (when he first began to govern without great ministers inherited from his father) and the revolution of 1258, after which the itinerary was at the mercy of political exigencies. Within this period, the analysis focuses on the years between 1234 and Henry's departure in 1242 for his campaign in Poitou, and between 1244 and his departure for Gascony in 1253.

In these seventeen years between 1234-1241 and 1244-1252, we find that Henry III spent 651 days at Windsor, amounting to 11% of his time. He averaged 7.5 visits a year, the average length of each stay being 5.1 days, although some were only for a day or so while others lasted for several weeks.

TOP LOCATIONS: HENRY III 1234–1241, 1244–1252	
Place	*Days*
Westminster	1746
Windsor	651
Woodstock	515
Clarendon	363
Marlborough	357
Reading	238
Winchester	202
Kempton	142
Guildford	89
Merton	83

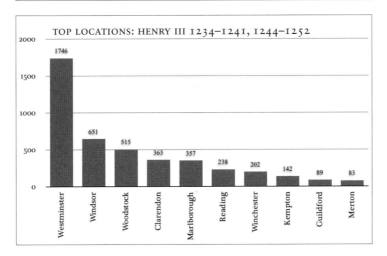

These tables and chart go some way to contextualise the place of Windsor in Henry's itinerary. Clearly that itinerary was dominated by Westminster, to which Windsor came a poor second. Clearly too, Henry liked to spend the bulk of his time at his palaces and palace castles in the south. Westminster, Windsor, Woodstock, Clarendon, Marlborough and Winchester all come into that category. Even Woodstock, the most northerly, was only sixty-five miles from London. The only other place to figure in the chart, Reading, was of course the site of the abbey founded by Henry I. Beyond his two campaigns on the continent, Henry was taken out of this congenial round chiefly by pilgrimages to Canterbury and the East Anglian holy sites, by his campaigns in Wales and by his journeys to the north to deal with the affairs of Scotland. Such excursions,

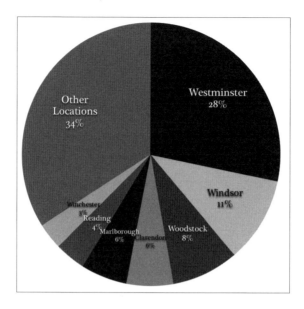

PERCENTAGE OF HENRY III'S TIME SPENT BY LOCATION 1234-1241, 1244-1252

together with the numerous stop-over places on all his journeys, account for the 34% of 'other locations' in the above chart.[10] This itinerary, and the place of Windsor within it, was very different from that found under Henry's father, King John. John spent just ninety-three days at Windsor during his seventeen-year reign, which makes it his ninth most favoured residence, where he spent only 2% of his time. The average length of his stays was 2.2 days as opposed to his son's 5.1. This was not because Windsor had been eclipsed in any significant way by more favoured locations. The fact was that John travelled his dominions with a speed and frequency quite unlike that of his son and dwelt nowhere long. Even Westminster and the rest of London absorbed only 9% of his time there, as opposed to Henry's 28%. The contrast was partly one of circumstance. The loss of the great continental empire meant that Henry did not have to shuttle back and forth across the Channel as his Angevin predecessors had. But it was also one of personality. Henry III liked a comfortable and easy life. The construction and adornment of the chambers and chapels at Windsor and his other palaces and palace castles was the result.

Our understanding of the place of Windsor in Henry's itinerary, and why it was so favoured, can be taken further by considering the circumstances of his visits.[11] These have two main patterns. The first shows how perfectly situated Windsor was between Westminster and Henry's favourite palaces and palace castles to the west. For beyond Windsor lay Reading and then the routes both to and from Woodstock (often via the castle of Henry's brother at Wallingford) and to and from Winchester, Clarendon and Marlborough. Again and again Henry's stays at Windsor were part of an itinerary going one way or the other along this east-west axis. Once Henry reached Windsor coming from the west, he very rarely went anywhere onwards other than to Westminster, a remarkable testimony to the latter's pulling power. The second pattern starts and finishes with Westminster, for it was Henry's frequent practice to leave his palace there, spend time at Windsor, and then go back to Westminster. Sometimes Henry made the journey to and from Westminster direct, but equally, he might make brief stays along the way at his small palace at Kempton or at Merton Priory. Occasionally too, the tour would take in Guildford Castle and reach out as far as Reading. Some combination of this Westminster-Windsor-Westminster pattern occurs at least thirty-four times during the period of Henry's personal rule.[12]

It is absolutely clear from both these patterns that Henry liked living at Windsor. Occasionally, when moving along the east-west axis, he might make merely an overnight stop, but more often he was there for longer, as he was also when he came out to spend time there before returning to Westminster. As we have seen, the mean average of his stays was 5.1 days, and often they lasted much longer. What then was the attraction? It is worth starting here by reflecting on what Windsor was not, because that also helps explain why it ran Westminster such a poor second. In the first place, Windsor was not an ecclesiastical centre with a great church and a saint to whom Henry could supplicate. Westminster, by contrast, had Edward the Confessor, and an abbey Henry was rebuilding in his honour. By the same token, Windsor was unsuitable for the great ecclesiastical festivals, and Henry rarely spent them there. Second, Windsor was not the seat of government. It was Westminster which was the home of the exchequer and the court of common pleas. It was likewise Westminster which was the usual venue for parliament. Indeed, in a new analysis by John Maddicott of parliaments and great councils held between 1235 and 1257, only three of the 54 met at Windsor, as opposed to over 40 at Westminster.[13]

This perspective helps to clarify Windsor's position. In Henry's peacetime years, it was not a place for great public events, religious or secular. Rather it was a private, domestic palace castle, for the king, his household and the immediate court. One suspects indeed, that the frequent visits to Windsor between stays at Westminster were to 'get away from it all', or at any rate to get away from the pressures of business and the ever present public eye. At Windsor Henry could relax in the privacy of chambers and chapels protected from clamorous petitioners by castle walls, as Westminster was not. He could also relax in the great park, again unparalleled at Westminster, using it perhaps less for hunting (for Henry was little known for that) than for promenades and picnics. Indeed, was it this rural aspect of Windsor to which the *Flores Historiarum* alluded when describing it as the 'most flourishing' of castles? The Latin word here, hard to translate, is *vernantissimum*, the superlative of *vernus* meaning verdant, blooming, flourishing, spring-like, and hence the English word 'vernal'. It was certainly not a term one could apply to the Tower of London.

Something of the relative quietude of Windsor is reflected in the household rolls, the documents which recorded the costs of the royal household's daily food, drink and stables.[14] Thus in July 1260 the average daily cost of four weeks at Westminster was £20. The daily cost of the week at Windsor which followed (Henry travelling via Kempton) was £13. This was equally the rate of Windsor's daily costs early in October before Henry moved to Westminster for the greatest event of his religious year, the feast on the Translation of Edward the Confessor on 13 October. The costs on that day approached £230.[15] Windsor's role as a cherished domestic residence helps, of course, to explain why the royal apartments were built and rebuilt to make them all the more comfortable and congenial. It also explains why the great hall in the lower bailey was left aisleless and comparatively modest in size. Since Windsor rarely hosted great public events, a larger one was unnecessary. The same considerations reigned at Dover, where the hall was similar in size and situation to that at Windsor, although Dover differed from Windsor in not being a regular royal residence at all.

This domestic role of Windsor castle was intimately bound up with Henry III's queen, Eleanor of Provence, whom, as we have seen, he married in 1236. The building of apartments for her in both the upper and lower ward was because Windsor, as a great deal of documentary evidence shows, became the primary base for herself and her children. (The first, the eventual Edward I, was born in 1239, and four more followed down to 1253.)[16] Almost certainly many of the visits Henry made to Windsor between periods at Westminster were to be with the queen. Just how much time Eleanor spent at Windsor on her own probably varied, but it could be considerable, as is shown by her own household rolls which cover part of 1252 and 1253 (the only ones to survive), the rolls, that is which record the daily costs of her own food, drink and stables. Thus in 1252 she was there alone from 23 August to 29 September before moving to Westminster to join her husband for the feast of the Confessor. In 1253, after Henry had left Windsor for Westminster, Eleanor, in the early stages of pregnancy, remained at the castle until 20 June, with Henry making two brief visits, on the first coming from and going back to Westminster.[17]

All of this brings us in conclusion to the impact of Windsor on contemporaries, and the encomium from the *Flores Historiarum* with which this chapter began: 'that most flourishing castle, of which at that time there was not another more splendid within the bounds of Europe'.

This striking claim is well known. What has not been appreciated is that it comes from someone well placed to make it.[18] It has been assumed almost universally that the *Flores Historiarum* was written at this point by a monk of St Albans who was continuing the chronicle of the abbey's great historian, Matthew Paris. In fact, as recent work has shown, the *Flores* at this point were being written by a monk of Pershore Abbey (Worcs.), who was himself deriving much of his information from his abbot Eleurius. Now Eleurius was a remarkable man. He was a monk of Fécamp in Normandy who had crossed the Channel to look after his abbey's interests in England. In the 1250s (and hence his promotion to the abbacy of Pershore), he rose very rapidly in the service of the king, becoming the escheator south of the Trent, and then a baron of the exchequer. Eleurius kept in close touch with Normandy, and also knew other parts of France, having been on a pilgrimage to Pontigny. He was thus a man of international experience, and almost certainly supplied the *Flores* chronicler with his detailed information about the 'European' dimension of the 1263-1265 English civil war. When, therefore, that chronicler commented that there was no finer castle than Windsor within the bounds of Europe, he knew what he was talking about.

What then impressed Eleurius? It was certainly in part the castle's military might. The very context of the comment was military, for it comes when narrating the Lord Edward's intention to make a stand at Windsor with his foreign mercenaries in 1263. The Pershore chronicler, moreover, again doubtless getting his information from Eleurius, was interested in castle fortifications for he comments on how Simon de Montfort had rebuilt Kenilworth in a remarkable fashion and had fortified it with 'machines' hitherto unseen in England.[19] If the physical strength of Windsor projected military power during war, it equally projected psychological power during peace. This was a period when castles were supposed to 'fight', an age when no one would have been impressed by the show castles of the later Middle Ages which merely looked the part.[20]

Eleurius, however, had done far more than simply gape at Windsor from without. Like any top royal official he had also been within. Indeed, we can see him there in September 1251 attesting a royal charter with other royal servants and favourites.[21] Henry III himself was acutely aware of the psychological effect of buildings. On one occasion he ordered Dover Castle to be shown off to visiting dignitaries 'in a courteous manner so that its nobility is revealed and no defects are seen.'[22] Dover certainly equalled Windsor in the nobility of its fortifications. Yet rarely visited by the king for any length of time, it was not in the same league when it came to the decoration and extent of its domestic quarters. At Windsor, for Eleurius, therefore, in terms of impact, Windsor's walls and wall paintings worked together. Both made it 'splendid'. We have said that Windsor was a private domestic castle, unaccustomed to great assemblies. Yet that did not make its projection of the majesty and mystique of kingship any less important. For the people who exercised in the verdant park, walked through the new cloister with its images of royal heads, worshipped in the new chapel with its doors by Gilebertus, and dined in the new hall with its golden figure of a king painted behind the royal seat, were those whom it was vital to impress – on the one hand the king's own servants, like Eleurius, and on the other the great and good of the realm who visited the king at the castle. The witness lists to royal charters show that most of the leading bishops and barons were visitors at one time or another, even outside the few parliaments which were held there. The castle's private nature made such access all the more privileged, and the king's guests were royally entertained. The costs of the daily fare may have been less than at Westminster, reflecting the smaller size of the court, but they were still considerable. The £13 a day averaged for the week at Windsor in August 1260 was only two pounds less than the annual income required to qualify as a knight. Not even the greatest earl lived on anything like this scale.

Henry also did his best to make up for Windsor's lack of church and saint. His new chapel, his great chapel, in the lower bailey was dedicated to Edward the Confessor and staffed by four chaplains. By the early 1250s there were as many as eight chaplains in the castle, although the number was later scaled down.[23] When Henry was at the castle, he continued his usual practice of feeding 150 paupers every day when the queen was with him (as she usually was). For the first three days after his arrival with Eleanor in August 1260, he fed 200 a day, a number which he increased to 300 on the vigil of the feast of the Assumption (the kind of lesser feast that might be celebrated at the castle).[24] On other feast days, when absent, the king could order all the halls of the castle to be filled with feasting paupers.[25] Thus Windsor was home not merely to the royal family, to ministers and magnates, but also, in Christ-like fashion, to the poor, praying assiduously for the king's welfare. At Windsor, as elsewhere, Henry made very clear that his was a kingship sanctioned and guided by the hand of God. And it had its effect. When the Montfortian captain, John fitz John, took over in 1264, a member of the displaced garrison refused to join him: he would take no oath 'save for the benefit of the king and his sons'.[26] One wonders too about the knights summoned to Windsor in 1261. They might certainly, as we have suggested, have been awed by Windsor's power, but they would also see at first hand the king's benevolent almsgiving. They would thus be all the more likely, as Henry put it, to 'see and understand that we propose to do nothing save what we know is for the honour and common utility of our kingdom'.[27]

Windsor thus projected both the might and majesty of kingship. It equally projected a powerful image of queenship. While at Windsor, Eleanor maintained herself in some state. Her household departments mirrored those of the king so that her rolls record the costs of her pantry, buttery, kitchen, scullery, saucery, almonry, hall and chamber as well as stables. The daily costs of her household's food, drink and stables seem to have run at half, or over half, that of the king, which meant they were a good deal larger than those of all but the wealthiest earls. On Whitsunday 1253, which Eleanor celebrated at Windsor without her husband, her costs rose to over £16.[28] What made the atmosphere all the more secure and sympathetic was that through much of this period, the castellans of Windsor were her own men, being drawn from her mother's house of Savoy or its servants and connections. One can understand Steven Brindle's comment that 'for the baronial opposition, Windsor must have been one of the principal symbols of the queen and her Savoyard faction, and their foreign grip on the government'.[29] Yet there was another side. The queen and her party integrated far better into English life than the king's Poitevin half brothers, and indeed were not marked out for attack until 1263. At Windsor, Eleanor, as many must have known, was surrounded by her offspring. Matthew Paris remarked quite naturally that she was living there with her children when a great storm damaged the castle in 1251.[30] The stained glass window with the tree of Jesse, which Henry had placed in the gable of one of her chambers, pointed to her duty to continue the royal line. At Windsor, Eleanor demonstrated her triumphal success in fulfilling this primary function of queenship.[31]

Windsor Castle under Henry III and Queen Eleanor, the castle Abbot Eleurius so admired, was thus both a palace as it has always remained, and also a castle in a real fighting sense, as it gradually ceased to be in the later middle ages. In the reign of Henry III, serving both functions in 'splendid' fashion, Windsor was at its apogee.

THREE

THE FIRST ST GEORGE'S CHAPEL

Steven Brindle

Sᴛ ɢᴇᴏʀɢᴇ's ᴄʜᴀᴘᴇʟ so dominates the Lower Ward at Windsor that it is difficult to imagine the castle without it. Yet the castle is almost 400 years older than the present chapel, and a visitor coming in through the main gate from the town in the twelfth century would have had a very different view. The focal point of the Lower Ward would have been the twelfth century Great Hall, long and high-roofed, sitting against the north curtain wall.[1] Henry III refurbished the Great Hall in the 1230s, and then added a group of buildings at its eastern end, to either side of what is now the Dean's Cloister. On 4 January 1240, the king ordered:

> ". . . to cause to be made in Windsor castle a chamber for our use next to the wall of the castle 60 feet in length and 28 feet in breadth and another chamber for the Queen's use 40 feet in length to adjoin our chamber and under the same roof along the said wall, and a chapel 70 feet in length and 28 feet in breadth along the said wall, provided that a suitable space be left between the said chambers and the chapel to make a grass plot."[2]

The next documentary reference is an order from Henry III, then on campaign in Gascony, dated 20 August 1243, in which he enjoined Walter de Grey, ArchBishop of York:

> ". . . to cause work to be done both in Winter and in Summer until the King's chapel of Windsor is finished, and to cause to be made a high wooden roof in the same after the manner of the roof of the new work of Lichfield, so that it resembles stonework, with good wainscoting and painting, and to cause the chapel to be roofed with lead and four gilded images to be made in the said chapel and to be set in the places which the king had previously arranged for them to be put and a stone turret at the front of the same chapel in which may be hung three or four bells."[3]

Despite the king's urging, the chapel was not finished for another five years.

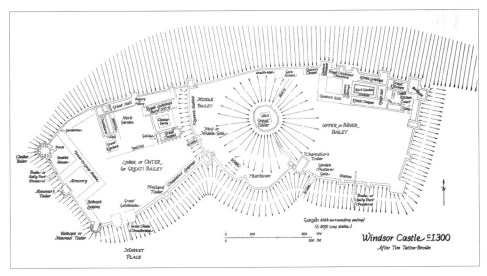

Fig. 8. Plan of Windsor Castle in *c.* 1300, showing Henry III's new buildings in the Lower Ward.

In December 1245 the sheriffs of London were ordered to buy ten wagonloads of lead for the chapel, and in July 1246 Henry de Farleigh was ordered to supply 30 oaks for that and other works.[4] In March 1248, Brother William the Painter, a monk of Westminster, was provided with 10 marks to buy colours for painting the chapel, and from then on there are numerous references to him working there, until 1256.[5]

The chapel was nearing completion in the autumn of 1248, for on 2 November Godfrey de Liston was ordered:

"... to find four chaplains to celebrate in the King's new chapel at Windsor, and to cause each of them to have 50 shillings for wages until Michaelmas next."[6]

On 19 December 1248 the keepers of the works at Windsor were given £200 to complete the chapel.[7] In May 1251 Edward of Westminster was ordered to send a series of books and vestments to Windsor, and in September 1251 he was ordered to have 'a large and beautiful basin made, with chains' for the new chapel.[8] A beautiful Purbeck marble font, part of which survives, may also have been made at this time, though no reference to it has been found.[9] In 1252-3 £200 was accounted for as having been spent on it: this was presumably the £200 which the king had ordered to be spent in December 1248.[10] By Michaelmas 1249 four chaplains had been appointed: they were to reside in lodgings 'opposite the King's chapel', and in 1251 the lodgings were given an extra chamber and a kitchen.[11]

The reign of Edward III (1327-77) saw the greatest transformation in Windsor's history, the central event being the foundation of the Order of the Garter, with its associated collegiate chapel of St George, in 1347-8. The king handed over the Lower Ward at Windsor with the two most important rooms, the Great Hall and Great Chapel, to his new foundation: the rebuilding of the Upper Ward was probably implicit in this decision. The chapel, hitherto dedicated to Edward the Confessor, was re-dedicated to St Edward and St George and the Virgin Mary. By 1352 there were to be 26 Garter Knights (including the sovereign), who would each have a stall in the chapel. It was served a warden (later a dean) and 12 canons and 13 priest vicars, who would also need stalls in the chapel, and a nearby chapter house, and lodgings. The Poor Knights were to receive lodgings and alms in return for attending services in the chapel and praying for the Garter Knights. This was to be a model of charity and piety, as well as chivalry.

Architecturally speaking, the project was a relatively modest one. The Great Chapel and Great Hall were to be refurbished rather than rebuilt. The warden and canons received new lodgings, all built c. 1350-55.[12] The lodgings for the Poor Knights were begun on the site of the chaplains' lodgings on the south side of the Lower Ward but they took a lot longer to complete, and were not finished until the mid sixteenth century.

As it happened, the new order and church were founded almost exactly at the moment that the Black Death reached England. Had William Ramsey, the king's former master mason, been alive, this important new project would probably have been entrusted to him, but he had died in 1349 probably of the plague. He certainly influenced the design for the College, and it is possible that he had begun them.[13] Work began on 26 April 1350 under the master mason John Sponle, possibly Ramsey's assistant, and the master carpenter William Herland.[14]

One of the first things to be done was the new stalls for the Garter Knights in the chapel. They must have been elaborate, for around twelve carpenters worked on them from April 1350 to July 1351, and thereafter several carpenters worked on them until November 1352.[15] Simon Hurley, probably the son of the famous William, was one of the carpenters from the outset and became their chief early in 1351. The stalls were made with boards (probably of oak) from the Baltic (termed *rygoldbords* and *estrichbords*), bought in London and presumably painted. A carver, Robert Burwell, was employed on the stalls from the outset.[16] In April 1352, Master Andrew the king's smith was paid for making 24 hooks with which to hang the Garter Knights' swords above the stalls, establishing that this tradition dates from the foundation of the Order.[17] Oddly enough, repair of the chapel roof only began after the stalls were complete – timber was bought for this on 16 April 1352, lead in July 1352, and scaffolding in August.[18]

In May 1350 work began on a stone-vaulted vestry and a chapter house, adjoining the north-east corner of St George's Chapel. The vestry is well-preserved, and is now the deanery chapel. The chapter house, much remodelled, is the deanery drawing room.[19] The first reference to the vestry vault is on 30 January 1351, and lead was being laid on its roof in November.[20] 5,000 tiles were bought for its floor and a marble stone for its altar in December 1351.[21]

Both the chapel and the new chapter house were to have painted windows, and in March 1352 a section of the royal glaziers' workshops at Westminster was set to producing glass for them. Most of it was bought in London, sent to Westminster, cut and painted there in the workshops which were producing glass for St Stephen's Chapel. On 12 March 1352, the first of several large consignments of 'white glass' was bought in London and sent to Westminster.[22] A team of craftsmen was assembled: the master-glaziers John Lincoln and John Athelard were responsible for 'drawing and ordering' the glass, with five glaziers to paint it, another ten to 'work on the breaking and laying of glass' and a labourer to assist them.[23] The finished glass was crated and shipped up river from Westminster in September 1353.[24] There are no references to the window openings being re-made to accept the new glass, which may have been set directly into the existing thirteenth-century openings.

Further furnishings for the chapel were added: first a splendid pew for the queen added to the Garter Knights' stalls[25], then a lectern.[26] Timber for a cross with figures of Mary and John (the Apostle) was made in July/August 1354: this was clearly a 'rood', though we do not know how it was displayed.[27] In 1362-3 a 'table' or painting was bought from John of Lindsey for 65 shillings. Finally, in 1367-8 a great alabaster retable was sent from Nottingham.[28] Henry III's chapel had been given a new role which elevated it above any other royal chapel except for St Stephen's at Westminster.

Edward IV resolved to enhance Windsor's role further by making it the place of burial for his dynasty, and the chapel would no longer suffice. The twelfth-century great hall was demolished in 1477, and the vast new Perpendicular chapel began to rise: Henry III and Edward III's building was to be preserved as its 'Lady Chapel'.

The next stage in this process of renewal was Henry VII's rebuilding of the thirteenth-century great chapel in 1494-8, with the apparent intention of making this the burial place of *his* dynasty, distinct from Edward IV's incomplete building to the west. The old chapel is said to have been pulled down, a new shell was built, and indeed the building's external character is largely Perpendicular. However, the king abandoned it in favour of the Henry VII Chapel at Westminster. It became the lady chapel to St George's, and, after the accession of Queen Elizabeth, the tomb house was remodelled for Henry VIII (1565), for James II, and finally in 1863-73 as the Albert Memorial Chapel: the interior today is entirely and spectacularly Victorian. Nevertheless, enough thirteenth-century fabric remains in the north and west walls to give us an idea of its design. There are also signs that the Perpendicular building followed the plan of the thirteenth-century chapel fairly closely. The remainder of this article will consider the architecture of Henry III's original great chapel.

The north and west end walls of the original chapel stand to about 15 feet in height, with their original surfaces surviving on the outer sides. The north wall, that is, the south side of the dean's cloister, has six bays of blind arcading, four wide bays flanked by two narrow ones, with richly moulded arches carried on brown Purbeck shafts with beautiful foliate capitals.

The west end of Henry III's chapel now forms the east side of the ambulatory at the eastern end of the present St George's Chapel. It is of three bays, again with richly moulded arches carried on Purbeck shafts, though here the capitals have been dressed back and their detail lost. There are blind arches to either side, but the doorway in the middle has a pair of thirteenth-century doors with decorative ironwork of the greatest elaboration signed by master 'Gilebertus'. The doors doubtless represent one of the chapel's original fittings, and are among the greatest masterpieces of mediaeval decorative metalwork in England.[29] A number of late mediaeval references to a 'Galilee' suggest that these arches and doors were sheltered by a porch.[30]

The Albert Memorial Chapel's internal dimensions are approximately 67 feet by 27 feet, close to the dimensions of 70 feet by 28 feet specified by Henry III in 1240. The survival of the thirteenth-century entrance door in the west wall demonstrates that the present chapel is on the same axis as the original building: the difference of one foot in its width can probably be explained in terms of the thickness of the Victorian linings. The blind arcading on the north side of the chapel, towards the dean's cloister, is aligned with the bay-rhythm of the existing Perpendicular building (though it is not aligned with the fourteenth-century cloister arcades). So it seems that the Perpendicular chapel reproduced the thirteenth-century chapel's bay rhythm as well as its width.

The Perpendicular chapel has shallow, slightly stepped buttresses on its south side. To the north it has shallow buttresses at upper level, sitting on the thick lower part of the wall. The north wall is much thicker than would be structurally necessary for a building of this scale: this would seem to be in order to present a nearly flat surface to the cloister, articulated by the blind arcading, while supporting shallow buttresses at the higher, window level, as at present. Here again, it seems likely that the Perpendicular building follows the outlines of its predecessor.

The east end of the present chapel has a canted apse with shallow buttresses. This undoubtedly dates from 1494-7, though it is much restored and refaced. We do not know whether this follows the footprint of the thirteenth-century building, but this seems likely for a number of reasons. Geometrically, a canted east end fits well with the narrow eastern bay, and makes for a generously-sized sanctuary. The idea of a canted east end is also supported by comparative evidence, discussed below.

The thirteenth-century fenestration is problematic: our only evidence comes in an account for repairs in 1294-5:

In a wooden circle bought for a round window in the chapel	1d.
In 12 great curved crooks for a round window in the chapel	6d.
In mending a gudgeon bar for a window beside the altar of the great chapel	5d.
In renewing five bars with 18 latchets and catches for a window at the head of the chapel towards the west	4d.[31]

The references are puzzling. The references to 12 great curved crooks suggest a large rose window: if the chapel had a canted east end, this could only have gone in the west wall. However, there was apparently another window at the west end, large enough to have 18 latches (which hardly sounds like a rose window): Sir William St John Hope interpreted this to mean a rose window above three lancets. Other historians have suggested that the reference to 'crokes' means that the windows had bar tracery, which would relate the chapel firmly to French precedents, in particular to Rheims. Windows with bar tracery of this kind would almost certainly have circular upper lights, and this might explain the references to round windows.[32] Certainly, the idea of the chapel having Rheims-style bar tracery is an attractive hypothesis, given its place in architectural history.

W.R. Lethaby first proposed that Henry III's chapel at Windsor was designed and built by Henry of Reyns, the master mason who designed and began building Westminster Abbey in 1245-53. Lethaby noted the similarity of the dean's cloister arcading to the work in St Faith's Chapel, the cloister, and other parts of the abbey. He noted the lack of drip-mouldings, the use of Purbeck shafts, and the profile of the bases, common to the two buildings. He noted the striking similarities between the beautiful foliate capitals at Windsor arcade and at Westminster, so similar that they are probably by the same carver. Lethaby's analysis seems impeccable, and his attribution has never been seriously questioned. [33]

The first documentary reference to Master Henry is as 'master of the king's masons' in 1243 when he and William le Brun, keeper of works at Windsor, were both given robes.[34] Master Henry's identity and origins have been the subject of much discussion, but a consensus has emerged that the Abbey represents an English interpretation of French concepts, and that he was probably an Englishman. This leaves open the question of whether 'Reyns' means Raynes in Essex (as Lethaby thought) or refers to him having spent time at Rheims, whose cathedral is the most important of the various sources for Westminster.[35]

The surviving elements of the Windsor chapel relate to and prefigure the 'English' qualities of Westminster Abbey more than the 'French' ones. Paul Binski noted the French character of the capitals,[36] but otherwise the depth and richness of the mouldings and the use of Purbeck shafts relate to well established tendencies in English architecture as seen, for example, at Lincoln (1200 onwards), the eastern arm of Worcester (1224 on), the transepts of York Minster, built by Archbishop de Grey from c.1225 on, and the presbytery of Ely (begun in 1234). So there are several places where Master Henry might have become versed in the elaborate English style, and developed his reputation to the point that he could secure the Windsor commission in 1240. However, matters were probably not that simple, for if the Windsor chapel had bar tracery, this would have been among the earliest dated uses of it in England. If Master Henry designed bar tracery at Windsor, it seems likely that he had already been to France and seen Rheims Cathedral by 1239-40.

There is another possible source for the design of the Windsor chapel in the vanished Lady chapel of Westminster Abbey, whose site is occupied by the Henry VII Chapel. It is thought, from fragmentary archaeological evidence, to have been a single vessel about five bays long with an canted east end, 28 feet in width and about 70 feet long: in other words, very similar in size and plan to the Windsor chapel, and also, significantly, to the rebuilt Lady chapel of Lichfield Cathedral. It was begun in 1220, but work proceeded slowly until the king assumed responsibility for it in 1240.[37] The completion of the Lady chapel in 1240-45 was the immediate prelude to the rebuilding of the abbey itself, starting in 1245.

Henry of Reyns died in 1253. If we suppose him to have been born around 1180-90, his career may have developed at one of the great cathedral projects of the early thirteenth century. It is possible that he designed the Lady chapel at Westminster or at least supervised its completion c.1240-45. He may have visited

Fig. 9. Mid-15th century drawing of Windsor Castle from the north in the 'Eton manuscript'.

France in the 1230s, and seen Rheims and Amiens. He must have returned to England by 1240, to have begun work on the Windsor chapel. He may have been appointed master of the king's masons around the same time. He may have been ordered to visit France again, in preparation for the start of work on the abbey in 1245. He was provided with a house at Westminster in 1246, and died there in 1253.[38]

So the Windsor chapel and Westminster Abbey are probably linked as the work of the same designer. He was probably an Englishman, of brilliant and original mind, responding by royal direction to the latest developments in French architecture, but interpreting them through a creative intelligence which had developed between 1200 and 1240, in contact with both English and French work.

How far can we reconstruct the lost elements of the Windsor chapel ? Our one view of it in the 'Eton manuscript' (Fig. 9) suggests that the building was proportionally tall.[39] It probably had shallow buttresses, similar to those of the existing building. The windows, as we have seen, are a difficult question. The 1295 document suggests a rose window in the west wall, though the Eton view seems to show a large arched window. Whether the side walls had lancets or bar tracery seems unknowable. It is likely that there was an outer porch or Galilee, sheltering the west arcade and the magnificent doors. The first bay was probably partitioned off as an ante-chapel, much as it is today. A gallery above may have given access to the windows with latches, referred to above. The walls of the ante-chapel and cloister were painted by Brother William, a monk of Westminster, with figures of apostles and saints: two painted heads survive from his scheme, one in the passageway and one in the cloister wall, incongruously isolated, and possibly not in their original location.

Inside, the lower part of the walls were probably articulated with blind arcading with Purbeck shafts, three or four per bay. We may imagine the use of tall Purbeck shafts rising the full height to separate the main bays. The chapel was 28 feet wide, and its proportions would have been tall for England, with window sills about 15 feet above the floor and the apex of the vault about 40 feet above the floor.

We know from Henry III's letter of 1243, quoted above, that the vault was of timber painted to imitate stone on the lines of one at Lichfield Cathedral, possibly over its north transept but more probably over its Lady chapel, which in plan and dimensions was very similar to both the Windsor and Westminster chapels.[40] Coming three years after the initial commission, this looks like a change of mind. It seems likely that the king had heard about the Sainte-Chapelle, and was moved to a frenzy of rivalry and cultural status-anxiety. Whatever the original design had been (probably some kind of open timber roof), it would no longer do. A stone vault could not be managed given the shallowness of the buttresses, but instead they could take a leaf out of Lichfield's book. If one was to hazard a guess as to its form, one might say a quadripartite plan with an English longitudinal ridge-rib: the Anglo-French scheme of the Westminster high vault.

Henry III's great chapel represented a stage in the complex dialogue between English and French architecture which reached a culmination in Westminster Abbey: it must have been galling for King Henry that his chapel should have been so swiftly trumped by Louis IX with the Sainte-Chapelle. Nevertheless, the Windsor chapel is one of the lost treasures of English mediaeval art: the cloister arcade and Master Gilebertus' magnificent ironwork on the doors survive to give us a slight idea of what we have lost. (see Fig. 12)

FOUR

ST GEORGE'S CHAPEL AND THE FOUNDATION
OF THE ORDER OF THE GARTER

Nigel Saul

A TURNING POINT IN THE HISTORY OF Windsor Castle and its chapel came in the late 1340s when the Order of the Garter was founded by Edward III. The Order, an elite company of 24 knights with the Sovereign and the Black Prince, was England's first national Order of chivalry. A notable aspect of its constitution was that it was associated with the chapel in the castle, originally dedicated to St Edward the Confessor, and now rededicated to St George. The establishment of the Order was a significant event not only in the history of Windsor but in the larger history of the English monarchy's engagement with chivalry. It is worth considering how this event came about and what objects it was intended to achieve.

Discussion of the origins of the Order is made difficult by the fact that the precise date of its foundation is not known. The earliest redaction of the statutes, which dates from the early fifteenth century, tells us, somewhat unspecifically, that the Order was founded in Edward III's twenty-third year as king. Since Edward came to the throne at the beginning of 1327, the implication is that it was founded sometime between 25 January 1349 and 24 January 1350. The possible date range can be narrowed further on the evidence of the king's Great Wardrobe account, which tells us that the first formal celebration of St George's Day at Windsor took place on St George's Day, 23 April 1349.[1] That occasion is likely to have witnessed the first proper meeting of the Order. It can probably be assumed that institutionally the Order was in existence by April 1349.

What is not so clear is whether the establishment of the Order was the result of a sudden impulse by the king or the fulfilment of ideas which had long been gestating in his mind. The documentary evidence, such as it is, tends to suggest that the idea of an Order associated with St George was one which occurred to the king fairly suddenly. It is known that as late as 1344 he was still considering the possibility of a much larger Order modelled on King Arthur's Knights of the Round Table. In 1344, as excavations in the Upper Ward have confirmed, he embarked on the construction of a massive circular hall for the ceremonial meetings of the proposed Order. This highly ambitious project was probably abandoned sometime in early 1346 when the king, anxious to finance his proposed invasion of France, decided that the project could no longer be afforded. The idea of a small, elite Order appears to have been one which occurred to him soon after his victory at Crécy in August 1346. As Sir N. H. Nicolas showed in the 1840s, the first evidence of the king issuing garters as royal emblems is found in the Great Wardrobe account already mentioned. This relates to the year-and-a-quarter period which followed the victory at Crécy and the capture of Calais. The implication seems to be that the establishment of the Order was the result of a sudden impulse, the expression of a desire by the king to celebrate the triumphant vindication of his cause.

It is possible, however, to take a very different view of events. The accounts of the medieval government are documents notoriously difficult to interpret. Typically, they were compiled over long periods, and not uncommonly they include payments for expenditure incurred before the actual period of account. These problems are evident in the account of the Great Wardrobe which Sir N. H. Nicolas published. It is clear that the account includes at least one payment for the distribution of cloth bearing the garter symbol made before the opening of the account in September 1347. It is suggested on the evidence of the size of this piece that it was a streamer on a ship taking the king's men to France in 1346.[2] This crucial evidence suggests that the formation of the Order was the outcome of a longer process of gestation than first impressions might suggest. Interestingly, it also points to the garter symbol originating in connection with the king's ambitions on the French throne.

We run into a further difficulty when we look at another aspect of the background to the foundation of the Order, Edward's relationship with Windsor Castle. It is apparent from the evidence of the king's itinerary that Edward took little interest in Windsor in the first nineteen or twenty years of his reign, only visiting the place some seven or eight days each year. His interest in the castle seems to have developed very suddenly in the first six months of 1348, when he spent significant amounts of time there – six weeks spread over six months – a period of residence probably occasioned by the choice of the castle for Queen Philippa's lying-in before the birth of her eleventh child. It has been observed that one of the king's visits in the first half of 1348 occurred very close to, indeed perhaps on, St George's Day, a coincidence of timing surely significant.[3] Quite possibly, the idea of setting up an Order of chivalry associated with St George and basing it at Windsor occurred to the king sometime around then.

One way of reconciling these conflicting evidential strands and appreciating their relation to the political and military achievements of the day is to separate the issue of the political and military background from the issue of the Order's connection with Windsor. It is certainly the case that the intensification of Edward's interest in Windsor in early 1348 points to the idea of giving the Order a spiritual home there taking root in that period. However, the Order's broader context in war and diplomacy points to a body of ideas going further back. On the evidence of the much quoted Great Wardrobe account, there can be little doubt that the conception of a knightly company identified by use of the garter emblem can be traced to at least the early part of 1346. Elias Ashmole, the first historian of the Order, showed three centuries ago that the motto of the Order (*honi soit qui mal y pense*) and the garter colours (blue and gold) must both refer to Edward's claim to the crown of France. The further point can be made that the choice of a French motto at a time when the court was making wide use of mottoes in English is also suggestive of a connection with the king's French ambitions. Successful Orders of chivalry in this period were almost always launched on the back of military success. Edward's victory at Crécy in 1346 was by far the most spectacular field victory of the age. The establishment of the Order both celebrated that victory and honoured the claim on the French kingly title which was vindicated by it.

Windsor appears to have been accorded a role in the king's great scheme for two main reasons. First, although this was not perhaps a matter of the highest importance, Windsor was the king's birthplace. He was Edward of Windsor; he had been born there in November 1312; and that meant something to him. Second, Windsor was a site rich in Arthurian associations, and Edward was an Arthurian enthusiast. The chronicler Murimuth associated Edward's Round Table of 1344 with the Round Table 'as Arthur, formerly king of England, had established it'. Froissart, writing a generation later and conflating the Round Table scheme with the foundation of the Order of Garter, spoke of 'the great castle of Windsor, formerly founded and built by King Arthur'.[4] Particularly striking in this connection is the evidence indirectly afforded by another site with Arthurian connections, the great hall of Winchester Castle. Sometime in the 1280s Edward I had commissioned and installed at Winchester a Round Table as part of a campaign to promote the already substantial Arthurian associations of that city. It has been suggested that this table was probably mounted on the wall of the hall – its present position – in Edward III's reign, in 1348-9, when the roof was remodelled and representations of sunrays or golden winds were carved on it. It is suggested that these golden rays were probably allusions to the Arthurian associations of Windsor (golden winds standing for 'winds' and 'or').[5] Even as the Round Table was being mounted at Winchester, then, Edward was mentally making connections between the Arthurian cult and Windsor. Even though the emphasis in the new Order was firmly to be on the person of St George, Windsor was still, for Edward, the new Camelot. Quite possibly, one element in its appeal was its spectacular setting on a hilltop overlooking the Thames. Nowhere in southern England could begin to compare with the drama of this site. Edward had a sharply developed sense of theatre, as his love of knightly ritual showed, and if he was looking for a site which could provide a theatrical setting for his new Order, Windsor certainly provided it.

When we speak of Edward as the founder of the Garter, however, a question is immediately posed. Was Edward solely responsible for the ideas which came together in the Order, or was he merely articulating the ideas of others? We know that in practice medieval kings acted on the advice of their counsellors; they did not come up with all the ideas themselves. There is a powerful case for believing that in this instance some at least of the key ideas came from the king's cousin, Henry of Grosmont, Duke of Lancaster, a one-time crusader and one of the most chivalrous men of the age.

It may well have been Henry who suggested the idea of replacing a larger Order with a small elite fellowship of 24 Knights. Only a few years before the formation of Edward's Order, Henry had visited the court of Castile, where King Alfonso had recently founded an elite company, the Order of the Band. This Order was a close model for the Garter in being a relatively small company, all of whose members were bound in close relation to the king. The Order was conceived, as the Garter was to be, as a buttress of royal power. Significantly, the Order also made use of an item of personal attire as its device, in this case a sash worn over the shoulder. In the course of his visit to Castile Duke Henry could hardly have failed to become aware of the new Order; indeed, it is very likely that many of its members were with him when he took part in the siege of Algeciras. The information which he brought back about the Castilian king's initiative could have been significant in shaping Edward's own ideas.

It is also possible that Duke Henry's influence is to be detected in a second area. It may well have been the duke who came up with the idea of making St George the Order's patron. The suggestion is prompted by the inclusion of St George on a brass with which he was associated, that of Sir Hugh Hastings at Elsing (Norfolk). Sir Hugh, the younger brother of the Earl of Pembroke, was another commander involved in the operations of 1346. Edward had entrusted him with the leadership of a force in Flanders charged with distracting and diverting the French while he himself invaded Normandy. Sir Hugh had died in July 1347 after contracting dysentery at the siege of Calais. Duke Henry acted as one of his two executors and was almost certainly involved in the design of the brass. This magnificent memorial, one of the most elaborate of its day, is rich in chivalric reference, and Duke Henry himself is represented in one of the side buttresses. The figure of St George is shown in the oculus of the canopy riding triumphantly over a stricken dragon. If the inclusion of the saint – remarkable for this early date – is indicative of the duke's interest in his cult, then it is conceivable that he was responsible for its encouragement at court. It may be worth remembering that the duke had visited the papal court at Avignon in the course of the peace negotiations of 1344. Almost certainly he would have seen Simone Martini's frescoes of St George and the dragon in the porch of the cathedral there.

How quickly did the Order of the Garter attain public and international recognition as a mark of supreme chivalric distinction? It is difficult to answer this question because the evidence is not only sparse but hard to interpret. One view is that the Garter only acquired the status of a token of esteem in the fifteenth century after Henry IV, the first Lancastrian king, reconstituted the Order as a branch of the Lancastrian affinity, so investing it with an *esprit de corps* it had previously lacked.[6] The evidence for this suggestion is largely negative. The point is made that the Garter only becomes regularly represented on the tomb effigies of knights from the early fifteenth century. Against this, however, has to be set the literary evidence, which points to much earlier recognition – to recognition in the later fourteenth century. How can the conundrum be resolved?

The literary evidence is fairly well known. First, there is the famous reference to the garter in the alliterative English poem *Winner and Waster*, a dream poem written sometime between 1350 and 1370. Garter imagery is used in the poem to identify Edward III, who is said to be dressed in a 'kirtle' and a 'mantle', the former embroidered with 'a grete gartare of ynde', and garter imagery is said to be a feature of his pavilion: it is decorated with garters of gold. The references to garters seem to imply the audience's familiarity with their use. It is also suggested that a garter context is to be envisaged for another late fourteenth-century poem, *Sir Gawain and the Green Knight*.[7] Gawain is said to wear a long blue mantle, surcoat and fur-lined hood when he is first seated in Sir Bertilak's hall: a costume very much like the ceremonial costume of the Order. At the end of the poem King Arthur's knights are said to adopt a green girdle as their emblem rather as Edward III and his knights adopted the famous garter. To the literary evidence may be added some artistic. In the Book of Benefactors of St Albans Abbey, c.1380, there is a striking drawing of Sir Nigel Loring shown dressed in his Garter robes. When these various shreds of evidence are taken together, there seems to be reasonable evidence of early recognition of the Order: that is to say, recognition in the later fourteenth century.

Yet there remains the problem of the lack of evidence of recognition from this time on monuments. Much later, companion Knights were regularly to be shown wearing the Garter on their left leg on their tomb effigies, a good example being provided by the effigy of the Earl of Worcester (d. 1526) in St George's Chapel itself. In the first half-century of the Order's existence, however, this does not appear to have been the case. The Earl of Warwick, a Founder Knight, was not shown wearing the Garter on his tomb in St Mary's, Warwick; nor was Sir Miles Stapleton, another Founder Knight, on his brass, now lost, at Ingham (Norfolk); nor, surprisingly, was the Black Prince on his magnificent tomb in Canterbury Cathedral. This evidence of omissions seems to tell against the argument for early appreciation of the Garter as a token of esteem and status. The evidence of church monuments seems to conflict with that from literature.

Part of the problem is found in the fact that so few early monuments of Garter Knights have come down to us. It is necessary to fill out the picture by looking not only at surviving tombs, but at the sources which tell us about lost tombs – antiquarian notes, wills, indents of lost brasses. When we look at these other sources, we come away with a rather different picture.

The extant monuments of late fourteenth-century knights with the Garter are three in number. The most notable of the group is the tomb of Reginald, Lord Cobham (d. 1361) at Lingfield (Surrey). Cobham was one of the first successor knights, elected in 1352; and significantly he is shown wearing the Garter on his left leg. Around the sides of his tomb chest, in an armorial celebrating chivalric companionship, are the arms of three other Garter Knights – the Earl of March, Bartholomew, Lord Burghersh, and Sir Walter Paveley. From the same year, 1361, comes the tomb, this a less distinguished one, of an actual Founder Knight, Sir William FitzWaryn, at Wantage (Berks), which again shows him with the Garter; while from a generation later comes that of Sir Richard Pembridge in Hereford Cathedral (d. 1375), again with the Garter.

To these examples can now be added a few others.[8] In excavations at Torre Abbey (Devon) the fragments were uncovered of the effigy of a Garter Knight, with the garter on the leg, which can be identified as the remains of the effigy of John, Lord Mohun (d. 1375), a Founder Knight, known to have been buried at Torre. At East Barsham (Norfolk) is the large Purbeck slab, despoiled of its brasses, showing a knight and his son surrounded by a rich array of Garter imagery. This has recently been shown to be the monument of Sir Thomas Felton KG (d. 1381), originally in Walsingham Priory and moved to East Barsham at the

Reformation. On the evidence of his will it can be deduced that the effigy of John, Lord Beauchamp, in Old St Paul's also showed him with the Garter, because Beauchamp asked for his tomb to be modelled on Pembridge's – and Pembridge's, as we have seen, had the Garter. The evidence of inscriptions is also of help. On his epitaph, now lost, in Old St Paul's, Sir Alan Buxhill (d. 1381) was described as 'Miles de Gartero'. Since terms of status in inscriptions (like 'knight') were always matched by appropriate attire on the effigy, it is likely that he too was shown with the Garter on his effigy.

In other words, when the evidence of lost tombs is taken into account, the picture begins to look more like that given by the literary and manuscript sources. This is not to deny that recognition of the Garter as a mark of esteem became much greater in the fifteenth century: it did so, partly because of the Lancastrian takeover of the Order and partly because of the military achievements of Henry V. Nonetheless there can be little doubt of the appreciation of the Order as a significant body as early as the late fourteenth century. Simply because of Edward III's greatness, simply because of the English success in arms, it was bound to be regarded as a prestigious company. It was considered an honour to be elected, just as it is today. Knighthood in the Middle Ages was seen as a Christian vocation. Edward III reinforced that perception by associating his Order with a chapel in a famous castle.

FIVE

WHY IS THE BISHOP OF WINCHESTER
PRELATE OF THE ORDER?

Martin Biddle

THE ROLE PLAYED by the Bishop of Winchester, in the person of William Edington, in the foundation of the Order of the Garter seems never to have been explored.[1] Edward III had returned from the Crécy campaign and the capture of Calais in the autumn of 1347; he landed at Sandwich on 12 October, and proceeded directly to London which he reached on the 14th.[2] The Garter badge and the Garter motto had been 'an integral part of [his] campaign from its inception, not merely a retrospective commemoration of its success'.[3] Eighteen months later the first formal celebration of St George's day took place in the chapel at Windsor.[4]

Edward's two collegiate foundations, St George's Windsor and St Stephen's Westminster, were founded on the same day, 6 August 1348. The chapel at Windsor was rededicated to the Blessed Virgin Mary, St George and St Edward the Confessor, that at Westminster to the Virgin and St Stephen. Each foundation was originally to have 24 secular priests, and in each case the arrangements were placed in the hands of the ArchBishop of Canterbury (John Stratford, d. 23 August 1348, formerly Bishop of Winchester, 1323-33) and the Bishop of Winchester (William Edington, 1346-66).[5]

Edward issued letters patent for the foundation of the college of St George in the chapel of Windsor Castle on 6 August 1348.[6] Since chapel and college were clearly intended to provide the setting for the annual celebration of the feast of the Order on St George's day, the foundation of the college can be taken as the earliest surviving indication of Edward's clear intention to establish the Order.

The buildings of the new college were not begun until April 1350, perhaps owing to the Black Death.[7] The repair and refurbishment of the existing chapel in the lower bailey, henceforth to be known as St George's Chapel, was completed by the installation of the new windows of painted glass in March 1353. The vestry and chapter house were completed by 1352, the warden's lodge by 1353, the treasury and the lodgings of the canons and vicars by 1355, and the cloister in 1356-7. To mark the completion of the college buildings, the feast of St George was

Fig. 10. Effigy of Bishop Edington on his tomb in Winchester Cathedral.

celebrated in the castle in 1358 with great splendour and solemnity.

Meanwhile, the statutes of the college had taken over four years to complete. The king petitioned the pope to confirm the consecration, endowment, and statutes in 1349.[8] Papal letters of approval, not dispatched until 30 November 1350, granted a faculty to the ArchBishop of Canterbury (now Simon Islip, 1349-66) and the Bishop of Winchester (William Edington) to settle the ordinances and statutes.[9] These letters were accompanied and followed by further faculties to the archbishop and bishop allowing them to appropriate certain benefices (31 January 1351) and grant exemption from ordinary jurisdiction to the college (12 February 1351).[10] The ordinances and statutes were finally completed on 30 November 1352.[11]

Although Windsor lay within the diocese of Salisbury, the existing castle chapel was apparently free from the bishop's control: the choice of the Bishop of Winchester to join the archbishop in settling the ordinances and statutes of the college was clearly deliberate and may have been indicated in Edward's petition of 1349.[12] Edington thus played a central role in the creation of the college – perhaps the key role after the king — and may have drafted the statutes himself.[13] A greater question is whether the bishop played a similar role in the foundation of the Order.

The original statutes of the Garter have not survived. A number of later copies are known, and six versions were published by Ashmole.[14] The first of these appears to provide the earliest surviving form of the text. It is in Latin and not earlier than Henry V's reign, but it does not contain the additional clauses promulgated by Henry V or the details of fees for marquises and viscounts, created in 1385 and 1440 respectively.[15] Although the foundation of the Order is stated in the prologue to this text to have taken place in Windsor Castle in the 23rd year of the king's reign (25 January 1349 – 24 January 1350), the members listed include Hugh de Courtenay (died before 2 September 1349), Richard Fitzsimon (succeeded in the Garter by the Earl of Suffolk in 1349), and Sanchet d'Abrichecourt (probably also succeeded in the Order during 1349).[16] In addition, several of the articles are written in the future tense,[17] a fact which adds to the impression that the body of this text dates from the first year of the Order and may be essentially that promulgated at or for the first formal celebration of St George's day on 23 April 1349.[18]

The Bishop of Winchester is named only in Article 18 and then in passing:

> . . . et istas denominationes scribet Principalis Praelatus Ordinis, scilicet Episcopus Vintoniensis qui pro tempore fuerit, et in sua absencia Decanus Collegii, vel Registrator, et in [eorum absentia] antiquior Recidenciarius Collegii supradicti . . .

Article 18 appears in the other surviving texts of the statutes, Latin, French and English. Since these were apparently derived independently from the missing original text (or texts), Article 18 probably formed part of the original text of 1349, albeit possibly in French.[19]

Edington's personal attendance at the St George's Day feasts might be followed in detail from his itinerary or from records of the annual issue to him of Garter robes from the Great Wardrobe. Both sources are incomplete.

The earliest occasion on which Edington's presence at Windsor on 23 April appears in his itinerary is 1360.[20] The accounts of the Great Wardrobe are missing for the years 1349-60.[21] By 1361 the issue of robes for the feast of St George had become an annual item, and from 1364 an issue to the Bishop of Winchester was a normal feature. These sources do not, therefore, provide a safe indication of practice, or of the bishop's presence, in the earliest years of the Order.[22]

Edington's gift to the college of £200 to endow his *obit*, received in 1361-2, provides another indication of his close association with both the chapel and the Order.[23]

Edington was, however, present at Windsor on one of the earliest feasts of the Garter. On St George's Day 1350, as recorded in the first notice of a feast of the Garter by a contemporary chronicler,

> A solemn mass [was] sung by the bishops of Canterbury, Winchester, and Exeter, and [afterwards the whole company] sat together at a common table, to the honour of the holy martyr to whom the noble fraternity was especially dedicated, calling their company 'St George de la Gartiere'.[24]

Edington's presence at Windsor on this occasion appears to be confirmed by the strictly contemporary evidence of entries on the fine roll warranted 'by bill of

Fig. 11. Bishop Edington's chantry chapel in the nave of Winchester Cathedral.

the treasurer' and dated on the 20 and 25 April 1350.[25] The bishop's register records institutions and admissions at Southwark on 21, 24, and 25 April, but these actions do not necessarily imply the bishop's presence there on those days, for he may have authorised them some days before and left it to his officials to issue the necessary documents.[26]

If Article 18 of the statutes is original, the Bishop of Winchester was prelate of the Garter from its foundation. The records of St George's chapel support this impression, and the presence of the bishop at the Garter ceremonies of 1350 appears to confirm it. The choice of the Bishop of Winchester to draw up the statutes of the college in association with the ArchBishop of Canterbury appears to be an indication of deliberate intent. This choice seems to have been an element in the shift of emphasis from Edward's still-born Order of the Round Table of 1344 to his successful foundation of the Order of the Garter in 1348-9.

For Edward I, as probably for Henry III before him, Winchester had been the city of Arthur. Now Edward's grandson wished to affirm that Windsor rather than Winchester was the castle founded by Arthur, the seat of chivalry, and (not incidentally) his own birthplace.[27] In such a transition, the choice of the Bishop of Winchester as prelate of the new Order would be both an expression of continuity with the ancient claims of Winchester and a validation of the status of Windsor.[28]

SIX

ST GEORGE'S CHAPEL AND THE
MEDIEVAL TOWN OF WINDSOR

David Lewis

THE FOUNDATION of the college of St George in 1348 could potentially have marked the beginning of a troubled chapter in Windsor's history. Tensions were apt to erupt when well endowed ecclesiastical institutions were founded in towns which were jealous of their traditions and privileges. To the people of Windsor, the establishment of the college in 1348 could have come as an unwelcome cuckoo in the urban nest.

Yet, remarkably, the evidence in large measure does not point to the college's rejection by the town: quite the contrary, in fact. Townsmen, as represented by the guild of the Holy Trinity, and members of the college appear to have mixed well together. The college proved an asset to Windsor as it not only employed a good number of townsmen, but also acted with the guild for their mutual benefit. Even the town's spatial arrangement was set to facilitate collaboration: Windsor's first guildhall was positioned immediately opposite the castle gates and formed part of the college's original setting. Both guildhall and college were built at about the same date, and this too was probably no coincidence. Clearly, the College of St George played a significant part in the development of medieval Windsor: a fact that has hitherto attracted little attention in either studies of the college and its chapel, or the town. An assessment of this aspect of Windsor's past is long overdue.

Windsor (or more accurately, before its name was changed in 1974, 'New Windsor'), is a royal town of some antiquity. Although established at the castle gates in c.1080, it had existed for at least four hundred years before the Conquest, but at a site three miles down river from its current location ('Old Windsor'). The town became a self governing community with its first royal charter in 1277. Most likely, it had forged some independence from the direct control of the castle for a generation before this date. We have little precise information about how the town was governed in this period, although some type of bi-partite control had clearly developed by the fourteenth century. This was composed on the one hand, of the town guild representing (roughly) mercantile interests, and on the other, the town bailiffs, representing the crown, as lords of the town. From the mid fourteenth century both groups were represented in the new post of town mayor, the senior civic official. Soon after this date the guild came to exercise additional responsibilities, relating specifically to Windsor's social and religious life. The body became known as the brotherhood or fraternity of the Holy Trinity, maintaining a Trinity chapel in the parish church of St John the Baptist, complete with a chantry priest. In accordance with the teachings of the Church, such priests were given the responsibility of remembering the dead and in the guild chapel, former guildsmen in particular. This was done through an annual obit or anniversary mass which it was believed would ease the soul's passage through purgatory. To procure the benefits of the chantry priest after death, townsmen endowed the guild with landed property in life, or alternatively, if their resources were more modest, left funds in their wills.

Windsor's medieval guild was extremely popular and this was reflected in the size of its prestigious guild-hall: a building which operated as the town court, council, assembly room and gaol, all rolled together. Undoubtedly, it was the town's largest secular structure, having dimensions perhaps four times that of the extant guildhall (or more accurately, 'town hall') built as its replacement in 1690.[1] The guildhall dominated the town's market place, but moreover its location near the castle meant it was also politically well connected. The close but informal relationship which developed between the town and college was no doubt aided by their physical proximity. Chantry priests, singing men, college officials and canons alike composed part of the select band of town worthies, merchants and artisans who were either members of the guild, or had links to those who were responsible for its control. The will of James Denton, a college canon of the early sixteenth century, provides one illustration of these ties.[2] Although Denton is most famous for building the 'New Commons' (accommodation for minor clergy) in the lower ward in 1519, significantly the terms of his 1526 will are almost entirely concerned with the provision of support for townspeople. The will begins:

> 'I will that the chantry priests [occupying the New Commons] shall distribute and deal in alms in lent season yearly for evermore to the poore people and needy inhabitants of this town of New Windsor only, and to no strangers, and that in herring, smoks, hose and shoes or other necessities as the chantry priests shall determine'.

Denton had purchased a substantial estate of land in the Windsor area for £45 from the guildsman John Heather, to pay for the provisions of his will, and this was given to the care of the college. His will goes on to provide for the bi-weekly provision of bread to twenty four poor men, and for other benefits to be distributed to the town's poor. If the chantry priests failed to honour his will, Denton requested that the endowment should pass to the mayor, bailiffs' and burgesses' control. Clearly Denton trusted the town's officials, indicating not only their direct interest in its terms but that he had become a well integrated member of the local community, despite having no previous connection with the town. His credentials as a Windsor townsman are further underlined by the will's restriction of benefit to fellow townspeople alone. Such limitations were a common feature of the many contemporary guild ordinances which sought to reserve the benefit of urban freedoms to those living in the town. Denton's repetition of similar restrictions would have had resonance within the guild; it emphasised his commitment to the town's well-being. Furthermore, it is interesting to note that the will was financed by means of local property of which the beneficiaries and guild would have had knowledge: more distant property would not have had this advantage.

Given the guild's focus on the town of Windsor, however, one might question why members of the College of St George would value its activities. Surely, its concern with *post mortem* remembrance represented, at least in part, a duplication of the college's own activities? It would appear, however, that by the sixteenth century some overlap could represent a distinct advantage. Excepting the special case of the Windsor martyrs of Henry VIII's reign, the town was separate from the shifting politics and changes in religious orthodoxy to which the college was subject.[3] It offered an alternative source of solidarity to which college clergy could appeal. Such considerations seem to be behind the will of another college canon, one James Mallet. Mallet had been the chaplain to Katherine of Aragon, Henry VIII's first Queen, but was executed at Colchester in 1543 for expressing his hostility to the suppression of the monasteries. Given his disgrace, there is (unsurprisingly) no record of his will or remembrance in the college; yet as a committed Catholic he would definitely have wanted elaborate and regular obit masses. His will was enrolled in the town's 'Book of Inrollment', kept in Windsor's guildhall, and this tells us of his requirements.[4] The wardens of the Guild of Holy Trinity were to be provided with £1 13s 4d 'to the intent that the said mayor, wardens [of the Trinity guild] and their successors shall keep and maintain yearly after his departure an obit with placebo, dirige and mass of requiem in the parish church of Windsor, after this manner and charges'. There then follows a long and comprehensive list of what was necessary, including the size and number of tapers to be used on his hearse, the singing men to be employed at the requiem mass, the bells to be rung about the town by the parish sexton prior to the mass, and importantly, the bread to be distributed to the poor of the town once the yearly mass was done. Mallet's emphasis on Windsor's guildhall, the parish church and the local community suggests that he was well known in the locality. Significantly, Mallet, Denton (and probably others from the college) relied on the people of Windsor as most likely to carry out their wishes after their death: evidence of the close relationship that must have existed between college members and their counterparts in the guild.

Despite the considerable information provided in wills such as these, a difficulty is encountered in reconstructing the relationship between the college and the town. Windsor's entire medieval archive was destroyed in the late seventeenth century, for reasons unknown, but which have nonetheless rendered much of the town's early history beyond recovery. Without these documents it is impossible to know the full extent of the provision in the townsmen's wills (or indeed, their other gifts) to the college, and conversely, the actions of college members intended to benefit the town. In consequence, it is impossible accurately to assess all the links which might have existed between the college and the town. The only surviving contemporary records are those held in the archive of St George's. Inevitably, these relate only to St George's and do not allow a balanced assessment to be made. Moreover, the archive consists mainly of property deeds, which give little or no information about the context motivating a particular transaction. A land transfer could simply have been the result of a commercial decision by the college and have nothing to do with charitable purposes. There is, however, a small, but significant, element of chance survival. We know that the town's archive was extant in the mid seventeenth century, as Elias Ashmole made notes from it as part of his work in recording the history of Berkshire. These notes still exist, providing a brief glimpse of the further information which might have been available had the archive survived. An example revealing the value of Ashmole's transcriptions is the will of James Mallet noted above, which would otherwise be unknown.

Despite the difficulties of the evidence, it is clear that the alienation of town property to the College of St George to endow masses of remembrance was a common occurrence in late medieval Windsor. Evidence can be found in many cases that the senior families of the town made post mortem provision of some kind. The will made in 1507 by Thomas Brotherton alias Hunt, a wealthy local man and probably a brewer, provided for land and tenements in Windsor to pass to the Dean and Canons, '[to] support and maintain the chantries of Master Thomas Passhe and Master John Plummer' [a college canon and verger, respectively] in the college, and for his wife and himself 'to be prayed for in the bede also within the same college when it is remembered or read'.[5] Interestingly, although the will is concerned exclusively with property left to the college to provide for obligations of remembrance, it is noted to have been executed in Windsor's guildhall before the mayor and burgesses. Although this may have arisen from the practical requirements entailed in transferring urban land, it also serves to emphasise the informal links which must have existed between the college and town. Indeed, the result of repeated alienation of town land in exchange for remembrance meant that by the mid sixteenth century the major part of all town property (probably over 60%) was owned by one or other of the local 'institutions'. These were several: the Trinity guild, the parish church or else one of the royal colleges in Windsor (either the College of St George or the College of the Blessed Virgin Mary at Eton).

It should be noted, however, that the college's ownership of land in the town was not without its difficulties. Property held by the church or college was not subject to pay national taxation and, as tax was assessed on a town as a whole, if there was an element of exempt property within the town, the amount due from the remaining properties not exempt necessarily increased. In Windsor's case, and owing to the unusual concentration of exempt land in the locality, the town's entire tax assessment came to fall on a relatively small number of local townsmen. Unsurprisingly, this issue was the cause of considerable friction between the town and the Exchequer over many years, if not also with the college. It was, however, eventually resolved by reducing the town's tax liability by the estimated value of the exempt properties. This amounted to £6 in the 1630s, or about 50% of the town's total assessment.[6] The size of this reduction underlines the extent to which Windsor by the seventeenth century had become part of the college's estate, the closures of the Reformation notwithstanding.

The greater part of property in the town alienated to St George's was rented out to third parties, providing the college with a rental income. This income was then used to employ chantry priests who performed the requested obit, any surplus being divided between the Dean and Canons. Not all property granted to the college was used in this way, however. Some was specifically given to the college to be used by the minor canons, vicars, chantry priests or other college staff as accommodation within the town. Property in this category included *inter alia* four tenements in the town's main thoroughfare, Peascod Street, and significantly several tenements in Gropecount Lane, near the parish church. One of these properties was gifted by Robert de Burnham, surveyor of the works and college steward in the mid fourteenth century.[7] Gropecount Lane (most often

Gropecuntelane) was a notorious street, known to be frequented by women of easy virtue, giving rise to its explicit name. Several medieval towns and cities including London, York, Reading, Oxford and Norwich had a street with the same name and purpose. These streets were particularly popular with the clergy, despite (or perhaps because of) the church's injunction that those in holy orders were to remain celibate. Quite possibly, action to reduce the temptation towards immorality may have lain behind Denton's gift of the New Commons to the college, noted above. The town archive, if it had survived, would probably have furnished details of the challenge which this street posed to the town's authorities.

Although of note, the activity in the town's back streets was of little real economic consequence. Immeasurably more important was the college's function as an employer of local artisans. This came about in several ways: the direct employment of those engaged in building and maintenance of the college's estate; from the requirement for college servants; and indirectly, through the purchase of goods sold on theWindsor market. Inevitably, those of low estate are most often omitted from the historical record, and it is impossible to say precisely how many local people of this type found employment in or through the college. Nonetheless, it is possible to hazard a guess. If two servants were employed by each college member, perhaps sixty or seventy people, or 10% of the town's fifteenth-century working population, were connected with the college in this way. If the effects of indirect employment are included, this figure could reasonably increase to 15%. If these figures are correct, then they suggest that the college was possibly of greater, and certainly of a more consistent, benefit to the town's economy than the wealthier, although intermittently occupied, royal castle.

More precise information about the skilled labour force responsible for the construction and subsequent maintenance of the residential buildings of the college in the 1350s is available from the castle building accounts. These records note the names and occupations of a number of Windsor men, such as John Bythewood (master lime burner), John Dunstaple (carpenter), John Cosin (glazier), Osbert le Taverner (carter) and John Lokier (lock maker).[8] Such skilled men would in turn have employed a number of assistants and apprentices, also presumably from the locality. Given the limited details which survive about the residents of medieval Windsor, the fact that so many local people can be identified from the accounts suggests that a good number of the workforce at the castle were of local origin. Indeed, the building programme at the castle, carried out in the wake of the Black Death, provided a major stimulus to Windsor's economy. In contrast to many other English towns and villages of the period which went into decline, Windsor at this time grew in prosperity.

In conclusion, no account of the relationship between Windsor and St George's would be complete without noting the effects of the many pilgrims who came to the college shrines between c.1480 and 1548, permanently changing the nature of Windsor's economy. Pilgrims travelling to the town came mostly from the capital and the south-east, and their need for overnight accommodation accounts for a remarkable increase in the number of Windsor inns mentioned in the sources in this period.[9] Inns and taverns are difficult to identify in the Windsor deeds before c.1480, although they no doubt existed. By the mid sixteenth century, however, they become numerous. The college became a major investor in these premises, some of them substantial in size, such as the Talbot Inn, taking up street frontage on both Peascod Street and the High Street. There may have been thirty or more inns in Windsor by this date, representing approximately one in every twelve properties in the town. With the inns came the need for beer and brewing, a feature of the Windsor economy which was to last into the twentieth century. The influence of the College of St George on Windsor after c.1350 was therefore profound. Not only did it greatly affect the medieval town, but these changes echoed through the centuries into the modern era.

SEVEN

MEDIEVAL DECORATIVE IRONWORK IN ST GEORGE'S CHAPEL

Jane Geddes

T HE DECORATIVE IRONWORK at St George's Chapel is remarkable for many reasons. Not only does it cover a wide time span, from the 1240s to the twentieth century. In terms of variety, it covers a range of objects rarely found elsewhere, from a decorated money box to architectural tomb gates, with splendid examples of the usual door furniture, hinges and lock plates as well. Above all, it is a showcase for the finest quality of decorative iron furnishings to be found anywhere in Britain. The following chapter will introduce this treasury of metalwork, explaining the intricate techniques employed, and the function of the objects. The rich royal accounts also allow John Tresilian, master smith to Edward IV, Henry VII and Henry VIII, to emerge as the outstanding ironworker of the late Middle Ages.

In 1240 Henry III instructed Walter de Burgh to begin work on St Edward's chapel, Windsor. It was complete by 1249. Of this structure, only the Galilee survives, with its doorway forming the east wall of St George's chapel (see Fig. 17). Although the bright red and gold paint on the doors is not original, contemporary manuscripts suggest that this was a likely colour scheme (see Figs. 12 & 13 on following page). The ironwork is like the Tree of Life, delicate leaves and flowers spiralling off central stems, enlivened by raised animal heads. Each scroll terminal is a precise stamped design. This was made using a die, similar to the tool used by coin makers. Although such a technique had been used somewhat earlier by blacksmiths to create repetitive patterns on hinges (as at Faringdon, Berks.) the controlled delicacy of motifs at Windsor was new. The foliage designs basically derived from manuscripts and had been translated into delicate metal appliqué by goldsmiths like Hugo of Oignies in the early thirteenth century. His work is found on objects like golden book covers. There are some clues that the innovation and accuracy seen at Windsor was also achieved by a goldsmith. One unique design appears among the foliage: a long-armed cross whose tips touch the edge of the disc terminal. In 1247, Henry III decided to change the design on

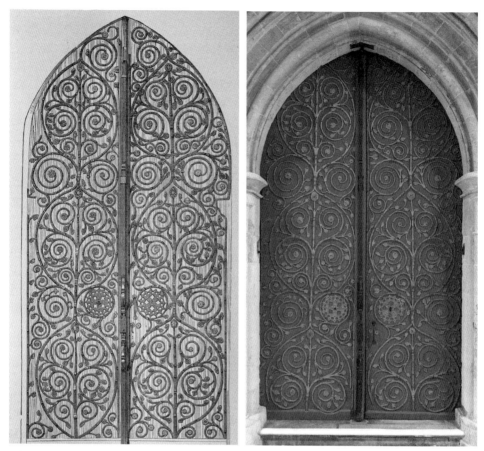

Above Fig. 12. Orlando Jewitt's mid-19th century engraving (based on C.A. Buckler's drawing) of the mid-13th century doors. Sadly the bottoms of the doors were cut off in the later 19th century.

Above right Fig. 13. The mid-13th century doors and doorway as they appear today.

the reverse of coins from a short cross in the centre of the disc, to a long cross whose arms touched the edges. This was to prevent the fraudulent clipping of coins. The long-cross issue appeared between 1247 and 1279, made by ninety-four named moneyers. One of these was Gilbert de Bonninton. Unlike almost all other medieval craftsmen, moneyers were accustomed to name their products for quality reasons. The Windsor doors are the only piece of medieval decorative ironwork in England which include a name: the prominent stamp +*Gilebertus*. Even the cross at the start of his name is a common feature on coin lettering. Of

Fig. 14. View south through Edward IV's gates into the sanctuary, as drawn by Wenceslaus Hollar in *c.* 1670.

course, Gilebertus could also be the name of a patron, but in view of the unique designs on the doors, it could well refer to the goldsmith Gilbert de Bonninton of Canterbury, inspired by the new coinage issued in 1247, and the completion of the chapel in 1249.[1]

Edward IV commissioned the next suite of ironwork, for furnishing his showpiece chapel. The building accounts indicate that between 1477 and 1484, John Tresilian was the 'principal smith'. His high annual wage of £24 5s was comparable to that of William Berkeley, the master carpenter responsible for carving the choir stalls. As a mark of their status in 1477-8, the two were awarded 10s each to purchase gowns, and they were paid double the wage of the master stone mason Henry Janyns. Later documents show that John Tresilian was also the royal clockmaker, paid 30s 5d in 1516 for his services. Thereafter, his name no longer occurs, but he was succeeded by Antony Trassilion, presumably his son, who received payments for royal clock making between 1519 and 1529, and dying in 1532. Antony's will provides additional detail about the circumstances in which a prestigious royal metalworker operated. His home was in Westminster, and Antony's will was signed by several skilled craftsmen from the Low Countries who lived nearby around the abbey. These historical details help to explain the extraordinary complexity, both in technique and design, of John's work.

Grimly black and spikey, the gates to Edward IV's tomb now face the choir across the north-east bay (Fig. 15). Originally they were gilded, to look like a glinting wooden Netherlandish altarpiece, and they faced the aisle side of the bay. They consist of the gates themselves and two half-hexagonal towers, composed of precisely fashioned mouldings and tracery so that they look like miniature architecture. The little canted bays on the gates echo the projecting bay of Edward IV's oratory above. Depth and perspective is given to the tracery by the application of pierced sheet-iron behind the openwork bars. The deeply articulated surface is built up by thousands of miniature mouldings and lancets riveted on top of each other. Once the major elements like panels had been constructed in this way, they were fastened to the internal iron frame by removable iron pegs. Celia Fiennes noticed this feature in 1698 when she wrote, 'to add to its rarity, it may all be taken piece by piece and put up in a box'. Fashioning countless accurate and repetitive components of wrought iron was precisely the skill of a medieval clock maker. Precedents for the design are to be found in the polygonal stone gate piers of Henry V's chantry at Westminster, and the flamboyant tracery of the Claude de Villa altarpiece made in Brussels around 1470. Not only were English craftsmen in close contact with their Netherlandish counterparts at this time, but Edward IV spent his exile during 1470 with Louis de Gruuthuse in Bruges. Gruuthuse introduced him to the niceties of Burgundian culture and began his own oriel chantry in Onze-Lieve-Vrouwekerk in 1472, just three years before Edward began his at Windsor.[2]

In spite of superficial resemblances to flamboyant Netherlandish work, Tresilian's designs remain uniquely English. On the door from the north aisle leading up to Edward IV's chantry is a suite of door furniture: a rectangular lock plate, a vizzy or spy-hole in the door which resembles a tiny exterior oriel window, complete with tiled roof. The plate for the door handle is an ingenious composition, using Tresilian's technique of layering one element upon another. The centre of the plate resembles the tracery of a rose window, but it is surrounded by the garter, looped softly around itself, and inscribed with the motto of the Order 'Honi soyt qi mal y pense'. On the north door to the choir is a rectangular lock plate framed by spiral columns and containing panels of openwork four-petalled flowers. The same flowers are found on the chantry lock plate and the royal gates, showing they are all by the same smith.

In the south choir aisle is an offertory box, a polygonal container made of stout iron places, standing on spindly moulded legs. The letter H is riveted on to each face of the box, for Henry VI. On the lid is an elaborate and guarded system for inserting coins: through slots covered with sliding lids, and through a series

Fig. 15. Edward IV's gates today, turned round and put on the south side of the arch by Henry Emlyn in *c.* 1787.

of miniature castle towers. It shows the same playful use of realistic motifs as the garter handle plate. Henry VI was murdered in 1471 and for political reasons his body was moved to Windsor in 1484, to promote the royal cult (See Chapter 11). Henry VI was renowned for his alms giving and coins played an important part in the thaumaturgic rites associated with his relics. Many miracles followed the bending of a coin in his honour and thus offerings at his tomb were of particular significance. Both its likely date, after 1484, and its method of construction using miniature symbolic architecture, place it in the group of Tresilian's work.[3]

In the late middle ages it became fashionable to illustrate one's name with a suitable pun or 'rebus'. The rebus was also a convenient device for identifying one's patronage, a timely reminder that money had been spent beautifying a church to speed the way through Purgatory. Sir Reginald Bray, a childless benefactor, wished to leave his mark at Windsor for posterity. His rebus, a hemp bray or crushing tool, appears extensively over the fabric of the chapel. His bequest helped to complete the nave and transepts between 1503 and 1509, and his bray appears in stone, wood, glass and iron. The lock plate to the Bray chapel in the south transept places a realistic miniature crushing machine on Sir Reginald's shield. The doors which form the south entrance to the nave have been reversed, leaving their plain cross-boarded face to the exterior. Now on the interior, their decorated face is carved with emblems of Henry VII while the moulded ribs of the door are studded with a rash of miniature iron brays. In terms of one-upmanship, this was a bold move by Sir Reginald, placing himself, may times over, on the very entrance to the chapel, alongside his monarch.[4]

Two further sets of railings, in every sense more normal and typical of their age, serve to highlight the exceptional quality of Edward IV's gates. In 1507, the Dean, Christopher Urswick, erected a chantry chapel for himself in the north-west corner of the nave. The stone plinth and stone door frame are surmounted by plain railings decorated with the painted shield of Urswick. The bars are topped by a decorative crest of trefoils set on openwork triangles. A more ferocious barrier was erected across the entrance to the Schorne chantry in about 1584, to protect the tomb of Edward , Earl of Lincoln (d.1584).[5] By this period, decorative iron in churches had slumped to a low ebb, mainly being used in a functional way and not reviving until the Baroque era. The Lincoln railings are tipped by sharp spear heads, the stanchions spiral upwards and the finials are somewhat coarse open fleurs de lys. The lock plate to the Oxenbridge Chantry in the south choir aisle, is symptomatic of this decline. John Oxenbridge was canon from 1509 to 1522. His lock plate is a plain sheet of iron with a simple raised rim and central rib concealing the key hole. The lock plate on the west door to the choir shows the influence of the Renaissance creeping in. The plate is divided into three panels by twisted bars. The plate is decorated with flat open-work patterns placed over a plain backing plate. The patterns are more like renaissance strapwork than medieval tracery, and the plate is clearly a mid sixteenth-century replacement, damaging the ribs of the 1478-85 choir doors.

The tour-de-force of medieval ironwork in the chapel was a hard act to follow, but a respectful effort was made for the King George VI chapel in the north choir aisle in 1969. Designed by George Pace and Paul Paget, spare modern bars with stripped rectilinear clusters at their tips recall their medieval predecessors in a modern evocation of the Perpendicular style.

The Gilebertus stamped ironwork set a new fashion for delicate scrolls and foliage in decorative ironwork, with later examples found at Merton College Oxford, York Minster Chapter House and the Eleanor Grille, Westminster Abbey (1293-4, by Thomas of Leighton). No smith came near to rivalling the meticulous and painstaking techniques of John Tresilian. Like the Windsor choir stalls, they do not bear comparison with any other English work although there are some fine tracery ring plates at Warwick, in the Beauchamp Chapel (1442-62) and the Dean's Chapel.[6]

EIGHT

THE BUILDING OF THE NEW CHAPEL:
THE FIRST PHASE

Tim Tatton-Brown

O N 21 MAY 1471 EDWARD IV arrived in London, having regained power in England after the two decisive battles of Barnet and Tewkesbury. Soon afterwards he had Henry VI killed in the Tower of London, and the House of York now attained sole control of the kingdom. Edward then proceeded to punish those who had resisted him, some by execution, many by the imposition of heavy fines. The situation was succinctly summed up by the *Great Chronicle* thus:

'Such as were rich were hanged by the purse, and the other that were needy were hanged by the necks, by means where of the country was greatly impoverished and the king's coffers some deal increased'.[1]

In the autumn of 1471 Edward and his queen, Elizabeth Woodville, visited Eton,[2] and authorised the work on Henry VI's new college there to start again under the supervision of the Bishop of Winchester, William Waynflete (1447-86), the founding provost. Some £16,000 had already been spent on the project under Henry VI, but work had stopped in 1461 after the king's deposition, and Edward IV decided to annex Eton to St George's; Edward had even procured a papal ball to enable him to do this.[3]

In 1471, however, Edward gave permission for work to resume, albeit on a reduced scale, perhaps because he was already thinking of a much bigger scheme for himself at Windsor. This new scheme was probably first worked out in 1472 with another bishop, Richard Beauchamp, his 'dearly beloved cousin'. Beauchamp, who had been Bishop of Salisbury since 1450, was like Waynflete a long-standing confidant of Henry VI from his earliest days.[4] However, early in 1461 he defected to Edward IV and was soon to be an even closer confidant of the new king.

By this time also, Beauchamp was completely refurbishing, and in part rebuilding the eastern end of his own cathedral at Salisbury, around the new shrine of St Osmund, whose canonisation he had secured in 1456 from the elderly and austere Spanish Pope, Callistus III. Beauchamp was also building himself a grand chantry chapel alongside the new shrine, and close to his palace in Salisbury, which he had also completely rebuilt.[5]

On 19 February 1473 letters patent were issued, saying that Beauchamp had been appointed, by the king, 'master and surveyor of works, both of the chapel of the Blessed Mary and St George within the castle of Windsor, and of divers other works there to be newly constructed'.[6] Beauchamp was then given *carte blanche* the power to acquire all the craftsmen he needed for the new work,[7] many of them probably foreigners from the Low Countries. As well as this, he was to obtain all the materials ('stones, timber, tiles, shingles, glass, iron, lead, etc.'), and put in hand their carriage to Windsor, and to make any payments relating to this.

Over the next two years, an extremely grand scheme was worked out that would take up much of the Lower Ward of Windsor Castle, with at its centre a huge new chapel that was perhaps intended to be some 240 feet long, and the project was agreed to by Edward IV, just before his invasion of France.[8] On 12 June 1475 the king who was then in Canterbury, sent Bishop Beauchamp letters patent for building 'a new chapel in honour of the Blessed Mary and St George the martyr within our Castle of Windsor'.[9] He was also given a free hand to demolish any of the buildings that 'are old and too worn away by age' or any other buildings that got in the way of the new scheme:

> 'from the west part of the chapel anciently built there to the walls of our castle, both to and upon the walls on the north side, and on the west in which the towers commonly called Cluer ys Towre and le Amener is Towre and Barner is Towre are situated, and also on the south as far as the belfry.'

A week later the king drew up his will (it is dated 20 June 1475), and in it he mentions the new chapel 'by us begoune of newe to bee buylded', making clear that work was already under way at this time. The first undertakings involved the demolition of the great kitchen and part of the chamber block, all of which were south of the great hall in the northern part of the Lower Ward[10] (see Fig. 8). Then all the almonry buildings and stables on the west (including the 'great stable') were pulled down to allow a very large new cloister (later called the 'Horseshoe cloister') to be laid out. We know that the main building work on the chapel got under way in the spring of 1477, and it seems likely that the two years before this were needed not only for the demolitions mentioned above, but also for the large amount of foundation digging, and terracing up of the hillside, on the clay and natural chalk, that was needed to create both the huge new chapel (some one hundred feet wide and 230-40 feet long) and the equally large new cloister (about

150 feet wide by 200 feet long). This proposed western cloister was so large that an area of the inner face of the massive thirteenth-century western curtain wall had to be hacked away to allow the south-western lodgings around the cloister to be fitted in (Fig. 16).

We can imagine Edward IV coming back to Windsor in 1476, after his great 'victory' in France at Picquigny (on 29 August 1475),[11] to see the ground works, and to plan fully the whole building scheme with Bishop Beauchamp and his new 'chief mason of the works', Henry Janyns. Janyns had earlier worked at Eton, and we know that he was now to be paid £12 a year (plus 10 shillings for his gown),[12] and that over the next six or so years he was buying large quantities of Taynton stone (9,755 feet of it, at 2d. a foot in 1478, for example) for the new building.[13]

The design of the new complex (choir, transept, nave and cloister) was laid out along a four-hundred-and-ten foot long axis, which ran westwards from just outside the original west doorway of Henry III's chapel. The alignment was determined by the old chapel (it is not quite east-west), and it was probably the polygonal east end (a semi-octagon) of the old chapel which inspired the unusual plan and form of the new works. Both the north and south terminations of the transept and all four of the outer chapels beyond the corners of the building,[14] as well as the western cloister, were made semi-octagonal in plan, and it is possible that the reason for this was to emphasise the 'royal' nature of the chapel, as first exemplified by the Sainte-Chapelle in Paris, and then by Henry III's new chapel at Windsor, as well as his new Westminster Abbey (with its polygonal 'chevet') and Lady Chapel.[15]

As we have seen, the main building work on the chapel got under way in the spring of 1477. Unfortunately the documented building accounts for this first year have not survived. After this, however, we do have the building accounts for the whole of the rest of the first phase of the work. The accounts continue until January 1484 (nine months after Edward IV's death), and indicate that during this period of eight years the whole of the choir was completed, with its lead-covered roof over the choir and aisles, and that the floor had been paved.[16] The elaborately-carved wooden stalls for the knights of the garter, and the dean and canons within the choir were also almost complete.

On 25 March 1477 Bishop Beauchamp was appointed dean of Windsor, in addition to his bishopric, and it is clear that right to his death on 18 October 1481 he was the main driving force behind the work. His role is touchingly commemorated in the extreme south-east corner of the chapel where the bishop and Edward IV are both shown kneeling on either side of the Cross Gneth, on the

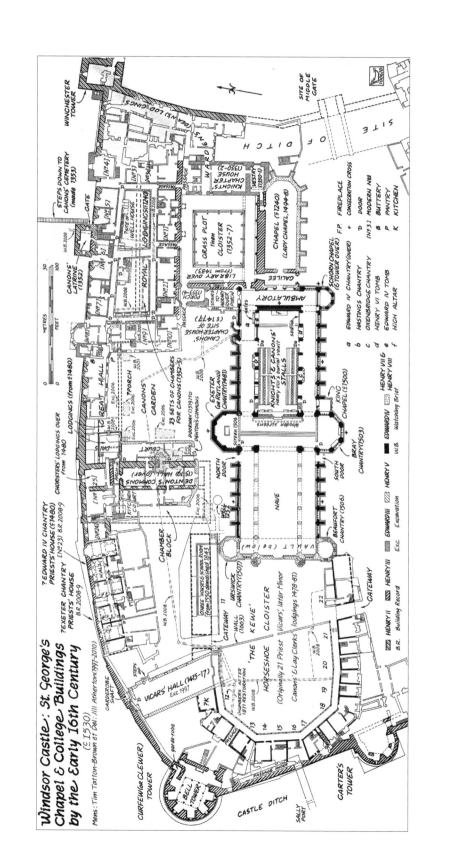

Windsor Castle: St. George's Chapel & College Buildings by the Early 16th Century

(c. 1530)

Mens: Tim Tatton-Brown et Del. Jill Atherton (1997-2010)

a EDWARD IV CHANTRY (C.1480)
b HASTINGS CHANTRY
c OXENBRIDGE CHANTRY
d HENRY VI TOMB
e EDWARD IV TOMB
f HIGH ALTAR

EDWARD IV CHANTRY (OVER)
SCHORN CHAPEL (6 TOWER OVER)
F.P. FIREPLACE
+ CONSECRATION CROSS
D DOOR
Nº 33 MODERN Nº1
B BUTTERY
P PANTRY
K KITCHEN

HENRY II
HENRY III
HENRY V
EDWARD III
EDWARD IV
HENRY VII &
HENRY VIII
B.R. Building Record
Exc. Excavation
W.B. Watching Brief

METRES 0 30 100
FEET 0 100

AMBULATORY
KNIGHTS & CANONS' STALLS
Henry VIII's burial vault
sacristy
KING EDWARD IV CHAPEL (C.1500)
Screen 1506
Wooden Screens
NAVE
VAULT (below)
BRAY CHANTRY (1503)
BEAUFORT CHANTRY (1506)
URSWICK CHANTRY (1507)
EXETER (or RUTLAND) CHANTRY (1481)
NORTH DOOR
SOUTH DOOR
WELL 1294
GATEWAY

CHAPEL (C.1240)
(LADY CHAPEL, 1494-8)
GALILEE
WESTRY (1350-?)
KNIGHTS' CHAPTER HOUSE (1350-2)
GRASS PLOT then CLOISTER (1352-7)
LIBRARY OVER (FROM 1483)
CANONS' CHAPTERHOUSE (1352-3)
SITE OF CHAPTERHOUSE (1353-4)
PORCH
STAIRS TO LIBRARY (OVER)
DOORWAY (1519) TO DENTON'S COMMONS
23 SETS OF CHAMBERS FOR CANONS (1352-3)
DENTON'S COMMONS (1519) HALL (OVER)
CHAMBER BLOCK
THREE HOUSES SCHOOL ROOM (from 1550, demolished 1843)

WINCHESTER TOWER
SITE OF MIDDLE GATE
SITE OF DITCH
WARDENS' LODGINGS
STEPS DOWN TO CANONS' CEMETERY (made 1353)
GATE
(Nº 4)
(Nº 5)
WELL HOUSE
CANONS' LODGINGS (1240)
(Nº 3)
(Nº 1)
(Nº 2)
PASSAGE
PASSAGE
CANONS' LATRINE (1352)
GREAT HALL
PORCH
CANONS' GARDEN
ROYAL LODGINGS (from 1480)
CHORISTERS' LODGINGS from 1480
EXETER CHANTRY PRIESTS' HOUSE (Nº 23)
EDWARD IV CHANTRY PRIESTS' HOUSE (C.1480)
EXETER CHANTRY PRIESTS' HOUSE

CURFEW (OR CLEWER) TOWER
BELL TOWER
CASTLE DITCH
SALLY PORT
GARTER'S TOWER
CASTLE DITCH

GARDEROBE SHAFT
CHAMBERS AFTER 1871 RESTORATION
VICARS' HALL (1415-17) Exc. 1997
'THE KEWE'
(Originally 21 Priest Vicars; later Minor Canons & Lay Clerks) lodgings 1478-81)
HORSESHOE CLOISTER
STEPS UP
garde-robe
KITCHEN COURT
HALL
DAIS
WALL (1053)
PASSAGE

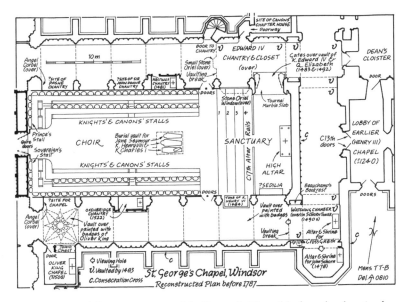

Above Fig. 17. Plan of the eastern arm of St George's Chapel before the drastic changes and additions carried out there in 1787-88 by Henry Emlyn. Note also the site of the Tudor burial vault at the very centre of the Chapel.

Opposite Fig. 16. Plan of the College of St George in the Lower Ward of Windsor Castle.

central boss of the vault. This cross, which was on the altar immediately beneath, contained one of the most precious relics in England, a supposed fragment of the true cross on which Christ died, which had been given to the college by Edward III.[17] To the bishop, this corner of the new chapel was the most sacred part of the building, counterbalancing the north-east corner of the chapel, where Edward IV's burial place and chantry chapel were being constructed. To enhance the sacredness of the south-east corner the bishop was also able to translate here the body of Blessed John Schorn, the saintly rector of North Marston in Buckinghamshire.[18] A Bull from Pope Sixtus IV (1471-84),[19] authorised this in 1478, and a shrine for Schorn's relics was made in the south-east polygonal chapel. The shrines were, of course, destroyed at the Reformation, but just to the north-west of them, on the north side of the beginning of the south choir aisle is a canopied niche for a book, beneath which is an inscription in English, which begins:

Who leyde this book here – The Reverend ffader in God Richard Beauchamp Bisschop of this Dioceyse of Sarysbury and wherfor to this entent that Preestis and ministers of Goddis chirche may have the occupation thereof seyging therin theyr divyne servyse.[20]

This text also commemorates the elaborate services and rituals, which the bishop inaugurated here, just as he had done at the east end of Salisbury Cathedral twenty years earlier.[21] It also records the '40 days of pardon' for those who came to the shrine (Fig. 17).

In his will of 1475 Edward had said that he wanted his body to be interred 'lowe in the grounde' of his new chapel with a stone laid over it. He goes on:

> We woll that overe the same Sepulture ther bee made a vowte of convenient height as the place wil suffre it and that upon the said vowte ther bee a Chapell or a Closet with an Autre convenient and a Tumbe to be made and sett there . . . [22]

His instruction is exactly what was done except that the 'Tumbe' in the chantry chapel appears never to have been made, though it was probably meant to fill the arch in that chapel on the north-east side, above the place of burial.[23] Edward IV died on 9 April 1483, and was buried in a stone laid vault, which was rediscovered below the chantry (Fig, 18) in 1789. It still contained his body in a lead coffin (as well as that of his queen, Elizabeth Woodville, who was buried there in June 1492).[24] Over the burial-vault, there lies (almost certainly still *in situ*), a large slab of black Tournai marble (or 'Touchstone' as it was then known) into which were set the superb iron gates that gave access through a Tournai marble lined arch from the north aisle to the sanctuary.[25] Unfortunately these gates were turned round and moved to the sanctuary side in 1789 (see Fig. 15), and the arch above was filled in with new decorated masonry designed by Henry Emlyn.[26] We do, however, have a fine pair of engravings by Wenceslaus Hollar, made in *c.* 1670, which show the sanctuary and choir from the west (see Fig. 28) and the gates in their original position, seen from the north choir aisle (see Fig. 14), before the 1789 changes were made.[27]

The two arches to the north choir aisle, on the north side of the sanctuary, are much lower than the other arches in the aisle arcades of the chapel. This was because Edward IV's chantry chapel (and closet) was built here from the beginning, as specified in his 1475 will. The building accounts for 1480 specifically mention 'Teynton stone called vowtynstone' for the aisles, and there can be little doubt that this 'vaulting stone' was used for the fan vaults below the chantry chapel, in the two eastern bays of the north choir aisle, as well as for the vaulting along the full length of the eastern ambulatory behind the high altar. All the other stone vaulting in the chapel was not put in until the later 1490s or later.[28] Recent cleaning work in the ambulatory has shown that the original Caen and Taynton stone vaulting is beautifully cut here, and very well-preserved.

Beneath the string course, just below the vaulting, is a remarkable concave

Fig. 18. Reconstruction of the proposed tomb for Edward IV in his chantry chapel. Note the gates beneath, with below this the actual burial vault.

chamfered course, made entirely of Caen stone. This is filled with a series of miniature carved scenes,[29] which must have taken several carver-masons many hours to cut. Similar miniature carved scenes were put into quatrefoils in the blind tracery of the relieving arches at either end of the ambulatory, and it is clear that in this first phase of work on the new chapel no expense was spared. This is hardly surprising, as we know that about £1,000 a year was being paid out by the Exchequer to the clerk of the works at St George's, one Thomas Chanceller.[30] Most of the money came from the income from the lands of the late Earls of Shrewsbury and Wiltshire, as well as those of Sir William Lovel and Lord Morley, all of which were in the king's hands at this time. Between 1478 and 1483 over £6,500 are documented as having been spent on the chapel.[31]

After Edward IV's death and the usurpation of the throne by his brother Richard of Gloucester, work continued on the building,[32] which was almost ready to receive Edward's body (he was buried there on 19 April 1483).[33] As we have seen, the documentary evidence suggests that the eastern arm was complete by the end of 1483, and it is very likely that the dean and canons had moved their daily services from the old chapel to the new choir by 1484.[34] One significant event in this year, which also suggests that the new chapel was in use, was the translation of the body of Henry VI from Chertsey Abbey to a new grave on the south side of the sanctuary in August[35] (see Fig. 23). Ironically the position was almost opposite the burial place of Edward IV, the man who had ordered his murder. More importantly, however, it was close to the two shrines – those of the Cross Gneth and John Schorn – in the south-east corner. By 1484 Henry VI's tomb at Chertsey was already becoming a place of pilgrimage, and in bringing the quasi-saint's body to St George's, Richard was clearly making a political statement, as well as trying to stop the unofficial Lancastrian cult at Chertsey.[36] Perhaps Richard III was beginning to think of his own burial in St George's Chapel, but when he died on Bosworth Field, a year later, nothing had been decided.

For about a decade from 1484-94 no building work seems to have taken place at St George's, except for some minor repairs to the temporary screen in the 'cros yle' (i.e. the transept) in 1492.[37] If we can imagine visiting the chapel at this time, we would probably have found that the Horseshoe cloister on the west had been completed (it was framed up in 1478-81), but that it faced into the empty shell of the nave, with at its far end the temporary screen in the transept, and within it a temporary west door and window above. The polygonal transept walls and the buttressed walls for the first six bays of the nave, up to window sill level, were probably all that had been completed. At the west end of this uncompleted nave a terrace wall must have dropped down about ten feet to the level of the cloister garth.

East of the new chapel, the old thirteenth-century chapel (as refurbished in 1350-1) was still intact but empty. In 1493-4 Henry VII started to think about his own tomb, and decided to place it in the middle of the old chapel, rebuilt as a Lady Chapel, close to a new shrine for 'St' Henry VI. Work on this new Lady Chapel commenced in the spring of 1494 and, as Leland tells us, Henry VII pulled down 'the old chapel of Edward III' and built 'from the foundations' a new one.[38] This is the building, now known as the 'Albert Memorial Chapel', which we see today, and payments of about £4,700 were made, on the king's behalf, for the cost of the work.[39]

In February 1498, however, just as the rebuilding of the Lady Chapel was nearing completion, the abbots of Westminster and Chertsey mounted bids to reclaim the body of Henry VI.[40] The abbot of Chertsey pointed out that his church had been Henry VI's original burial place, while his counterpart at Westminster cited the depositions of the now-elderly men who had witnessed Henry VI himself visiting St Edward's chapel in the abbey to mark out the exact place for his burial.[41] This last evidence won over both the council and the king himself, and the work at Windsor abruptly stopped, and preparations were made to transfer 'St' Henry's body to Westminster. In the event, the move never happened; Henry's body remained at Windsor. As is well known, however, a superb new Lady Chapel was created at Westminster which was to become Henry VII's own burial place and that of his queen.

Once royal interest in St George's had ceased in 1498 (and the money had dried up), it was left to senior figures around Henry VII, among them Dean Christopher Urswick, Bishop Oliver King and, most notably, Sir Reynold (or Reginald) Bray, to supervise and pay for completion of the chapel. It is perhaps ironic, therefore, that it was Henry's son and successor, Henry VIII, who should have expressly chosen to be buried in the chapel beside his queen, Jane Seymour, in the small vault at the centre of the choir (Fig. 17). It is also ironic that no monument survives today to this most famous of English kings, though large parts of a monument in the Lady Chapel were made for him, and then destroyed. [42]

APPENDIX

The Site of the Tudor Burial Vault in St George's Chapel

In the middle of the quire of St George's Chapel is a large black marble slab, placed there 'by command of King William IV, 1837,' which records that Jane Seymour, Queen of King Henry VIII (1537), King Henry VIII (1547), King Charles I (1648, *recto* 1649), and an infant child of Queen Anne are buried in a vault *beneath this marble slab*. Recent research, however, has shown that this cannot be correct. The vault almost certainly lies some four meters to the east of this in the middle of the next bay, which itself is the central bay of the quire and sanctuary in the eastern arm of the chapel (Fig. 17). This is exactly where it is described as being in Henry VIII's will, in which he directs 'that our body be buried and interred in the quire of our College in Windsor, midway between the stalls and the high altar, with the body of our true and loving Queen Jane and there be made and set as soon as conveniently may be done after our diescease by our executor, at our costs and charges . . .'.

The vault is midway between the stalls on the north and south sides, but also midway between the high altar on the east, and the return stalls (including the

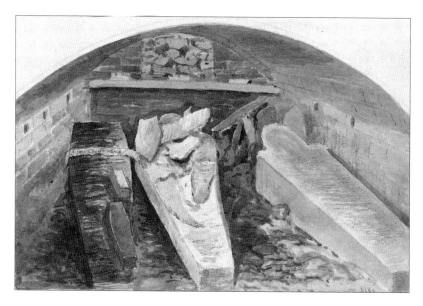

Fig. 19. A.Y. Nutt's watercolour of the Tudor vault, looking west, in 1888.

Sovereign's and Prince's stalls) on the west. This brick burial vault was probably constructed in the quire, beneath the original Purbeck marble paving soon after 24th October 1537, when Jane Seymour died, in childbirth, at Hampton Court Palace. By the time of Henry VIII's death, almost ten years later, he had long decided to have an elaborate tomb for himself, and his queen, in the Lady Chapel to the east, and that a new burial vault would be made there for them beneath this tomb (as happened with Henry VII, and his queen, in the Lady Chapel at Westminster Abbey[43]). This never happened.

By the time of Charles I's execution on 30th January 1649, and subsequent burial in St George's Chapel on 9th February, the position of the vault seems to have been lost (no large slab is then known to have marked its site), but by 'beating gently upon the pavement with a staff in the quire', a hollow sound was heard, 'and ordering the stones and earth thereunder to be removed, discover'd a descent into a vault, where two coffins were laid near one another'.[44] Charles I's coffin was then probably inserted into the vault, with little ceremony, through an opening on the vault's west side, and soon afterwards it was again concealed beneath the floor (Fig. 19). In about 1686, Dr. William Child, the long-serving chapel organist, paid for new black and white paving to be laid in the quire,[45] and the tudor burial vault may have been re-exposed at this time, as ten years later (in 1696), it is recorded that a

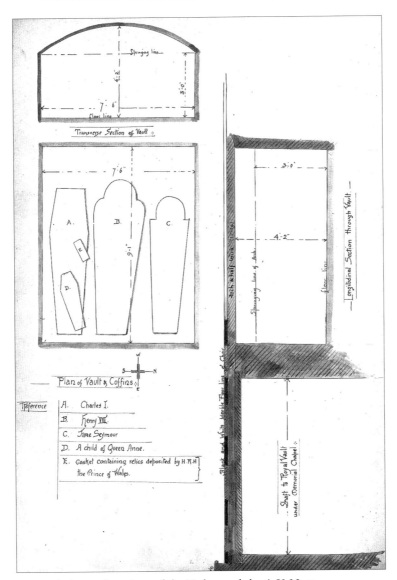

Fig. 20. Measured plan and sections of the Tudor vault by A.Y. Nutt.

stillborn son of Queen Anne was put in the vault in a coffin.[46]

In 1813, during the construction of the shaft, cut through the natural Chalk, for access to the tunnel into the west end of George III's new burial vault under the Lady Chapel (or Tomb House, as it was then called), the Tudor burial vault was again accidentally uncovered. When the Prince Regent was told of this, he ordered an official examination of the vault, and this was carried out on 1st April 1813 in his presence, and a full record of this examination was published soon afterwards by a witness, Sir Henry Halford, who was the king's, and Prince Regent's official physician.[47] In his account, Halford describes the vault and its contents, and says that it 'is situated in the centre of the choir, opposite the eleventh Knight's stall, on the Sovereign's side'. This is what may have misled those responsible for laying the new black marble stone in the floor in 1837, as at that time the Tudor vault was apparently not opened, or even located.

In 1861, possibly in connection with work for the Duchess of Kent's or the Prince Consorts' funerals, A.Y. Nutt (see below) records that the eastern end of the vault was again exposed 'during certain structural works then undertaken in connection with the passage that leads thence beneath the choir pavement, on under the altar, into the larger Royal Vault of George III'. He also tells us that a sketch of the four coffins within the vault was also made at this time.

The final, and most recent, opening of the Tudor burial vault was carried out on 13th December 1888, when relics of Charles I, which had been removed in 1813, were returned to the vault in a new box. This was overseen by the Prince of Wales (later Edward VII) and the Dean, with Queen Victoria's permission (on condition that no one entered the vault or disturbed the coffin). A written report, as well as a series of measured drawings (Fig. 20), were made at this time by the chapter surveyor, A.Y. Nutt, which locate the vault precisely in relation to the 1813 shaft into the George III burial vault, already mentioned.[48] This leaves no doubt of the position of the Tudor vault. A.Y. Nutt also says in his report that 'the vault is in the centre of the chapel midway between the Sovereign's stall and the high altar, at the fourth bay from either end of the seven bays of the choir'. He then goes on to describe how six of the small black and white marble squares in the floor were raised on the south side, (and not the black marble slab) followed by the removal of mortar bedding and about twenty bricks in the brick vault, all done 'with the greatest care, so that no debris should fall on the coffin (of Charles I) beneath'. Surprisingly, despite all these accounts of the rediscovery and opening of the Tudor burial vault, none of the many books published on St George's Chapel in the last century or so record that the black 1837 slab does not accurately mark the site of the vault.

NINE

THE ARCHITECTURE OF ST GEORGE'S CHAPEL

Peter Kidson

B Y THE STANDARDS that apply to most medieval monuments, we may consider ourselves well informed about the building of St George's Chapel. Letters patent of King Edward IV, his own and other wills, various accounts submitted to the royal exchequer, and miscellaneous items from sources beyond the court, allow us to offer plausible and even definitive answers to many of the questions that are likely to be asked about it. Thus we can say roughly when the scheme was first mooted, and we are given some idea why the king thought it desirable to have a new chapel at Windsor. The men who controlled the finances are named in the records. So are some of the craftsmen who designed, built and furnished the chapel. For its early stages, the year to year expenditure listed item by item has survived so that for a while at least we can follow with some confidence the progress of the work.

All this has been set out in such exemplary detail elsewhere that it is tempting to suppose that nothing further remains to be done.[1] It is true that written documents are unlikely to yield any further information which will seriously alter what we already know about the chapel and there are unlikely to be any unknown buildings that would shed further light on the origins of the style. Nevertheless there are matters on which the Windsor documents have always been silent, matters which must have had a profound bearing on its design, and about which we are bound to speculate if we wish to understand it properly. Moreover, the building itself, though it has been meticulously examined, has perhaps not yet yielded up all its secrets.

Edward IV, like the first founder of the college, Edward III, was cast in the heroic mould. His contemporary, Philippe de Commynes, was full of admiration for his courage in fighting eight or nine battles on foot, i.e. without a chance of flight. This was real dedication to St George. It is true that Edward's invasion of France in 1475, ostensibly intended to reopen the Hundred Years' War, ended with a comfortable French subsidy instead of glory; and this was not at all in the great tradition. However, by then the chapel was started, and the ignominious pension did at least offset the prodigious expense.

In general terms the chapel can be seen as the thank-offering of a man who had been stretched to the limit by the hazards of civil war, and who survived by the narrowest of margins. Yet by the same token, it was also a monument to the glorious future of his dynasty. From yet another point of view it could be construed as a temple of pageantry and a gesture of appreciation toward the military aristocracy whose preoccupations the king shared and admired, and with whose support he had won and kept the crown. Edward did not refound the Garter, but its self-esteem must have been wonderfully inflated by what he did for it. Some reflection of this is to be seen in the privilege which was extended to some of the Garter knights of being buried in the chapel with the king.[2] In a more precise sense, however, Edward brought together two ideas of a knights' chapel and a mausoleum. This was the essential novelty, and whether or not he was conscious of what he was doing, the notion that they could be combined was full of symbolic implications. In no sense was the identification casual or superficial. The thirteen places over Edward's tomb were almost certainly intended for specially appointed bedesmen. Presumably they were either to replace or augment the traditional weepers, whose presence graced royal tombs of previous generations. Their professional services cannot have been required all at the same time; and though the combined prayers of the thirteen would no doubt benefit the king's soul in purgatory, it is difficult to resist the impression that they were to be there not so much in their own right as to represent the knights. In other words it was the order rather than the clergy who gave meaning to the whole arrangement.

While there was nothing improper or irregular about the idea of a king being buried among his knights, whether living or dead, it was undeniably a departure from custom in the direction of Romance or even folklore. Legendary kings, Arthur among them, were supposed to be sleeping with their warriors, awaiting a future call to battle. There is no need to suppose that Edward entertained any such wild fancies on his own account. But he subscribed wholeheartedly to notions of kingship in which the pursuit of fame and the practice of chivalry were declared motives of policy. Charles the Bold of Burgundy, the most romantic and flamboyant ruler of the fifteenth century, was Edward's brother in law. His nephew by marriage was the Hapsburg Emperor Maximilian – the 'last of the Knights'. All of them would have acknowledged the inspiration of the great conquerors of antiquity, the Old Testament, and the Christian past, who supplied most of the subject matter for medieval secular romances, and who came to be known collectively as the Nine Worthies. North of the Alps it was not easy to disentangle Romance from history; and for most uncritical minds, the Romances were history. So they were taken seriously. They provided the only standards by which men of action could measure themselves. What this amounts to, put into the language of historians, is that Edward and his kinsmen belonged to two worlds. In part they were still men of the Middle Ages; but in other respects they shared the outlook of the Renaissance. Maximilian's tomb in the Hofkirche at Innsbruck, around which statues of the Worthies still stand guard, was in a sense the monument which most perfectly expressed their ambiguous ideal. But a generation earlier, Edward's chapel at Windsor had been conceived in a similar spirit; and it has a claim to be regarded as a tentative anticipation of the great visionary funeral chapels of sixteenth-century Europe.

If Edward had lived longer on the continent, he might have commissioned a more cosmopolitan work on his return, one that gave full expression to the complexities of his character. As it was, however, despite his exile, he ostensibly remained thoroughly English, his taste circumscribed by preferences as yet little modified by influence from abroad. Apart from the ceremonial surrounding the Order of the Golden Fleece, which made a deep impression on him, things that he had seen appear to have left only one lasting memory: of the watching loft, high up in the choir of a church at Bruges for the use of the ducal family, a feature which duly found its way into his new chapel. When it was finished, the chapel looked entirely at home among English churches of its time, which was as it should be if one of its purposes was to provide St George with his only great church in the country of which he was the patron saint. For this to be done effectively it had to be outstanding by the standards of existing monuments, and that is precisely what it was: the most expensive English church of the fifteenth century, and in style among the most up to date. There were echoes of other buildings, some obvious, others less so. This makes it all the more puzzling that in certain respects St George's is quite unlike any other great church of its time in the country. The vista of the nave is very grand, but Gothic purists would say that it is either too wide or too low, in other words that there is something odd about the proportions. This can be demonstrated by comparing it with its nearest equivalent among the recipients of royal bounty, and one with which it might be expected to have close connections, i.e. Westminster Abbey. The width of the nave at Windsor, whether measured edge to edge or centre to centre of the arcade piers, is actually greater than at Westminster, whereas the height of the abbey church, c.102ft, is not far short of twice that of the chapel, c.54ft. Admittedly Westminster was an extreme case, but so also was St George's.

Architectural historians have seldom failed to comment on this peculiarity, or to suggest explanations, though none has been so conclusive as to put an end to all further discussion. Here, the design will be approached not as an aspect of style but the product of working methods that architects habitually used in the selection of dimensions for their buildings. In a sense this merely restates the problem in a different language, but it puts the design into a context where connections of a non-stylistic kind can be perceived, which may shed unsuspected light on its origins. In order to do so, something must first be said about these methods. The subject is both complicated and unfamiliar, and this is not the place to set out the argument in full, but a brief summary should at least make what follows intelligible.

The preamble to any major commission in the Middle Ages was probably not much different from what it is today. There would be a meeting between the patron and his architect in which the general character of what was required would be clarified. The architect would then convert this into a design, i.e. a set of shapes and dimensions, and submit it for approval. Work could not proceed until there was agreement, tacit or contractual, about something that could only become a practical proposition for an architect when it was quantified, that is, turned into numbers. The basic principle of the art of design was that every dimension except one should be taken from another, the exception being the baseline that was usually, though not always, one of the constituents. The connections took the form of ratios which had been familiar to the masonic profession, if not the rest of the world, from time immemorial. The approved list was not long, but its brevity was not felt to be constricting in an age that had minimal use for diversity.

The ratios were not an arbitrary collection. The core group were features of regular geometrical figures, for instance the ratio of the side to the diagonal of a square ($1:\sqrt{2}$), or that between the side and the perpendicular of an equilateral triangle ($2:\sqrt{3}$), or what is perhaps best known to us as the Golden Section, which was involved in the construction of the pentagon and its derivatives. It is a feature of all these ratios that none of them can be expressed exactly in terms of whole numbers. On the other hand, the mathematicians of classical antiquity had worked out and handed down to posterity certain standard approximations which were recognised to fall within reasonable limits of practical accuracy. Indeed there were formulas for calculating whole series of these approximations so that it was seldom difficult to find one that would fit a given situation. Thus for $\sqrt{2}$, there was 5:7 or 7:10; 12:17 or 17:24; 29:41 or 41:58 etc; for $\sqrt{3}$, there were 4:7; 11:9; 15:26 etc. There was also $\sqrt{5}$, which could be represented by 4:9;

13:19; 17:38; 21:47 and so on. It was from these $\sqrt{5}$ numbers that the so-called Fibonacci Series was deduced, i.e. 1, 1, 2, 3, 5, 8, 13, 21, 34, 55........in which each sum is the same as its two predecessors, with each successive pair edging closer to the exact value of the ratio without ever getting there. That was true of all these approximations. Not that architects could ever hope to achieve extreme precision, and they attached no great value to it. It may be that they excused the imperfections, especially in the design of churches, because they symbolised man's inability to encapsulate the infinity of God in material form; but essentially it was the conviction that their ratios had been revealed, and were not arbitrary inventions, that mattered. By the end of the fifteenth century they no longer knew that the mathematical underpinning had been worked out in the ancient world, and could only point to tradition to justify what they did, but so long as no one asked awkward questions, that was a strength rather than weakness.

Around this nucleus a mass of subsidiary know-how accumulated, much of it well founded, like inverted forms of the original version, e.g. 45/26 for $\sqrt{3}$, or compound ratios such as $\sqrt{2} \times \sqrt{3}$ for $\sqrt{6}$, $\sqrt{2} \times \sqrt{5}$ for $\sqrt{10}$, or $\sqrt{7}$ which could be got from the relation between every other term in the Fibonacci Series. But some of it was just convenient rules of thumb that were strictly false, and this got architects into bad odour with serious mathematicians, who were beginning to resurface in the fifteenth century. For the designer of St George's, however, the tradition was still sacrosanct.

It follows from the short list of ratios that it should not take long to deduce both the unit measure of the design, and the sense of its principal dimensions. Up to a point that is the case. St George's being a royal building, it is never in doubt that the architect used the standard English foot, and the deceptive ease with which the plan can be read as a set of interlocking ratios is reassuring on that score. John Harvey, who was not put off by the quirky proportions, and saw it as 'the last great building of the Perpendicular style' or 'the finest of all Perpendicular interiors of the fifteenth century',[3] clearly felt that it was a masterpiece. There is no need to dissent from that opinion – so long as it does not demean King's College Chapel, Cambridge – but it does need qualifying. As a one-off commission that fell into none of the recognised categories of 'great church', being neither cathedral, nor abbey, nor orthodox collegiate foundation, nor just a funeral chapel, but a conflation of aspects of all four, it was perhaps inevitable that the design should also be out of the ordinary, and its high repute should not conceal the fact that it was a 'royal peculiar' in more senses than one.

As built, the plan could be described as an elongated rectangle, with additions at the corners that resemble the oriels of secular halls. In shape these are five sides of an octagon, and there are similar but larger octagonal attachments to the longer sides, not quite in the middle, which indicate the presence of a transept. The setting out seems to have been done with exemplary care. Errors of the kind that were always unavoidable were never more than a few inches. It is therefore disconcerting to find that what looks like the most promising line of enquiry is ostensibly marred at the start by a quite exceptional inaccuracy. Despite this flaw, however, the argument is worth following through since it leads to what, in a different form, was almost certainly one of the contributory factors in the formation of the design, if not the complete solution.

It starts from the width of the choir, which from side to side measures almost exactly 36ft. The wall to wall width of the church when the side aisles are included, is uniformly c.71ft throughout the building. There is an obvious temptation to read this as 36 x 2, i.e. 72ft. On a small-scale plan the difference is imperceptible. If the overall width of St George's really was meant to be 72, a fruitful idea leaps at once to mind. 72 is the given width of the nave and aisles of Westminster Abbey. Moreover it has sometimes been asserted that the nave proper at the abbey is also 36ft wide. That is not the case: notionally it is 38ft from centre to centre of the arcade piers. Though similar, the cross section ratios of the abbey could not be repeated at St George's without another fudge. But the idea that there might have been a token connection between the two buildings gets unexpected support from the overall length. St George's as built is in the vicinity of 230ft. How long the abbey was before Henry VII's Chapel replaced the Lady Chapel that was begun in 1220, turns on the implications of an excavation in 1923,[4] which uncovered meagre traces of what has been construed as part of the apse. If it was, it can be worked out that the end of the chapel would have been in the vicinity of 510ft from the west end. There is confirmation for this inference in the manifest affinity between 510 and the rest of the design, most notably the 2:5 ratio with the breadth of the transept, and the 1:5 ratio with the height of the vaults. The great unit of the Westminster design was 17ft. 510 is 30 x 17, or 60 x 8.5. St George's is all but 27 x 8.5 (strictly 229.5, a possible reading of the length, but no doubt rounded up to 230). 27:60 reduces to 9:20, which is the reciprocal form of 9/4 for $\sqrt{5}$. Thus the sense of the length of the chapel was in all probability that of a $\sqrt{5}$ ratio with that of the abbey. Related dimensions were an accepted way of conveying the idea that there was some kind of continuity between them, and Edward IV's evident intention that his new church should succeed Westminster as the mausoleum for future royalty made a connection of

Opposite Fig. 21. Phased plan of St George's Chapel and the Albert Memorial Chapel.

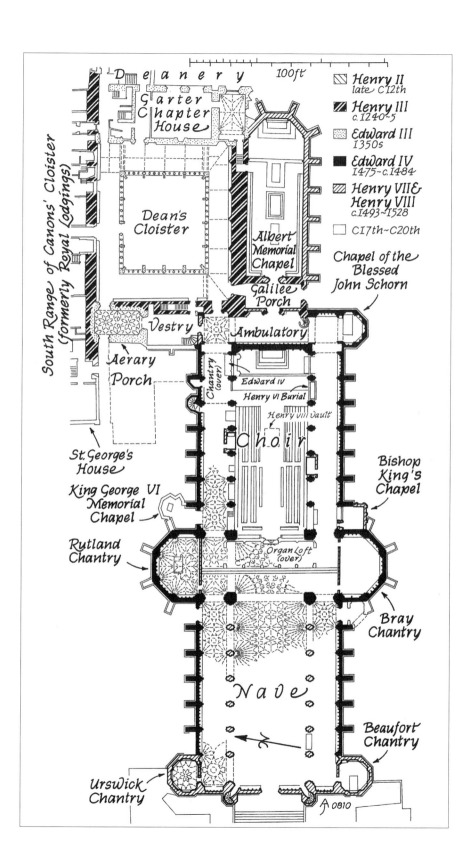

Deanery

Garter Chapter House

100ft

Henry II
late C12th

Henry III
c.1240-5

Edward III
1350s

Edward IV
1475-c.1484

Henry VII &
Henry VIII
c.1493-1528

C17th-C20th

Dean's Cloister

Albert Memorial Chapel

Chapel of the Blessed John Schorn

Galilee Porch

South Range of Canons' Cloister (formerly Royal Lodgings)

Vestry

Ambulatory

Aerary Porch

Chantry (over)

Edward IV

Henry VI Burial

Henry VIII Vault

Choir

St. George's House

King George VI Memorial Chapel

Bishop King's Chapel

Rutland Chantry

Organ Loft (over)

Bray Chantry

Nave

Beaufort Chantry

Urswick Chantry

N 0810

some kind a virtual necessity. It was, however, a very esoteric way of spelling out the message, imperceptible to the world at large. To make the point clear a more substantial link would be required, such as a royal chapel that could be identified with the choir of St George's, but that is precisely what cannot be found.

The choir of St George's is in effect a self-contained entity within an entity, 36ft wide and 90 or 92ft long, depending on whether the measurement is taken from the west wall to the reredos, or from the threshold to the east wall. If there was a model, a likely choice in view of the Westminster connection might have been the Lady Chapel, but that was a complete non starter. If the arcades of Henry VII's Chapel stand on the old foundations, as they are thought to do,[5] the width cannot have been much more than 33ft, and was probably the same as in the nave, i.e. 34. Moreover the Lady Chapel was far longer than 92ft. St Stephen's Chapel would have been closer to the mark. Published plans seem to agree that the length was c.90, and given figures for the width vary between 26 and 38, though no one else agreed with Carter's estimate of 38.[6] The rest fall well below 36. There may be others, but even if a comparable plan does exist somewhere, there is still the problem of the height and the vexed question of the space frame.

In Brakspear's section of the choir of St George's (Fig. 22) the height is shown as c.54ft, which makes a ratio of 3:2 with the width. This was not unknown in church architecture, but it was seldom if ever found in churches of high regard, more appropriate for unpretentious parish churches, which is not where to seek analogies for St George's. In fact ecclesiastical buildings of any sort are unlikely to produce the answer. The place to look is among secular halls. Not least of the oddities of St George's is that at first it had a timber ceiling rather than a masonry vault, and part of this was actually in place over the east end when Edward IV was buried there in 1483. Before the work was finished, however, it was replaced by the present equivalent in stone, which is a clue to its approximate form. The shallow profile of the span is quite exceptional among late Gothic vaults – it rises no more that 14ft over a distance of 36.[7] The obvious explanation is that it occupies the dimensions allocated to its timber predecessor, from which it follows that the latter could not have been a vast hammer beam affair. Some idea of what it might have looked like can perhaps be seen at Crosby Hall, now in Chelsea, which was built shortly before St George's.[8]

Crosby Hall is worth a closer look. The man for whom it was built, Sir John Crosby, was a wealthy City of London luminary who backed the Yorkist side in the Wars of the Roses, and was especially helpful to Edward IV in their later stages. This procured a knighthood for him in 1471. His house in Bishopsgate, of which the hall is the only surviving part, dated from the late 1460s. It was

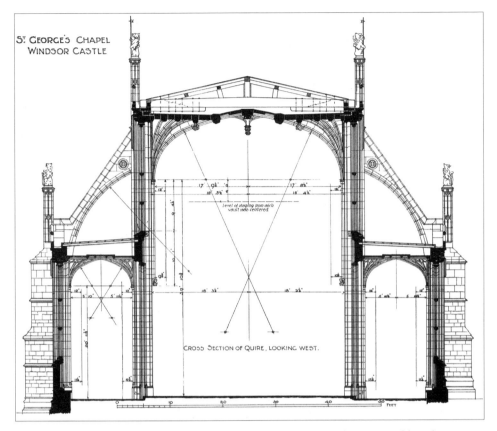

Fig. 22. Cross-section of the quire of St George's Chapel, drawn by Sir Harold Brakspear.

then the loftiest hall in the city, being all of 40ft high, on a plan that was c.27 x 69. If these dimensions are compared with those of the choir of St George's, the correlation is all but consistent: 27 and 36 are related as 3:4; so are 69 and 92; and three quarters of 54 is 40.5. This coincidence was almost certainly no accident. The name of Crosby's architect is not recorded, but on the strength of stylistic similarities with Eltham Palace, Harvey thought that he might have been Thomas Jurdan, who was 'sarjeant of the king's masonry' in 1461, and was still in royal service when he died in 1482.[9] In his capacity as the king's mason, it is highly probable that Jurdan was responsible for the great hall at Eltham (36 x 101 in plan, 55 high), built between 1475 and 1480,[10] and it would not be stretching credibility unduly if at an earlier stage of his career he had been seconded to Crosby to design his great hall for him as one of a series of perks that he got from the king. The house was royal enough for Richard III to use after

Crosby's death. Nor is it out of the question that his specifications for Crosby Hall were upgraded for use at Windsor by the Oxford mason Henry Janyns, who is known to have been in charge there between 1478 and 1484.

The conclusion to which these various lines of thought lead is that the design of St George's is likely to have been the work of someone very well acquainted with both Westminster Abbey and Crosby Hall, an unusual combination of sources, access to which by masons whose names are known to us appears to have been confined to the king's mason Thomas Jurdan. The design of the chapel was essentially a fusion of two rectangles: the overall plan and the separate plan of the choir, which was possible by virtue of their fortuitous possession of a common factor: i.e. a unit of 23. This was one tenth of the length that linked the plan to the abbey, and one quarter of the length that linked the choir to Crosby Hall. Apart from that, it almost certainly did not escape notice that half the breadth of the transept, which itself was half the length of the chapel, i.e.57.5, was all but the geometrical mean to which the length and breadth of the choir were related as 8/5 and 5/8. Otherwise there is no sense of the design emanating out from a seminal nucleus; it was more like a case of an extraneous organ successfully transplanted.

Lengthwise 230 was divided in the ratio of 7:8 at the line of piers in front of the choir screen. This was the axis of the transept. The extensions of the transepts on either side of the core rectangle were 22ft deep and 31ft wide, in other words they were constructed around a $1:\sqrt{2}$ ratio, which though not very accurate, was one of the few for which there is medieval documentation (31/22 being 24/17 + 7/5).[11] It follows that, in theory if not exactly in fact, the extensions formed five sides of octagons. On the west side of the dividing line the length of the nave was notionally 107.33ft. If the width was 71, the ratio of the shape was 1:1.51174.... As the dimensions of the nave were the product of ratios imposed on the plan as a whole, it is hardly surprising that this looks like a nonsense. But in design terms there was nothing random about it. It has the sense of being as the golden section to $\sqrt{6}$ times a common term, 43.81..., which was related to 115 as 5:13, i.e. two steps on the Fibonacci Series. At the west end where the façade broadens out to include the 'oriel' chapels, the internal width becomes almost exactly 100ft, which is $c.71 \times \sqrt{2}$.

On the other side of the dividing line the east end in theory takes up 122.666...ft. Most of this is occupied by the 92ft of the choir. 92 is three-quarters of 122.666. The position of the choir was not symmetrical. It was probably fixed by the high altar, which was often, as it may have been here, at the apex of an equilateral triangle whose baseline was in the transept. The fourth quarter of 122.666..., i.e. 30.666...., was divided in the ratio of 3:2 between 18.4 and 12.2666..., of which the former is one fifth of 92, and the latter one tenth of 122.666.... 18.4 was assigned to the ambulatory beyond the choir, and 12.2666... to the screen in front of it.

The cross-section ratios of the choir appear to have the singular distinction of defeating the system. The Westminster model does not work: the choir proper is wider, the overall width slightly narrower than at the abbey, and alternatives prove hard to find. The notional breadth of the arcade piers is ostensibly one tenth of 36, i.e. 3.6, making the centre to centre distance 39.6. This would normally be construed as 40; but if so the aisles would be 15.5, and the ratio 1:2.580..., which would almost certainly be invalid. If 39.6 was used instead of 40, the ratios would become 1:2.5223...:1, which is no better. What probably happened is that appearances were saved by the simple expedient of declaring the width of the choir to be 37.5, which would allow it to be claimed that the Westminster ratios of 1: $\sqrt{5}$:1 were in fact used; but what this really means is that the designer preferred to bend the rules rather than tamper with the integrity of the Crosby Hall model.

There is confirmation of a kind for this conclusion in the elevation, where the single design ratio focuses on the height of the vault springers. This is given in Brakspear's section as all but 40ft. The ratio between 40 and 54, i.e. 1:1.35, is perhaps noteworthy as an indication of the shallow profile of the vault, but the diagonal of the rectangle 40 x 36 is much more interesting, for it is 53.814..., i.e. in effect 54. In other words the height of St George's was in a sense already present at Crosby Hall, and the difference between them became the rise of the chapel vault.

The recognition that a shape with secular connotations has been woven into the design of a major ecclesiastical foundation can perhaps be said to solve the problem of the peculiar proportions of St George's, but it does so only by restating it in a form that takes it on to a different plane: what did it mean, or did it mean anything at all? Normally the choir of a great church was the preserve of the clergy, and in a collegiate chapel the proper place for the laity was at the west end. If there was a distinction between vaults and no vaults, the choir was the part that was vaulted. Yet at St George's the fan vaults were in the side aisles, and the choir started with a timber roof. It looks almost like a deliberate inversion of the normal order. There is no question of the clergy not using the choir: they were in regular attendance, the Garter Knights only on rare occasions. Nevertheless, it is in the choir that the secular element was to be found, as though to be a perpetual reminder that it was for them that the chapel had been built.

Could this have been the mainspring of Edward IV's project? St George's was his only pious foundation. He gave no college to either university, and one of his first acts on becoming king in 1461 was effectively to halt work on King's College chapel. It was not until 1479 that, under pressure from Bishop Waynflete of Winchester, he relented to the extent of restoring enough funding for it to be continued. But by instinct he was no patron of scholars. His heart was with the noble order of knighthood, and it would be in line with his contempt for his unmilitary predecessor if he insisted that his chapel for the Knights should be as unlike Henry VI's as possible, even defying all the conventions by allowing his architect to incorporate a secular theme into the design.

There is of course no hard evidence to confirm this speculation, only its apparent consistency with aspects of Edward IV's enigmatic character that can perhaps be taken for granted. It may be way off the mark, but in the absence of serious competition, it is worth an airing.

TEN

THE FEAST OF THE ORDER OF THE GARTER AT WINDSOR, 1476

Anne F. Sutton and Livia Visser-Fuchs

BY THE TIME OF Edward IV the Order of the Garter, with its select membership of the sovereign and twenty-five companion knights, and its ceremonies at Windsor, was well established. Edward made a few changes to the Order's ordinances, including certain services honouring the Virgin Mary, patron of the Order with St George, and the establishment of the office of chancellor in 1475. Most important, Edward strengthened the endowment of the College of St George and rebuilt its chapel. The feast day of St George, 23 April, was celebrated by the court and household at Windsor each year. In theory, the sovereign and the knights should all have attended. In practice, however, attendance during Edward's reign was often very low, as few as two or three. The sovereign himself could appoint a deputy if he was unable to be present. The knights were expected to assemble on the eve of the feast and meet together at terce, with strict regulation of dress. They attended vespers on the eve and on the feast day itself and made offerings. The celebrations concluded with a requiem mass for recently deceased knights on the day after the feast. The dates of the meetings might be changed to accommodate Easter and the days of the week (as they were in 1476), but a chapter was held on the feast itself wherever the king was. It was one of the most important dates in the king's calendar, but despite his devotion to the saint and his undoubted respect for the Order, Edward IV was only able to attend six feasts at Windsor during his twenty-two year reign: in 1463, 1467, 1472, 1473, 1476 and 1477.[1]

The records describing the ceremonies of the Garter during Edward's reign are poor, although they improve in the 1470s. There is the narrative by Bluemantle Pursuivant of events in 1471 and 1472, which includes the feast of St George and the ceremonies surrounding the reception of Louis of Gruuthuse and his creation as Earl of Winchester in 1472.[2] Bluemantle would have been expected to take a particular interest in the Order of his title like his superior, Garter King of Arms, both offices created by Henry V with titles referring to the two most distinguishing elements of the regalia, the garter and the blue mantle. The original narrative of the festivities of 1476 seems likely to have come also from the pen of Bluemantle; it survived in two copies of which an abbreviated version was printed by John Stow in his *Annals* and a slightly longer one was printed by Anstis in his *Register*.[3]

1476 was a comparatively quiet year for Edward compared to the previous one, during which he had invaded France. He had achieved an annual pension from Louis XI and had money to spend. He planned the reburial of his father and eldest brother, Richard, Duke of York, and Edmund, Earl of Rutland, at Fotheringhay in July, and his plans to rebuild St George's Chapel to enhance the surroundings of the Garter and to house his own tomb were at an advanced stage, under the direction of Richard Beauchamp, Bishop of Salisbury, a close friend of the king. Demolition of the old buildings had begun in June 1475, but work on the foundations probably only began in March 1477 and the narrator of the 1476 ceremonies gives no hint that they were inconvenienced by the works. It can be suggested, therefore, that the original stalls, choir and the roodloft where the ladies sat were still in place. It is likely that the ceremonies of 1476 were the last to have taken place in the old chapel. The new choir stalls were to be adorned with the text of Psalm 20, 'a prayer for the king going to war', and Edward's own misericord in the stalls was to be carved with a representation of his meeting with Louis XI at Picquigny in August 1475, when they made peace: Edward's glorious and bloodless victory.

In 1476 the feast of St George was kept in a 'most royall manner', partly no doubt to celebrate Edward's return from France. Only one of the king's brothers was present, the Duke of Clarence. The Duke of Gloucester was in the north, Henry Stafford, the young second Duke of Buckingham was presumably on his estates, William, Lord Hastings (elected 1461; died 1483), was in Calais as the king's lieutenant, and Sir William Parr (1474-84) was also presumably in the north where he was a useful administrator. Three of the English knights were in foreign parts: Anthony Woodville, Lord Rivers, the queen's eldest brother (1466-83), was in Italy, and John, Lord Scrope of Bolton (early 1463-98) was with him. The Gascon, Gaillard de Durfort, Lord Duras (elected 1463), Edward's regular envoy to Brittany, was also overseas and was shortly to decide to return to French allegiance and resign from the Garter, when Sir Thomas Montgomery replaced him. Other absentees were the kings of Sicily (Naples) and Portugal, and the dukes of Urbino and Burgundy.

There was one particular duty to be undertaken at the feast of 1476: John, the last Mowbray Duke of Norfolk, had died and his sword and helmet had to be offered. The ceremonies opened before noon on the Saturday, 27 April, when the king was joined by five knights, the Marquess of Dorset, the earls of Arundel and Essex, and the lords Maltravers and Dudley, and they continued the chapter into the afternoon in order that late-comers among the knights should not incur any penalty. The ceremonies then resumed before evensong with a full complement of knights accompanying the king: the dukes of York and Clarence, Marquess of Dorset, the earls of Arundel, Essex and Douglas, lords Maltravers, Dudley, Ferrers and Howard, and Sir John Astley, now all safely arrived. They rode on horseback from the king's lodgings in the castle to the chapter house, probably leaving the Upper Ward by its main gate and passing the orchards and gardens on the outskirts of the town and re-entering the castle by the Lower Ward's main gate, no doubt watched by a crowd of on-lookers. The short journey was undertaken on horseback in order to emphasise the honour and ceremony of the occasion. The knights were dressed in their blue mantles, the great roundel of the garter surrounding the arms of St George on their shoulder. The Chancellor of the Order, an office newly created the year before, was Richard Beauchamp, Bishop of Salisbury, the Prelate was William Waynflete, Bishop of Winchester, William Dudley was dean of St George's Chapel (from 1473 until May 1476, when he became Bishop of Durham) and the Order's Register, Thomas Danet (canon of St George's 1472-81); all these officers also rode in the procession. The chapter meeting lasted until almost vespers or evensong, when they went on foot to the choir. After evensong they again went on horseback to the castle and had their void of spices, that is a serving of hippocras (a spiced wine) with appropriate sweetmeats and spices.

On Sunday morning, 28 April, the king and his knights rode to matins in the chapel. They enjoyed breakfast at the dean's house afterwards and then returned to the choir. There they were joined by the queen, the Lady Elizabeth, eldest daughter of the king, the Duchess of Suffolk, the marchionesses of Montagu and Dorset, Lady Hastings, and probably other ladies unknown to or unmentioned by the chronicler but very possibly all the wives of the knights present this year. The ladies also rode on horseback, dressed in gowns made of the Garter livery of that year, which consisted of murrey cloth powdered with the number of garters to which their individual rank entitled them; the narrator noted, however, that the marchioness wore a gown of silk, perhaps because she was a widow, and the marchioness of Dorset wore no livery. The ladies were seated in the roodloft, where they watched, but did not take part. The same ceremonies were observed in the afternoon for evensong.

That evening the king dined in his great chamber with the new chancellor of the Order on his right hand, the Bishop of Salisbury. On his left hand sat George, Duke of Clarence, the king's erratic eldest brother destined for execution in 1477, and John de la Pole, Duke of Suffolk (1472/3-1491/2). A table on one side of the chamber accommodated Thomas Grey, Marquess of Dorset, the eldest son of the queen (1475-1501), William Fitzalan, Earl of Arundel (1471-87), Henry Percy, Earl of Northumberland (1474-89), Henry Bourchier, Earl of Essex and the king's uncle (1452-83), and James Douglas, Earl of Douglas, disloyal subject of the king of Scots (1463-91); and also Thomas Fitzalan, Lord Maltravers, son and heir of the Earl of Arundel (1474-1524), John Sutton, Lord Dudley (by early 1459-87), William Devereux, Lord Ferrers, and John, Lord Howard, both elected 1472 and both dying on the battle field of Bosworth fighting for the last Yorkist king; and finally Sir John Astley, famous for his feats in tournaments and an authority on chivalric protocol (1461-86). A table on the other side of the chamber seated William Dudley, dean of St George's Chapel, and his canons, who wore murrey mantles provided by themselves, bearing the 'roundlet' of St George (that is a cross of St George within a 'roundel'). All ranks and personages associated with the Order had their own dress down to the poor alms-knights, who wore red cloaks with a shield of the arms of St George without the garter. The infant Duke of York had apparently been sent early to bed and the ladies did not dine in the king's chamber, but would therefore have dined with the queen in her chamber.

On the Monday, the day after the feast day, the sovereign and his knights entered the chapter and had a short meeting, They then passed to the choir and every knight stood in front of his stall while the king offered a rich suite of vestments for the chapel, undoubtedly something like the suite of six copes of white damask embroidered with angels and 'divers minstralsies' supplied at Whitsuntide 1480 by the workshop of William Morton, mercer and vestmentmaker of London, at a cost of £53 6s. 8d., also destined as a gift to St George's Chapel. Edward IV was accustomed to give such lavish works to the chapel: in 1479 he gave a cope embroidered with the royal arms within a white rose and the orphreys embroidered with the Seven Joys of Mary. The dean received the gift and the king returned to his stall. The knights sat until the offering of the achievements –– sword and helm – of John, Duke of Norfolk; all such ironwork was the perquisite of the College. Edward IV planned that his second son, Richard, should have this additional title and the hand in marriage of the infant heiress, and appropriately the infant Duke of York was present to witness the offering of the achievements of his future father-in-law. It is likely he was carried on someone's shoulder in the same manner as the young Duke of Buckingham and his infant wife had attended the coronation of Queen Elizabeth in 1465. The sword was offered by Dorset and Suffolk and the helmet by Maltravers and Howard. Obeisance was done and all the knights offered at the altar in turn, two by two including the little duke. If the holder of the stall opposite was absent then the knight present offered alone. Once the requiem mass and *de profundis* had been sung, the knights went to the chapter. All deceased knights were entitled to a certain number of masses for their souls depending on their status, 600 for a duke as in this case, 300 for an earl, 100 for a knight, and so on.

Display was an important element in every Garter ceremony and a livery was issued for each year's feast from the king's Great Wardrobe – clothing at the king's expense was a traditional form of payment or reward to his servants and Garter knights were no exception.[4] The livery consisted of a gown, as it was called in the fifteenth century (now surcoat), and a hood. The distribution did not include the mantle which was the original garment of the knights companion and presented to them on their election along with their garter. The mantle was the sole garment mentioned in the statutes of the Order, at first of blue woollen cloth, later of velvet, usually blue with a white damask lining. It was tied at the neck with a mantle lace with knop and tassle, all of silk, and a large embroidered garter with the arms of St George was worn on the left shoulder. The long gown might be of scarlet (the most expensive woollen cloth available, dyed with the rare kermes dye); it was garnished or powdered with garters, and furred with miniver and ermine; the hood would be of the same cloth and also powdered with garters. There are so few details for the Yorkist period of the annual garter liveries that the 1476 narrative is of prime importance. Scraps of information survive in the enrolled accounts of the Great Wardrobe for 1461-65 which record laconically that the livery was of blue cloth in 1461 and of scarlet in 1462. The Great Wardrobe accounts of Henry VI and Henry VII give some idea of the issues which the knights expected and how colourful and lavish were the ceremonies. In 1422-23 five ells of scarlet, with miniver and a number of embroidered garters appropriate to the rank of each knight were issued as powderings for their gowns and hoods. The king was entitled to 240 garters to powder his gown, a Prince of Wales 200, another son of the king 160, all other dukes 120, earls 100, barons 80, and knights bannerets 70. In 1438-39 the livery was scarlet again, but in 1443-44 there was a change to blanket cloth, presumably white as no colour is specified. In 1456-57 the issue was blue cloth, with miniver and garters.

As stated there are few details of annual Garter liveries for the reign of Edward IV, but in 1478 it is known that liveries were ordered for the Queen, the Prince of Wales, the Duke of York, and the princesses Elizabeth, Cecily and Mary, the dukes of Gloucester, Buckingham and Suffolk, the Duchess of Suffolk, the Marquess of

Dorset, several earls led by Essex, Hastings and other barons, Sir John Astley, and the bishops and officers associated with the Order. In 1498-99, there exist exceptionally good details: blue cloth was issued to the king for a gown and hood lined with white damask, both powdered with 240 garters with gold letters, costing 7d. each from William More, embroiderer; George Lovekyn, the king's tailor, made the gown and hood and supplied a roll for the latter at 13s. 4d.; the Prince of Wales received the same, with some miniver and 200 garters; the Duke of York received 160 garters; the Bishop of Winchester, as an official of the Order received the livery cloths but no garters; the Duke of Buckingham received 120 garters of silk, with no gold letters; earls received 100 silk garters each, barons eighty, and knights banneret seventy silk garters with which to powder their gowns and hoods.

One of the most important aspects of the 1476 narrative is its reference to the ladies. There has been much dispute over their role and degree of association with the Order, but it is certain that ladies were accepted as members of the fraternity of St George: that is, they shared in its religious aspect as women did in other religious fraternities.[5] They were observers of the male ceremonial, never had any formal status, were never formally admitted and did not receive the mantle of the Order although they received the annual livery and might wear a garter given to them by the king. They relied on the sovereign's favour for their association: relationship to the sovereign or marriage to a knight were the essential requirements. The first known lady associated with the Order was Edward III's daughter, Isabel, Countess of Bedford, in 1376. Liveries of cloth and powderings of garters to the ladies of the Order became usual from the reign of Richard II, the yardage of cloth and the number of powderings regulated by their rank in the same way as that of the knights. In 1422-23 the Duchess of Gloucester received scarlet, miniver and garters, and in 1438-39 she and the countess of Suffolk received the same. In 1443 the countess of Suffolk received blanket cloth and powderings of garters like the knights. Margaret of Anjou became the first lady of the Order upon her marriage and received, for example, blue cloth, miniver and garters in 1457-58. The 1476 narrative shows that Edward IV's queen was naturally the first lady of the Order and was joined by their eldest daughter, Elizabeth, the king's sister, Elizabeth, Duchess of Suffolk (died 1503-04) – and presumably the duchesses of the dukes of Clarence and Gloucester would also have been ladies of the Order in which their husbands were knights. Katherine Neville, the wife of William Lord Hastings, a knight companion since 1462, and Katherine's daughter by her previous husband, Cecily Bonville, second wife of Thomas Grey, Marquess of Dorset, were also accorded the livery, Dorset being one of the newest knights created by Edward (elected 1475). Lastly, the marchioness of Montagu was the widow of another knight companion, John Neville, Marquess Montagu, who had died at Barnet in 1471; she was Elizabeth Ingaldestone and had remarried Sir William Norreys in 1472, but like other remarried peeresses retained her rank; she was to die this same year in May. Edward IV's younger daughters, Cecily and Mary, joined their mother and eldest sister at Garter ceremonies by 1478. Under Henry VII, however, the numbers of ladies apparently dropped and may have been limited to his mother. It was usual for a lady to wear her garter on her left arm: the monument of Alice de la Pole, Duchess of Suffolk, at Ewelme, shows her wearing it as a bracelet on her forearm, and the widow of Sir Robert Harcourt is shown wearing it above her elbow. The narrative of 1476 indicates that a certain variety could be maintained among the ladies for the marchioness of Montagu was in a gown of silk possibly not powdered with garters, perhaps because she was a widow of a knight. It remains likely that the ladies wore their liveries in the surcoat and kirtle styles adopted by Alice Chaucer and Lady Harcourt on their tombs, styles which were no longer fashionable but adopted to show rank.

ELEVEN

THE BURIALS OF KING HENRY VI
AT CHERTSEY AND WINDSOR

Ralph Griffiths

THE BURIALS AND REBURIALS of medieval monarchs and modern dictators alike are often touchstones of political revolution. The planned interment, the actual burial, and the translation and reburial of Henry VI offer a framework of reference for the several phases of the Wars of the Roses. In 1498, twenty-seven years after the king died, three religious institutions were still claiming his body: Westminster Abbey, where he planned his tomb; Chertsey Abbey, where he was buried in 1471; and St George's Chapel, Windsor Castle, to which his remains were moved in 1484 – all not many miles distant from one another on the banks of the Thames.[1] The circumstances of Henry's death in the Tower of London during the night of 21-25 May 1471, and his posthumous reputation and religious cult, were of political, dynastic and religious interest to the Yorkist kings who supplanted him and the early Tudor monarchs who claimed connection with him. They have also commanded the attention of historians.

There is no dispute among contemporary writers or later historians that by the time of his death, the health of the 49-year-old king was fragile in mind and probably in body too. He had suffered a mental collapse in August 1453 and his recovery at Christmas 1454 may have been only partial. The political and personal disputes that resulted in civil war in 1459-61 seem to have weighed heavily on him. In the years that followed, he was a fugitive in northern England or Scotland until, in 1465, he was captured; thereafter Edward IV, who had deposed him, confined him in a small room akin to a religious cell (*ergastulo*) in the Tower of London.[2] His last six months (1470-1) – 'this quesy season', as the early sixteenth-century chronicler, Robert Fabyan, described them – were spent in the Bishop of London's palace, adjoining the north-west side of St Paul's Cathedral, during the king's brief restoration before the triumphant Edward returned him to the Tower in April 1471.[3] During those final weeks, Henry VI's fate is bound to have been in the mind of both the hapless monarch and his captor.

In 1498 it was recalled that Henry had expressed his wish to be buried in Westminster Abbey, close to the tombs of his royal ancestors and the chantry chapel which he completed in the 1440s in honour of his father and mother, Henry V and Queen Katherine. According to several men who accompanied him to the abbey in the mid-1450s to discuss his tomb, he measured with his feet the proposed tomb-vault, and a stone-mason used a crowbar to mark the spot.[4] It is not surprising that a king in his thirties should have planned a Westminster burial for himself: Richard II and Henry V had done as much when they were no older; and Henry VII, when told of his uncle's visits to the abbey, believed that burial there was his intention. A new group of feoffees was appointed in November 1459 to implement Henry VI's plan, and signs that a start was made on the tomb before 1461 have been located on the floor of Edward the Confessor's chapel.[5] There is no evidence that Henry contemplated interment in his new college of Eton, either during his reign or later, for its buildings (including the chapel) still stood incomplete in 1471. Nor would he have thought of St George's as his last resting place, for no noble or royal burial took place there before Edward IV began to rebuild the chapel as his (Yorkist) mausoleum in 1475.[6] Whatever concerns Henry may have felt during the 1460s that his earlier plans might be frustrated, his restoration to the throne in October 1470 would have removed them. All that was to change again in April 1471.

The precise circumstances of Henry's death are now unfathomable – they could hardly be otherwise. Those who wrote about him soon after his death suggest that in the weeks immediately before he died he was in a state of pathetic passivity, which generally aroused sympathy rather than hostility or derision. However, this does not seem to have prevented him from riding short distances in London or to Westminster. When he appeared in public, he was noted as being dressed in a long blue velvet gown, in contrast to the military garb of his noble supporters and his enemies as they approached the city. Few contemporaries equated this with poverty or personal neglect; rather should it be interpreted as the king's preference for the robes of royal mourning or as appropriate to royal and religious ceremonies at Eastertide. His experiences over the past decade and the slaughter at Barnet and Tewkesbury in recent days are ample explanation of that.[7] The news of his only son's death at Tewkesbury (4 May) and the beheading of his cousin Edmund Beaufort, Duke of Somerset after the battle, and of his queen's capture a few days later might easily have deepened his depression.

Just hours after the arrival of Edward IV in London on 21 May, Henry died during the night while still in the Tower. There is no contemporary suggestion of suicide – which would have been a major scandal – and sources close to the Yorkist regime imply that his life slipped away (*feliciter moriens,* 'of pure displeasure and melancholy') after the triumphant Edward returned to London.[8] The most dispassionate contemporary chronicle, associated with Peterhouse, Cambridge, records that Edward's brother, Richard, Duke of Gloucester, and other lords were in the Tower when Henry 'was putt to dethe' – but it goes no further than that, possibly because it was written soon after Gloucester became king in 1483.[9] The suggestion that one of the king's keepers was responsible for the deed is pure speculation. Only much later, in Henry VII's reign, did rumours about the manner of his death openly identify Gloucester as personally responsible for murder, acting with or without his elder brother's knowledge, and culminating in Sir Thomas More's description of Richard slaying the king 'with his own hands' – though even some sixteenth-century writers (like Polydore Vergil) could not be certain.[10] There was a strong incentive for Edward IV to contrive Henry's death; but there was something to lose too in inflaming public opinion, as Henry IV had judged when he deposed and at first imprisoned Richard II in 1399. What may have been decisive in May 1471 was the threat from Thomas, Bastard of Fauconberg's soldiers, ships and guns, with the aim of freeing Henry from the Tower. Moreover, not many days before 21 May, opinion in the city had been volatile and not everyone concurred with the city fathers in supporting Edward.[11] However Henry VI's death occurred, its pathos encouraged the religious cult that developed in the 1470s: the hardening belief in his martyrdom at Edward's hands, or on his order, is part of that cult, even to the extent that a dagger with which he was supposedly slain by Gloucester was venerated at Caversham, near Reading, in the 1530s.[12]

Once dead, Henry's body was treated with greater respect than chroniclers and historians allowed; even Edward IV acknowledged that he had been a king in reality if not by right. The choice of burial site may reflect this and Henry's own wishes. Suggestions that his corpse was treated perfunctorily and buried at Chertsey Abbey at night are wide of the mark, though the arrangements were swiftly executed without the chivalric formalities recorded by heralds for Henry V's funeral – and which they would later record for Edward IV's. Materials were purchased to preserve the body and wrap it in 28 ells of Holland linen, and the cortege, which included torch-bearers and an armed escort from the former Calais garrison, passed on 22 May from the Tower through Cornhill and Cheapside to St Paul's Cathedral, where the coffin lay for all to see, the body's face uncovered. (Ironically, other Calais soldiers had been with Fauconberg in the attack on the city's gates.) The body was seen to bleed – a not uncommon phenomenon soon after death – on the cathedral pavement before being taken next day, Ascension

Day, for funeral services at Blackfriars; only later was the bleeding at St Paul's and Blackfriars regarded as a sign of the king's martyrdom. The cortege was accompanied by friars drawn from the main friaries of London – Franciscans, Dominicans, Carmelites and Austin Friars – and by some Crutched Friars from the Holy Cross Friary near the Tower. As they did for prominent citizens and some noblemen, these friars performed the obsequies and masses for the dead at Blackfriars and accompanied the funeral barges upriver to Chertsey. The interment probably took place the next day, the 24th.[13] These arrangements were made by two of Edward IV's servants from the Tower, Hugh Brice, a London goldsmith and deputy-master of the royal mint, and Richard Martyn, rector of St Peter's ad Vincula, the chapel in the Tower, and archdeacon of London. Both men would have been acquainted with the imprisoned king.[14]

Henry's burial place, Chertsey Abbey (and its Lady chapel), was identified by contemporaries as standing beside the Thames in the diocese of Winchester. No one at the time (in contrast to later writers) suggested that this Anglo-Saxon foundation, which had been patronised by medieval monarchs, was chosen for its obscurity, for it was easily accessible by road and river. Given that the king's preference for Westminster Abbey was out of the question in 1471, as presumably was St Paul's Cathedral where his great-grandfather, John of Gaunt, was buried, and Canterbury where his grandfather, Henry IV, lay, Chertsey may have become Henry's own alternative choice after his capture in 1465. From the time of his seclusion in Windsor Castle during his illness in 1453-4, Henry visited Chertsey on a number of occasions, and more frequently than at any other time in his life. Moreover, William Waynflete, in whose diocese the abbey stood, was Henry's most intimate advisor among the bishops; he also had close connections with Chertsey and its abbots and had sometimes rented their London inn when he was provost of Eton. Waynflete was imprisoned with Henry in the Tower in the weeks before 21 May, as were several other bishops who had been appointed by Henry in the 1450s, and could have offered the king solace and advice.[15] Moreover, Chertsey was less than ten miles from Windsor so that the king's grave could be closely supervised. Nor was it far from Woking, the favourite estate of Margaret, countess of Richmond and Henry VI's cousin, and her husband Henry, Lord Stafford; their meetings with King Henry and Waynflete in October-December 1470 may have helped to crystallize the idea of Chertsey as the king's burial place should an alternative to Westminster Abbey be needed.[16] In short, the former king may have had a say in his own burial, just as Richard II, in his last months, may have contemplated an alternative to the tomb he had prepared for himself in Westminster Abbey: Richard had often stayed at the royal palace at King's Langley, where he was buried in the Dominican friary on Henry IV's order in 1400.[17]

Nothing is known about the burial itself, except that the friars who accompanied the coffin from London were in attendance for the funeral masses on Friday, 24 May. Abbot John May and the convent of Chertsey would surely have been present and it is possible that Waynflete and some of the other bishops may have travelled from the Tower with the corpse. Edward IV and his brothers had business elsewhere, quelling Fauconberg's rising in Kent. It was presumably the expectation that Henry VI's body would remain in perpetuity at Chertsey, where a vault is likely to have been built for the coffin. As a foreign observer commented within weeks of the deaths of Henry and his only son, Edward IV 'has in short chosen to crush the seed'.[18]

Edward doubtless hoped that the burial would bring dynastic uncertainty to an end. Yet within a year, Henry VI was being venerated as a martyred king of blameless life, and his grave began to attract pilgrims to Chertsey. Edward IV and the abbot sought to suppress the cult, though the monastery would likely benefit from gifts by the faithful. Within a decade, miracles were reportedly taking place at Henry's tomb or in his name.[19] This development had a worrying political dimension for it might bestir Lancastrian resentment and produce rumour and sedition, or worse. By the time Edward died in 1483, the king's efforts to suppress the veneration had not been successful.

It is ironic that it should have been Richard III, the man close by when Henry died, who was responsible for removing the venerated body on 12 August 1484 to grander quarters in the new St George's Chapel that Edward IV had begun to construct. Thomas Pygot, abbot of Chertsey since 1479, may have regretted the move. There is no reason to doubt that the removal (which cost the Chapel £5 10s. 2d.) was reverent and honourable, or that the exhumed body was (as John Rous reported a few years later) largely uncorrupted. Richard would have been able to view the result when he visited Windsor a week later. His motives for translating the body to St George's are unclear, yet for the next half-century the earthly after-life of Henry VI had implications for the English monarchy much more complex than those of the king's death and burial in 1471.[20]

Richard was aware that Chertsey Abbey was not far from Lady Margaret Beaufort's house at Woking; by 1484 he also knew that Margaret's son (and Henry VI's nephew), Henry, Earl of Richmond, was preparing an invasion from Brittany to challenge Richard for the crown. To bring the grave under yet closer supervision at Windsor might have seemed prudent to Richard lest its popularity as a pilgrim centre be manipulated by Lady Margaret in her son's interest; she is certainly known to have made endowments to St George's later on, and may have done so to Chertsey before 1484. Other factors may also have weighed with Richard. Windsor was not one of his favoured places: he visited the castle infrequently both before and after he became king, despite the fact that Edward IV's building works were transforming St George's into an imposing Yorkist mausoleum. Richard was not present at the funerals there of Edward's two children, George and Mary, in 1479 and 1482, and as king he did not even attend the Garter celebrations; indeed, in April 1485 he pointedly left Windsor a day or so before St George's day.[21] Nor did Richard see Windsor as his own burial place: when his queen died in March 1485, she was buried in Westminster Abbey, near the doorway of the Confessor's chapel, which suggests that he contemplated restoring Westminster as the pre-eminent royal mausoleum.[22] In brief, Richard wanted to have as little to do with Windsor as he could.

This attitude may be reflected in the positioning of Henry VI's new tomb and altar. Closer supervision was one thing, but to place them before the entrance to the choir directly opposite Edward IV's new chantry, which was largely complete by the time Edward died in 1483, seems quite another. Pilgrims to the re-located tomb of Henry VI, which was acquiring an aura of sanctity and approaching Thomas Becket's shrine at Canterbury in popularity, would upstage the memorial to the brother whose birth and marriage Richard had recently slandered and whose son, Edward V, he had deposed. Moreover, in the year between the translation of Henry's body and the battle of Bosworth in 1485, Richard may have taken steps to provide the new tomb with a suitable shrine, whereas work on King Edward's tomb stopped. Indeed, it was probably Richard who ordered his brother's former craftsman and smithy, John Tresilian, to make an elaborate offertory box for pilgrims to Henry's shrine which still stands beside the grave.[23]

Apart from the disdain shown towards Edward IV, and a wish to direct the passage of pilgrims, Richard in 1484 may have wished to fortify his uncertain kingship by reconciling the factions of Lancaster and York and so reduce the threat from Richmond. The removal of Henry VI's body was a symbolic act of reconciliation akin to Richard's establishment, three months earlier, of the first public memorial to the dead on both sides in the Wars of the Roses, namely, a chantry chapel built near the site of the bloodiest battle of the wars, at Towton (1461). As Henry V had shown in 1413 when he translated Richard II's corpse from King's Langley to Westminster Abbey, such ostentatious acts could have significant political merit.[24]

Richard may even have planned an elaborate new chantry whose design – another irony this – Henry VII probably approved after he killed Richard at

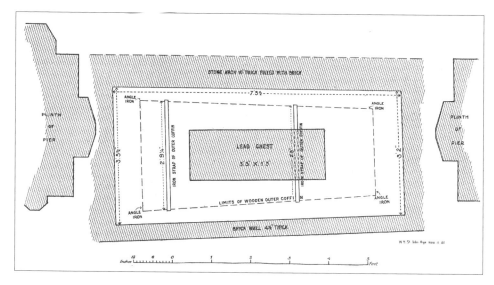

Fig. 23. Plan of the grave of Henry VI, as excavated in 1911.

Bosworth. The sixteenth-century drawing of a tomb and heraldic achievements associated with Henry VI represent the tomb-chest and effigy of the king planned after the translation of his body had taken place in 1484. That they are Henry's is indicated by the chivalric accoutrements (without the spurs which were kept elsewhere for pilgrims to kiss), the heraldic beasts at the figure's feet (the antelope and leopard) and the angel often associated with the venerated king. The effigy wears the closed crown which Henry popularized during his reign and with which he came to be identified in later representations. [25]

Miracles were recorded at the new tomb with growing frequency, and Henry VII planned his own burial at Windsor close to his revered uncle. At the end of 1497, however, Henry VII changed his mind and made plans to move the body yet again to a new Lady chapel at Westminster, with the intention of harnessing his uncle's burgeoning reputation. Westminster's Lady chapel – Henry VII's Chapel, as we know it today – was at first constructed with space at its eastern end for the shrine of Henry VI. There are still signs there of this intent, including niches for statues of Henry VI and his birth-saint, St Nicholas, to whom he was attached. The last Lancastrian came within a whisker of having his original burial plan fulfilled. [26] Both Henry VII and Henry VIII petitioned a succession of popes to have the venerated king canonized prior to the second translation – unsuccessfully, as it proved. And, so, Henry VI still lies in St George's (Fig. 23).

Henry VI's first burial was intended to end one royal dynasty and enhance the security of another. His second burial symbolised a desire for political reconciliation which Henry had ineffectually advocated during his life. Henry VII sought to enlist the dead monarch in his own interests, even to the extent of planning a third burial and pursuing sanctification. By contrast, those who invoked his name and visited his graves at Chertsey and especially Windsor expressed a personal devotion to Henry VI that focused on what they understood to have been the king's compassion, piety and fellow suffering whilst he lived.[27]

TWELVE

THE BURIAL OF BISHOP OLIVER KING

Robert Dunning

'THERE IS SOME DEGREE of uncertainty as to the real burial place of Bishop King'. So wrote John Britton in his *History and Antiquities of Bath Abbey Church* (1825) though his statement was qualified by the suggestion, reaching back to Bishop Francis Godwin in his *De Praesulibus Angliae Commentarius* at the beginning of the seventeenth century and repeated many times since, that he lies in St George's Chapel, Windsor. More specifically, it was assumed that King lay in a tomb of grey marble in the chapel of St Saviour there that he himself had built in the angle between the south transept and the south choir aisle. The evidence is strong: outside the little chapel, in the south choir aisle, are portraits of a royal prince and three kings, all of whom Oliver King served as secretary; and an inscription bearing the dates 1489 and 1492 inviting prayers for the founder seem to make clear his intentions.[1]

A bold and somewhat contradictory voice was heard when Sir George Gilbert Scott was leading the restoration of Bath Abbey in 1860-73. It was that of his chief assistant J.T. Irvine, a man of considerable archaeological expertise, who frequently shared his discoveries in the local press, read a detailed paper on the subject to members of the British Archaeological Association in 1881, and published in the Association's *Journal* in 1890 a shortened version of his conclusions about the earlier building on the site and its relationship with the new cathedral priory church Oliver King had begun. Irvine's papers relating to Bath, deposited in the city's library by the National Museums of Scotland, include two drawings that mark what he believed to be the end of a vault prepared for King's burial.[2] The architectural historian E.M. Hick, knowing of Irvine's work, still remained 'uncertain' about an actual burial there in his Bath Abbey guide book of 1913[3] but at least a slight doubt about Windsor was introduced. S.J. Gunn, Oliver King's most recent biographer in the *Oxford Dictionary of National Biography*, remained 'unclear' on the subject, but in a lecture at Bath in 2000 published by the Friends of the Abbey the then Dean of Windsor (and former

Dean of Wells), Patrick Mitchell, had no doubts: 'the evidence is clear: Oliver King was buried in Wells Cathedral; but where his grave may be is a continuing puzzle for future scholars to solve.'[4]

In the years around 1490 Oliver King was evidently intent on creating for himself a burial place at Windsor as the dates 1489 and 1492 in the inscription near his chapel there indicate. It was a natural place for him to choose after so many years of intimate royal service that included membership of St George's chapter from 1480 and the office of Register of the Order of the Garter. Promotion to the see of Exeter in 1492 made little if any difference to his administrative work either in Windsor or London but translation to Bath and Wells in November 1495 was followed in December by a letter issued by Pope Alexander VI whose terms suggest that King's personal commitment to his chapel might be weakening. The pope's letter, which must have originated in some contact between King and the papal chancery, was issued to encourage visitors to the chapel. It suggested to its founder that he might endow it further but also offered remission to visitors on the fourth and sixth day of each week wishing to pray for the founder's soul, and by implication making offerings for its maintenance.[5]

Already King may have seen his translation to the see of Bath and Wells as pointing to retirement from his government post, but he remained in Henry VII's service for a few more years. From the Spring of 1499 onwards, however, he spent most of his time in Somerset, more often than not in Bath, dating official documents either at his palace there or more generally at the monastery, the cathedral priory that formed part of his episcopal title.[6] He was the first Bishop of the diocese to care much for his co-cathedral for three centuries. The last to be buried there was Roger of Salisbury in 1247.[7] If not staying at Bath King lodged at his nearby manor houses at Chew Magna or Banwell (where he spent the last month of his life), with very occasional forays to his palace at Wells or elsewhere in his diocese. He was not the active, assiduous diocesan that some of his predecessors had been,[8] but the famous dream he is said to have experienced certainly gave him a reforming vision for the dilapidated cathedral priory church at Bath.[9]

Clearly, Bath absorbed his interest. The need to rebuild had become obvious at his visitation in 1499[10] and his proposals to limit the monks' domestic spending in order to create a building fund were quickly put in place. Letters discovered in the Westminster archives dating from 1501[11] reveal how King drew on contacts from his Crown service, finding support from Sir Reginald Bray and through him of Henry VII, and thus the expertise of Robert and William Vertue. Both King and Bray planned to be commemorated in the new building.

But both died in August 1503, which must have been a huge blow to progress. King had hoped, so he had told Bray, that the new church would be roofed by the winter of 1501, and thus he could perhaps confidently declare in his will (the precise date of which is not known) that he wished to be buried 'with no great pomp' in the choir of the new church next to the first arch on the north side nearest the high altar.[12] It was the place of honour befitting a founder. It was presumably knowledge of the bishop's will that led J.T. Irvine to identify a stone slab he found in the north arcade of the choir as probably one end of his burial vault.[13]

What happened immediately after King's death is not certain, but interment obviously took place but only a very modest sum of 1s was received by the cathedral's escheator at Wells on the day as compared with 1s 10d offered when Dean Cosyn was buried there in 1525.[14] Might the ceremony at Wells have marked a temporary burial there or elsewhere pending re-interment at Bath when progress on the building should be sufficiently advanced according to the bishop's wish?

Having supervised the burial of the bishop and submitted his last will and testament for probate, Oliver King's executors were obliged to carry out its provisions. They were an interesting group of people: the bishop's sister Elizabeth Cosyn, his nephew William Cosyn, dean of Wells, Bishop Thomas Cornish, a bishop *in partibus* who served as suffragan in the diocese and was precentor of Wells, Thomas Beaumont, archdeacon of Wells, and Thomas Grene, whom King had appointed some years before as keeper of his manor and park at Banwell,[15] a man in the bishop's confidence who had been entrusted with at least one letter to Sir Reginald Bray on the delicate question of a promise King had made to Henry VII on his appointment as bishop.[16] Here were people representing King's family, his household and the Wells chapter.

Most of these people had acted as fellow trustees with King at least once before when John Poulet wanted to alter the legal settlement of his estate at Goathurst, Wells and elsewhere. That was in October 1502 when they were joined by Sir Reginald Bray, William Cosyn's brother Robert, and two other members of the Wells chapter.[17] Bray might have been expected to be among King's executors, not only through personal friendship but also in his role as steward to the Wells chapter.[18] His personal interest in the new building at Bath would have made him a natural choice to balance the interests of what were too often rival communities. Instead, the Wells interest was dominant among the executors, for Bray had died before King drew up his will.

The bequests in King's will were relatively straightforward. £33 6s 8d to

New College, Oxford, and £20 to Robert Shirborne, his successor as the king's secretary and, among his many other posts, archdeacon of Taunton. These two bequests were in the first paragraph of his will written in Latin. The rest, because not all would understand, King ordered to be written in the vulgar tongue. Plate was specified for the cathedral churches of Bath and Wells (Wells to have second-best candlesticks) and gifts of cash to each of the Bath community for singing masses for thirty days after the bishop's burial – a reasonable gift from a man who expected to be buried in their church. Plate was also reserved for a few relatives and wages were given to members of the bishop's household. The plate for Wells cathedral was duly delivered just over seven months after the bishop's death[19] and there is no reason to suppose that the plate destined for Bath was not also handed over. In fact, by the beginning of January 1504, just over four months after King's death, his executors led by Bishop Cornish, received a grant of pardon and release 'for all matters relating to the said bishop'.[20]

The wills of Thomas Beaumont and William Cosyn indicate that this was not a statement of dismissal from a task fully executed. Clearly there were problems in carrying out King's wishes. Plate actually held in the bishop's treasury could be handed over without undue delay but cash bequests might not so easily be fulfilled, for wealth of that kind was as likely to be represented by debt as by coin. The problems experienced by at least two of the executors may be one reason why the bishop's last resting place is a matter of doubt.

Thomas Beaumont in his will drawn up in 1507 asked to be buried in Wells where he had been a member of the chapter since Bishop King appointed him archdeacon of Bath in 1499.[21] He left a sum of money to establish a commemoration in the cathedral choir, naming himself and the bishop as the chief beneficiaries. Another bequest was cash, a horse and bedding to John Warforde 'above his bequest of my lorde of Bathes'. King had left to a man named John Wardeford, surely the same and presumably a member of his household, his wages for a year and the sum of £20. Beaumont evidently felt that in some way he was responsible for a bequest that may not have been fulfilled. He also gave gold rings to 'Maistres Cosen and Robert Cosyn hir sonne' the late bishop's sister and executor, and another nephew. Dean Cosyn and Thomas Grene, two more of Bishop King's executors, he appointed to act for him in a similar way, and Bishop Cornish he made the supervisor of their activities. This tight-knit circle implies very close cooperation and perhaps a continuing struggle to fulfil King's wishes. Bishop Cornish's will of 1513 makes no mention of any connection with King, nor does it name Dean Cosyn.[22] Perhaps by then a negligent dean and an assiduous precentor had ceased to be close friends.

The final settlement of Bishop King's estate thus may not have been completed by the death of Thomas Beaumont, and was clearly still a serious personal concern of Dean Cosyn when he made his will in 1522.[23] He wanted his brother Robert to be his executor, to bury him in his cathedral, and to dispose of his goods 'at his owne mynde', excepting a single debt for an estate where the dean had been executor with inadequate funds to operate. The dean then went on in his will to declare that the late Thomas Beaumont had withheld Bishop King's goods during his lifetime, that is for some three and a half years after the bishop's death, with the consequence that he, the bishop's nephew, had had to pay for the burial:

> 'I have been much at cost for my lorde of Bathe and have buryed my lorde of Bathe at my owne charge and could never come to any of my lordes goodes till the Archdeacon [Beaumont] was disceased, I bere all the charges and the Archdeacon was possessed of all the goodes'.

The location of the bishop's grave is still not certain. The grey marble tomb in the entrance to the chapel he founded at Windsor (Fig. 24) has never been archaeologically examined but the vault beneath its floor was subject to considerable disturbance when the foundations of the chapel had to be stabilised and under-pinned in the 1920s.[24] The circumstances revealed by the wills of Oliver King's executors suggest a possible scenario that seems unlikely to involve Windsor. In spite of his hopes for progress on the new church at Bath, its choir may have been sufficiently complete to receive his body, but hardly ready to house a tomb suitable for one who was a founder. The building may have been roofed, as the bishop had hoped, but it may not have been vaulted and the tower arch forming its western end might have been closed only with a temporary screen while work on the tower and nave continued.

A temporary grave at Wells, or possibly at Banwell where he died, would therefore have been a reasonable temporary solution – if at Wells, either a site in or around the choir where other bishops were buried, or in the new Lady chapel by the cloister. The statutes drawn up in 1495 allowed for burials of dignitaries there.[25] Could it be that Bishop King was laid to rest in that magnificent building as a temporary measure until such time as the new church at Bath was far enough advanced for his wishes to be carried out? The illegal management of the bishop's estate by Thomas Beaumont clearly limited Dean Cosyn's ability to act to the capacity of his own pocket, whatever family loyalty dictated. And by the time the new church at Bath was ready to receive its founder, the dean may well have been dead, the estate dissipated and the incentive to translate the episcopal bones gone.

Excavation of the site of the Lady chapel by the cloister at Wells by Warwick

Fig. 24. Engraving by Orlando Jewitt of the north side of Oliver King's Chapel in the mid-19th century.

Rodwell revealed many unidentified burials disturbed when the chapel was demolished after 1552.[26] Rodwell's belief that King had added a sacristy or vestry to the north side of the chancel of the chapel, and perhaps also a bridge linking the body of the chapel to the staircase of the cathedral's south transept, would make it an entirely suitable place for his burial, temporary or not. The thorough demolition of the chapel and the destruction of the graves has made identification of graves without other evidence impossible.

An alternative outcome must be that Bishop King had his way, on the initiative and at the personal cost of his nephew. The vault identified by J.T. Irvine could well have been constructed under the bishop's direction. In that case a simple covering slab would not have been unduly vulnerable while construction work proceeded not far away. Only archaeological examination can test the theory, but should his bones lie where he had wished, then Dean Cosyn probably also found the money to pay the Bath monks to sing masses for the bishop's soul. What he did not provide was a memorial that might have matched that which records, on the other side of the choir, the achievement of that other great Bath builder, Prior Birde.

THIRTEEN

THE WEST WINDOW OF ST GEORGE'S CHAPEL:
A RESTORATION HISTORY

Sarah Brown

IN 1497, as the work of rebuilding the fire-damaged royal palace of Richmond got under-way, King Henry VII appointed the Netherlandish artist Barnard Flower as his chief glazier.[1] The appointment was official recognition of the growing importance of immigrant artists in the English craft. Foreign glass-painters, especially those from the Low Countries, had begun arriving in England in significant numbers in the 1470s. In 1474 the London Glaziers' Company had first petitioned the king for protection against 'aliens', a struggle that continued into the sixteenth century.[2] While large numbers of immigrant artists and craftsmen were active in England by the end of the fifteenth century, their impact on stained glass was especially marked and it is no exaggeration to say that, working in collaboration with native artists, they were to have a transforming effect on English stained glass at the end of the Middle Ages.[3]

Unfortunately much stained glass from documented royal projects undertaken by Barnard Flower and his collaborators, notably Richmond Palace, the Tower of London and the manor of Woking, has been lost. Other major glazing schemes, such as the new Lady chapel of Westminster Abbey and the west window of St George's Chapel itself, are largely undocumented.[4] However in 1515 Flower, who died in 1517, was contracted to make the earliest windows at King's College, Cambridge, and it has been strongly argued on stylistic grounds that Flower was also involved in the earlier work at Westminster and Windsor.[5]

The west window of St George's was probably glazed soon after the completion of the masonry of the west wall and the insertion of the nave vault, believed to have been completed by 1506.[6] Work was certainly sufficiently advanced by the summer of 1503 for Sir Reginald Bray to anticipate completion and to include provision for glazing in the bequests made in his will.[7] While the identity of the workshop entrusted with the work is not known, it seems reasonable to conjecture that this most prestigious of projects would be entrusted to a team led by the King's Glazier, who only a few years later was to be commissioned to glaze

Fig. 25. Wenceslaus Hollar's engraving of the west front of St George's Chapel in *c.* 1670.

the chapel of King's College at Cambridge.

The complex post-Reformation history of the Tudor glass of the west window has been explored before in print, most recently by the late Dr Hilary Wayment.[8] The examination of the window from an external scaffolding by Dr Sebastian Strobl of the Cathedral Studio, Canterbury, in 2000 and the compilation of a recent condition report and conservation proposal by Stephen Clare of Holy Well Glass provides the occasion to revisit the subject and to consider the impact of past restorations on the current state of the window, one of the most extensive surviving glazing schemes of the early sixteenth century.[9]

The earliest depiction of the west window, by Wenceslas Hollar, of c.1659-60 shows the west window plain glazed with rectangular quarries (Fig 25).[10] This suggests that the sixteenth-century painted glass was removed to safety during the Civil War and Commonwealth, and may explain the survival of a large number of medieval figures of popes, a subject surely unacceptable to Puritan sensibilities. The loss of all the medieval canopies and backgrounds which must once have accompanied these figures may also be explained by this circumstance: that is, the figures were made smaller for ease of storage and concealment by the removal of extraneous decorative and close up elements. The castle was occupied by parliamentary forces until the Restoration of 1660 and it was not until 1692 that the west window received attention. The Chapter Acts of 6 May that year record an agreement that the west window of the chapel be repaired.[11] It is likely that it was at this date that painted glass was returned to the window, although it cannot be assumed that all the glass returned to the west window at that time had originated there.

Our next insight into the condition of the window comes from three-quarters of a century later, in 1767. In that year the Chapter resolved to repair the masonry of the west window and decreed that the window should also be 'repaire'd [my emphasis] with such painted glass as can be collected from other parts of the chapel'. The work was implemented by the Windsor glazier William Kimberley, under the general oversight of Canon John Lockman who had gathered glass from elsewhere in the chapel for the purpose. Kimberley was also engaged in the repair and releading of quarry glazing throughout the chapel.[12] Kimberley's bill, later challenged by the Dean and Chapter, and reviewed by two other local glaziers who confirmed that his demands were reasonable, reveals that sixty-nine figures were newly leaded, repaired and made good at a cost of £1 3s per figure, with new coloured glass added 'to the Borders and Podistalls' of the figures. The same bill also records a payment of £12 10s for the manufacture of '10 lights made with the arms for the sides of the west window'.

Sixty-nine figures of historic glass and ten new panels of decoration of an armorial nature would have been sufficient to fill every one of the seventy-nine major openings in the window. While there can be no doubt that Kimberley charged for the repair of sixty-nine figures of medieval or substantially medieval origin, there is some confusion as to how many of the figures were actually returned to the west window, and how they were arranged across the available openings. If ten armorial decorations were used to fill 'the sides of the west window' – taken here to mean panels 1a – 5a and 10 – 50 – the sixty-nine figures would have been sufficient to fit the remaining main lights, extending into the four large openings flanking the stone shield of the arms of Henry VII at the apex of the window panels, now filled with armorial glass of 1840 by Thomas Willement). While this fits the description of the work for which Kimberley was paid, it does not fit the

Fig. 26. Internal view of the west window at the beginning of the 19th century by F. MacKenzie.

visual evidence contained in the engraving of the west elevation of the chapel, drawn by F. MacKenzie and published on 1 July 1810 (Fig. 26).[13] This fine view of the west wall, in which shadowy outlines of figures are clearly discernible, suggests that only fifty-nine figures were displayed in the window by this time, with twenty openings, not ten, filled with armorial decoration (clearly discernible in panels 1a-5a, panels 1e – 5e, panels 1k – 5k and panels 1o – 5o). In 1777 Henry Emlyn undertook further extensive repairs to the window and a glazier was paid £15 18s 3d for his work.[14] The size of Emlyn's overall estimates (£250 18s 71/2d) suggests that this was a significant intervention and his annotation of a drawing of the window makes this clear; 'the principal and other mullions, heads and tracery were decayed in several parts, some of which were made new'.[15] It is possible therefore, as Wayment has suggested, that ten figures were removed from the window at this time in order to facilitate stonework repair, barely a decade after their installation by Kimberley.[16] It must be assumed that these are the ten figures which were to be retrieved from store by Willement in 1842. In 1815, William Webb was paid £49 3s 10d for further cleaning and repair of the west window.

It was at the end of the eighteenth century that the greatest threat to the medieval glass of the window was to come. This was in 1796, when King George III commissioned a large enamel-painted Crucifixion from the painter Benjamin West, to be executed in glass by Charles Forrest. Although substantial progress was made on it, the project was never completed or installed and was subsequently donated in 1846 to Calcutta Cathedral.[17]

Henry Emlyn's work had not been sufficiently durable to safeguard the stone tracery of the window, and by 1841 another major restoration had become necessary. The architect Edward Blore reported to the Chapter in June that year and drew up a specification for the work, which was implemented by Samuel Cundy.[18] Between March and September 1841 all the stained glass was removed to facilitate the masonry repair, and the work of restoring the Tudor glass and creating a new setting for it was entrusted to Thomas Willement, a long-time friend of Edward Blore, an artist-antiquarian not without his own associations with members of the Chapter, particularly the Canon Steward, Revd the Hon. Henry Cockayne Cust.[19]

Willement's earliest proposal, described in a letter to Cust on 6 April 1842, had suggested creating only one new figure, with five new 'compartments' dedicated to the arms and badges of Queen Victoria.[20] He quickly revised his ideas, proposing only a month later that six new figures be created.[21] Willement's final scheme involved the banishment of all eighteenth-century decorative glass and the filling of the window with medieval figures set under new architectural canopies, with pedestals and enriched backgrounds in sixteenth-century style of his own devising.[22] The fifty-nine figures already in the window were restored, ten figures were retrieved from the chapel stores,[23] and seven entirely new figures (not six as first proposed) were created. Four new panels of royal heraldry were installed in the principal upper tracery openings,[24] and a new inscription: 'God save our gracious Sovereign, and all the companions of the most honourable and noble Order of the Garter', was introduced at the base of the window. This enabled him to fill all seventy-five main-light openings with a standing figure, the new ones based on medieval models elsewhere in the window. Wayment identified seven figures as being wholly by Willement (3f, 3o, 4f, 4j, 5f, 5k and 5l), suggesting that a medieval figure was 'cannibalised' in order to create one of the five medieval composite figures today in the window (1j, 2i, 4d, 5e and 5o).[25] Wilfred Drake, entrusted with the removal and reinstallation of the glass in 1940 and 1945, argued that sixty-six figures were of ancient glass, with nine of eighteenth-century vintage (presumably mistaking Willement's work for that of Kimberley).[26]

Willement greatly admired the stained glass of the west window, recognising that it belonged to the reign of Henry VII. Despite the white quarry backgrounds against which the figures had been set in the eighteenth century, he observed that 'still, with all its defects, this window, particularly towards the time of sunset, had from its great dimensions a very imposing and pleasing effect'.[27] It is clear that he found the task of restoring the window difficult: 'I find more trouble than I expected with the glass – the several parts have been so ridiculously mismatched in former leading together'.[28] The plain backgrounds were replaced with what he described as 'ancient diaper patterns', while rich canopies, columns and bases were added to each figure, drawing upon Willement's extensive study of late medieval models. Some of the tiled pavements beneath the feet of the figures are medieval. R.H. Essex's view of 1844 shows that each figure stood before a 'cloth of honour' with alternately blue, red or chequered grounds glimpsed at the head of each light. These decorative features had a unifying effect on the rather disparate collection of figures, disguising visual discrepancies, particularly by 'equalising' their variant scales. The plinth forms are particularly important in this respect, especially for those figures of significantly shorter stature. The window as restored by Willement was characterised, however, by a subtle variety in the disposition of figures by posture, gesture, attribute, identity and scale. Popes, kings, saints, civilians and figures in armour were intermingled in an impressive and richly coloured tableau. Willement's arrangement was protected from external damage by the installation in 1880 of iron guards costing £57 10s.[29]

Willement's arrangement of the window survived unaltered for less than a century. Once again, it was the structural repair of the building that was the spur to the alteration. In 1926 the architect Harold Brakspear expressed his concern for the stability of the nave vault, which had been strengthened by the introduction of extra braces, tie rods and brick piers in the vault pocket in about 1883.[30] The condition of the west window glazing was also revisited in this period, the advice of M.R. James, provost of Eton and authority on medieval art having been sought. It is clear that James had, in turn, sought the advice of G. McNeil Rushforth.[31]

The advice received was thus of impeccable provenance, as these two scholars were of immense reputation. After what seems to have been a fairly brief perusal of the glass, James proposed a re-ordering of the medieval figures, abandoning Willement's varied arrangement in favour of one in which figures were grouped by 'type' in the three principal divisions of the window. Thus an academically-driven iconographic approach was substituted for an aesthetic response to the glass. James suggested, for example, that the twenty-four figures of popes, with one other figure for good measure, should be grouped in the first major division of the window, with the fourteen kings, three archbishops, five bishops, and what James termed the 'George-figures' in the second. The remainder – six knights, two armoured men, six garter knights and twelve saints (with one figure deducted to join the popes) were to be arranged in the third. In addition, he suggested that the 'more interesting and identifiable figures' be placed in the lower compartments of the window where they would be more visible.[32] James's scheme was approved by Chapter in April 1929, although it was decided that the Willement heraldry at the top of the window and the prayer at its foot should be retained. The glass was sent away to be re-leaded in the Birmingham studio of Pearce and Cutler, not a company renowned for its expertise in restoration. The reason for their selection for the task remains unclear. While Willement's canopies were retained, his backgrounds were replaced with plain quarry glazing, presumably in order to lighten the window. Apparently, aspects of James's scheme were not executed in 1929, although which aspects are not specified. In 1940, after the outbreak of war, the Exeter glazier Wilfred Drake was instructed by the Dean to remove the glass into safe storage in the Curfew Tower. Shortly afterwards a bomb fell near the Great Western Railway Station, a fate from which the window would be unlikely to have survived. In 1945 it was also Drake who repaired and reinstalled the glass, at the same time completing James's proposed reordering.[33] The work undertaken by Drake at this time is unlikely to have been extensive, as he began the task on 1 October 1945, and the fixing of the window had been completed by 3 November (Fig. 27).

The recent enquiry into the condition of the window has highlighted the need for a better understanding of the conditions contributing to its current condition and longer term outlook. Environmental monitoring has contributed significantly to present-day understanding of the impact of the heating and ventilation of the chapel, while an overall condition survey has picked out some differences in the state of preservation of individual figures.[34] What follows is an attempt to explore the degree to which art historical factors may assist in explaining these anomalies.

Fig. 27. A recent view of the west window from the nave.

Two factors could account for the variable state of preservation of the glass:

1. Differences in the chemical composition of the glasses used in the make-up of individual panels. This could reflect the use of different batches of glass or preferences for certain colours which are more poorly durable. These differences can reflect differences of workshop identity or practice, or be suggestive of different chronological phases of glazing activity.

2. Differences in the environmental conditions experienced by the glass at various times between its original installation in the chapel and the present. This could reflect differences in the location of the glass in the building for significant periods of time, or shorter term exposure to conditions likely to accelerate decay mechanisms.

It cannot be assumed that the glass restored to the west window in 1692 had all originated there, although all the medieval glass now in the west window appears to date from the early sixteenth century. Differences in style and scale were recognised by Willement, Drake and Wayment, and Drake and Wayment both suggested that some of the figures are of earlier date than the rest. James singled out certain figures as being of particular quality (e.g. St Katherine and St Martin of Tours, which he argued were the work of the same artist). Knowles suggested that some of the glass may have come from the chapel's east window.[35] The paucity of documentary evidence for the glazing campaigns within the chapel as a whole make these distinctions difficult to substantiate without the much closer scrutiny that a conservation programme might make possible. In the meantime, a number of more objective observations may be made, some of which may be of relevance to our understanding of the current condition of the glass.

Recent examination of the figures from scaffolding has substantiated the differences in scale observable between groups of figures. By far the largest group, comprising the popes, most of the other ecclesiastical figures, the kings, armoured figures and the two male civilians measure in the range of 101cm-109cm in height. A group of 16 medieval figures (and three Willement figures copied from medieval originals) are noticeably shorter in stature, measuring between 89cm and 99cm in height. Within this group are the smallest figures of all, a group comprising six 'Garter knights' (1i, 4l, 4m, 4n, 5m and 5n) and three 'George' figures (4g, 4h and 4i) with dragons at their feet, ranging from 89cm to 96cm in height. The difference in scale and the distinctiveness of the subject matter, with a very specific reference to the Order of the Garter and its patron saint, St George, suggests that these figures originated in the same window or group of windows and did not originate in the same window as the larger figures of popes, kings and other ecclesiastics. A location at the east end of the building, in the devotional heart of the chapel created for the celebration of the chivalric Order of the Garter might be considered. Five of the figures (4g, 4i, 4m, 5m and 5n) have suffered moderate paint loss on much of their internal surface, although the remaining three figures are very well preserved. At least two of the members of this group (4i and 4m) are faintly discernable in the 1810 view, suggesting that they have been in place in the west window since at least the 1770s if not earlier. Of similar size is a small group of figures including that of St Katherine (1m), an unidentified male saint (2m) and St Louis (3i) all measuring in the region of 94cm – 96cm in height, a stature that also separates them from the larger series to which the popes belong.

Of the largest group of the bigger figures, the largest single group depicts popes. The survival of St Peter, vested in papal tiara shows this to have been a series depicting the papal succession. Of this series of twenty-five surviving figures,[36] five can be identified by name (Peter, Evaristus, Eleutherius, Calixtus and Cornelius). The size of the series of papal figures is noteworthy. As M.R. James noted, it is sufficient to fill one of the three principal partitions of the west window. The survival of such a large number of subjects which would have been objectionable in the post-Reformation period is in itself remarkable. A large number of the papal triple tiaras show signs of deliberate defacement, probably in order to make their popish associations less noticeable and to make them look more like conventional mitres. When this was done is impossible to say. The outline of a large number of ecclesiastical figures can be seen in the c. 1810 view of the window, so it is most likely to have been done when the papal figures were first reintroduced to the west window some time after 1692. The high church proclivities of St George's Chapel, a royal chapel where the canons revered as a quasi-relic the table on which the executed body of King Charles I had lain, perhaps explains why this contentious subject was acceptable with only minimal disguise. It should be recalled, however, that even in the early 1840s a great display of popes would have been objectionable to certain brands of Anglican churchmanship and is unlikely to have been tolerated outside a royal peculiar.

Of the other identifiable figures of comparable size, five can be identified as English saints – Alban, Oswald, Edmund, Dunstan and Edward the Confessor. It is notable that three are also royal saints, with Edmund and Edward the Confessor famously depicted as patron saints of monarchy in the Wilton Diptych image of Richard II. Alban was England's protomartyr, suggesting that another sequence of figures in succession was intended, with English saints, royal and ecclesiastical, matching the papal series in succession to Peter. The literature surrounding Alban's life and cult enjoyed revision and augmentation in the late medieval period, with three new vitae being composed between 1400 and 1539.[37] The fifteenth and early sixteenth century witnessed a revival of interest and the renewed promotion of the cult of Anglo-Saxon saints, whose heroic aspects were emphasised. An illuminated text of Lydgate's new life of St Edmund (BL Harley Ms 2278) had been presented to the young Henry VI and subsequently belonged to Henry VIII.[38] In 1439 Lydgate was commissioned by Abbot Whethamstede to compile a new life of Alban and Amphibalus.[39] Dunstan of Canterbury, somewhat eclipsed by Becket, also enjoyed a revival of status in the early Tudor period, when in 1508 the rival claims made for relics preserved at Glastonbury were comprehensively quashed by Archbishop Warham, just as the Windsor glazing was being created.[40] A significant number of armoured saints also survive, albeit now unidentified, a third subject appropriate to a great window in a chapel dedicated to a chivalric order.

This kind of subject matter – a display of historical figures redolent of legitimacy and succession – would have been appropriate to a great west window, over the chapel's principal ceremonial door. Similar iconography is found in this location in both stained glass and sculpture, but here at Windsor the size of the window precludes any significant display of statuary. Comparable displays in English stained glass survive in the west walls of Canterbury Cathedral and York Minster.[41] The great west window of St George's Chapel would have been the rival of any of these other late medieval displays in terms of both variety and splendour.

FOURTEEN

THE RESTORATION OF THE DEAN
AND CANONS IN 1660

Stephen Taylor

WINDSOR CASTLE fell to the parliamentarians in October 1642, shortly after the outbreak of the civil war. Subsequently, Charles I returned there only once, and then briefly, while awaiting trial at the end of December 1648. During the eighteen years that St George's Chapel was used as a garrison and prison, there can be little doubt that it suffered considerable damage at the hands of the soldiers of parliament and the Republic. The treasury was broken open by Captain Fogg almost immediately after the seizure of the castle, and the plate and vestments were removed. In September the following year many of the furnishings were destroyed, including the metalwork for the unfinished tomb of Henry VIII, and at some point lead was stripped from the roofs of the deanery.[1] However, while the chapel and the surrounding buildings undoubtedly suffered damage, it is clear that St George's escaped the worst depredations of many of the English and Welsh cathedrals at this time. This good fortune was partly the result of the fact that, after Prince Rupert's brief bombardment, Windsor was never the scene of any fighting, and partly the result of the parliamentary order of 21 April 1643 'that there be no disorders and disturbances made in the chapel'. Even allowing for these considerations, given the extent of puritan iconoclasm elsewhere, it is remarkable that the glass of the west window survived.

One reason why it is difficult to catalogue in detail the destruction of the 1640s and 1665s is that little documentary evidence survives of the process of restoration in the 1660s and 1670s.[2] Hollar's engravings of the chapel, published in Elias Ashmole's *Institution, Laws and Ceremonies of the Order of the Garter* (1672), suggests that the interior of the chapel was already in good order in the early 1660s (Fig. 28). Certainly, thanks to a series of gifts the altar was lavishly decorated at service times, as the inventory of 1667 makes clear: there were a pair of large candlesticks, embossed with foliage and Biblical subjects; a large basin commissioned by Princess Mary of Orange (though ultimately paid for by the chapter); a pair of large basins, the gift of the Duchess of York; a tapestry copy of

Fig. 28. View of the quire looking east in 1670, by Wenceslaus Hollar.

Titian's 'Supper at Emmaus' from Lady Mordaunt to hang above the altar, and, covering the east wall behind it, twenty-two panes of gold and purple damask from the king himself. On the other hand, work on the canons' houses was still continuing into the 1670s and 1680s.

Cathedrals and collegiate chapters, however, consisted of more than buildings and furnishings; they were also communities of people. Here, too, St George's fared at least a little better than the average chapter during the civil war and interregnum. It has been calculated that across the country, by the time that the monarchy was restored in 1660, approximately two-thirds of all canonries and prebends were vacant.[3] At St George's five of the twelve canons were still alive and returned to claim their dignitaries, as were four minor canons.[4] All of these men, of course, were 'sufferers', that is, episcopalians who were deprived of one or more of their livings or were otherwise persecuted by parliament; and all can be traced in John Walker's *Account of the … Sufferings of the Clergy of the Church of England … in the … Grand Rebellion* (1714).[5] As might be expected from a body of men who owed their preferments to the king, there were some fervent royalists among them. David Stokes (third canon), for example, 'deserted his fellowship' at Eton and 'resided in the King's quarters and garrisons in open hostility' to the forces of parliament. William Brough (fifth canon) also joined the king in Oxford, serving as chaplain to Henrietta Maria's protestant servants, having been sequestered in March 1643 after denouncing parliament, 'especially lawyers among them', for meddling in spiritual matters. The movements of these men during the 1650s are unknown, though Brough continued to publish works defending the worship of the Church of England, including the popular *Sacred Principles, Services and Soliloquies* (1650). Two other canons, however, illustrate the different strategies open to episcopalian nonconformists, that is, those churchmen who refused to make any accommodation with the regimes which ruled the country following the defeat of Charles I. Herbert Croft (ninth canon), who had distinguished himself in royal service, carrying messages between the king and his generals, found a refuge in the household of Sir Rowland Berkeley at Cotheridge in Worcestershire, supported in part by income from the family estates. By contrast, Thomas Browne (first canon), a former domestic chaplain to Archbishop Laud, appears to have followed the royal family into exile, finding service as chaplain to Princess Mary, Charles II's sister, who had married the Prince of Orange.

While in exile Charles II showed little interest in nominating to the vacancies in the chapter at Windsor or, indeed, anywhere else. The only exception was the deanery, to which he appointed Edward Hyde, the cousin of the Lord Chancellor, on the death of Christopher Wren in 1658, though Hyde did not live to enjoy it, dying himself in August 1659. Following the Restoration, however, the king moved remarkably quickly. All of the vacancies at Windsor, with the exception of the deanery, were filled in July – no other chapter, not even Westminster, the other major royal peculiar among the collegiate churches, was filled so fast. It seems difficult to explain this process simply in terms of the clamour of expectant clergy petitioning for preferments; it is far more likely that the king took a particular interest in the restoration of a church which had especially strong links with the monarchy, as the home of the Knights of the Garter, and with the Stuart dynasty, as the resting place of his father.

Whom, then, did Charles II appoint to the restored chapter? As might be expected, prominent among the new canons were men who had distinguished themselves in the royalist cause in the 1640s and 1650s and who had suffered for their loyalty to church and king. A stall at Windsor would have appeared a particularly appropriate reward for men like Bruno Ryves, who filled the last vacancy in the chapter when he was appointed to the deanery on 25 August 1660. A former Lent preacher at court and chaplain to Charles I, Ryves committed himself wholeheartedly to the king's cause right at the beginning of the civil war, joining the royalist army and even serving on the council of war. Then, in the 1650s, he appears to have acted as an agent for the exiled court, carrying money to the continent on at least one occasion. He is best known, however, for his journalism, notably the influential newsbook, *Mercurius Rusticus*, which appeared irregularly through 1643 and 1644. Unsurprisingly, he was sequestered from his livings of St Martin Vintry and Stanwell and, in a classic account of clerical suffering, it was later recorded that he and his family were 'taken out of their beds at midnight, turned out of doors, all his goods seized, and all that night lay under a hedge in the wet and cold'. Other canons could make similar claims of loyal service: John Lloyd (fourth canon) and Anthony Hawles (eighth canon) both served as chaplains to the king in exile, while Edward Fulham, having been imprisoned by the House of Commons as early as December 1640, later fled to Italy, where he served as chaplain to the British Factory at Leghorn in the 1650s.

While negotiating the terms of his return to England, however, Charles II had made it clear that he was determined to rule as the king of all his people. His declaration issued at Breda on 4 April 1660 promised 'a liberty to tender consciences; and that no man shall be disquieted, or called in question, for differences of opinion in matters of religion'. As proof of this intent, two of the king's very first ecclesiastical preferments, announced while he was still at Dover, on 25 May 1660, were the appointments of two Presbyterians, Edward Reynolds and Edmund Calamy, to royal chaplaincies. His government remained committed, publicly at least, to a broadly-based church settlement for some months: at the end of September 1660 Reynolds was promoted to the bishopric of Norwich and, in October, the Worcester House Declaration renewed Charles's commitment to a church settlement which would accommodate Presbyterian consciences. This policy was reflected in the filling of the vacancies at St George's with the appointment of another Presbyterian, George Evans, later a distinguished antiquary, to the tenth canonry. Evans's promotion to a dignity in the burial place of the royal martyr was, perhaps, easier for the old royalists to bear as he was still a young man. He had been born in 1630, and had played no part in the conflicts of the 1640s. Admitted to Jesus College, Cambridge, in 1646, the year in which the first civil war ended, he received his first preferment there as a fellow in 1650. Thus, while he conformed to the new regime, he had not opposed the old. The canonry was not the only symbol of royal favour granted to Evans; he was presented to another living of symbolic importance, the vicarage of New Windsor, on 7 July 1660, though there is no evidence that he ever received a royal chaplaincy.

Of course, not all of the new canons fit neatly into the categories of episcopalian royalist and Presbyterian. The events of the 1640s and 1650s posed for churchmen a whole series of challenges, both practical and intellectual, and individuals responded in a variety of different ways. The decision to go into exile or retreat into internal retirement had serious consequences, both personal and financial, but those who adopted this course of action were at least able to maintain a sense of ideological purity. For many clergymen in the 1640s the decision-making process was complicated and messy. Some clearly resolved to keep their heads down and to try to hold onto their preferments for as long as possible. One such was William Chamberlain, a domestic chaplain to the Duke of Ormond, who was appointed to the sixth canonry in 1660. While he was sequestered from the rectory of Duxford St Peter during the first civil war, he managed to hold on to his fellowship at Trinity College, Cambridge, until he was finally ejected in 1650 for refusing the Engagement. It should not be assumed, however, that Chamberlain had to make any kind of submission or accommodation with the authorities in order to retain his fellowship – at Emmanuel College William Sancroft, who was as uncompromising as any episcopalian, also managed to hold on to his fellowship until presented with the Engagement. George Evans, however, was not the only one of the canons to have embraced – or, at least, to have accepted the necessity of – some kind of conformity to the new regime, especially in the 1650s. Both George Hall (seventh canon) and Ralph Brideoake (eleventh canon) and, among the survivors from the pre-civil war period, George Gillingham (twelfth canon) served in the national church of Cromwell and the Republic.

George Hall was the son of Joseph Hall, Bishop of Exeter and Norwich, a moderate Calvinist, who continued ordaining ministers according to the rites of the Book of Common Prayer right through to his death in 1656, despite having been deprived of his bishopric in 1646. George received his early preferment from his father, including the vicarage of Menheniot, a prebend of Exeter, and the archdeaconry of Cornwall, from all of which he was sequestered by parliament in the 1640s. Regular payments were made to his wife by order of the Committee for Compounding in the late 1640s and further evidence that he had made his peace with the new regime came in November 1651, when he was appointed lecturer at St Bartholomew by the Exchange in London. Although the keepers

Fig. 29. Ralph Brideoake's effigy on his tomb in the Bray Chapel.

of the great seal would not accept his election as rector of that parish in 1654, he was, in the same year, admitted by the Cromwellian Triers, the committee created to vet ministerial appointments, to the rectory of Berwick in Sussex, and in 1655 he became rector of St Botolph, Aldersgate. A clear indication that, like his father, he remained episcopalian in inclination and practice is provided by his appointment as lecturer at St Clement Eastcheap, one of the centres of episcopalianism in the City in the later 1650s.

Hall's political sympathies in the 1640s are obscure. Ralph Brideoake's, by contrast, were clearly royalist: appointed to the mastership of Manchester Grammar School shortly before the outbreak of war, he found a patron in Lord Strange, later Earl of Derby, and was present at the sieges of Lathom House in 1644–5. After the king's defeat, he found a new patron in William Lenthall, Speaker of the House of Commons, through whose influence he was made Preacher of the Rolls, despite opposition to him as a Cavalier and a dull preacher, and then rector of Witney. Unlike Hall, however, Brideoake appears to have moved away from his episcopalian roots, being elected as an elder in the Manchester Presbyterian classis in 1647 and then appointed as a 'Trier' in March 1659. Later he was to gain promotion to the deanery at Salisbury (Figs. 29 & 30) and then the see of Chichester and was to be buried in the Bray Chapel at Windsor.[6] Our knowledge of George Gillingham's career is more fragmentary. During the 1640s, according to Walker, 'he was persecuted from place to place, and took shelter for some time at Southampton; but was at last driven thence likewise'. However, he resurfaced, in 1653, as a lecturer at St Gregory by St Paul's, one of the other major centres of episcopalianism in Cromwellian London.

Perhaps the most interesting case, however, is provided by the new dean, Bruno Ryves. As indicated above, Ryves had been a prominent royalist in the first civil war, and he maintained close contacts with episcopalian nonconformists through the 1650s, continuing to present himself as a sufferer. On completing a new edition of the works of Bishop Grosseteste in 1658, he wrote to Gilbert Sheldon, the heart of the royalist episcopalian network in England and future archbishop of Canterbury, explaining that, 'being deprived of Liberty to exercise my Calling, I have entertained myselfe by this diversion'. But Ryves's career after the fall of Oxford in 1646 was more complicated than this statement might suggest. He had compounded on the Oxford articles, though his fine was still unpaid in 1653. There is evidence of him preaching in London, perhaps unofficially or even clandestinely, in 1649. Then, in 1654, he was elected Preacher at Lincoln's Inn, a post which he filled until he was replaced, on Cromwell's order, in 1656. Finally, in 1659, he was granted £5 by the Trustees for the Maintenance of Ministers in

Fig. 30. The top of the dean's stall, made for Salisbury Cathedral in 1672, with Ralph Brideoake's punning rebuses on it.

respect of the deanery of Chichester. None of this can be adduced as evidence that he made peace with any of the regimes that governed England following the execution of the king, especially in the light of his role as a courier to the court in exile. Cumulatively, however, it reveals that he negotiated a finer line between conformity and nonconformity than his self-presentation as a royalist sufferer might suggest.

Two points may be highlighted as a result of this discussion of the composition of the dean and canons of the restored chapel. First, even this small sample of clergy reveals strikingly the wide range of responses to the events of the 1640s and 1650s.[7] In particular, conformity to the regimes that exercised power in England following the defeat of the king took a wide variety of forms. Different individuals not only accommodated themselves to the disappearance of monarchy and episcopacy in different ways; more than that, it seems clear that conformity meant different things to different people. Second, while there is a notable diversity of experience in the new dean and canons over the previous two decades, it is important not to exaggerate this characteristic of the chapter at St George's. Despite the attention which has been given to the episcopalian sufferers of the 1640s and 1650s, these men were no more than a minority, amounting to perhaps 15 per cent of clergy beneficed in the Church of England in 1640, and the nonconformists, those forced, in Bishop Duppa's memorable phrase, to eke out an existence, like the primitive Christians, 'in dens, and caves, and deserts', were a tiny minority of that minority. Most of those ordained before the abolition of episcopacy in 1646 were conformists. In addition, over 3,000 men received episcopal ordination clandestinely between 1646 and 1660, most of whom served in the interregnum church, and they were joined, between 1660 and 1662, by enormous numbers who sought orders, whether reluctantly or enthusiastically, from the restored bishops. In other words, the body of the clergy of the Church of England in the early years of the Restoration was composed overwhelmingly of conformists. St George's Chapel, however, was not. It has only been possible to identify five members of the restored chapter as conformists, one of whom was the highly ambiguous figure of the new dean.

In fact, the tone of the Chapel in the early years of the Restoration was distinctly high church. George Evans, the former Presbyterian, found it an uncomfortable place and, during a period of illness, lamented to a friend: 'if you lived among them as I doe, you wold say as the Queen of Sheba to Solomon the one half has not been told; if I live, I'le come as little among them as I can'. The priority given to the acquisition of new communion plate and furnishings for the altar provides one insight into the attitudes of the dean and canons. The appointment of four new minor canons in October 1660 offers another: the three who were not yet in orders were required to obtain them by Christmas 1660, despite the implication of the Worcester House Declaration that episcopal ordination was not to be imposed as a condition of preferment in the Church. Indeed, even Evans felt obliged to be re-ordained well before the deadline of St Bartholomew's Day 1662 imposed by the Act of Uniformity. Bearing with him a dispensation from Archbishop Juxon allowing him to be ordained deacon and priest on the same day, he presented himself in Henry VII's Chapel, Westminster Abbey, as the only candidate to Humphrey Henchman, Bishop of Salisbury, a hardliner and an emergent leader of the restored Church. The symbolism of the occasion could hardly have been lost on him.

Charles II's religious beliefs are notoriously opaque, even to his biographers. By turns, he backed toleration for dissenters and the imposition of an exclusive and repressive Anglicanism. He also promised to convert to Catholicism as part of the Treaty of Dover and was actually received into the Church of Rome on his deathbed. Yet, for all the studied ambivalence, there seems little doubt that the character of worship at St George's owed much to Charles's own preferences. Kenneth Fincham and Nicholas Tyacke have observed that, whatever his personal faith, Charles as king 'steadfastly remained a Laudian at his devotions'. He was personally involved in choosing the new dean and canons and he contributed liberally to the new furnishings. Other chapels in which he had a personal interest, such as Whitehall and the private chapel at Windsor, were organized in similar ways. And, while it might be necessary to give a canonry to a Presbyterian, George Evans was left in no doubt about how he had to behave:

> At the King's coming thither, he [Evans] was against bowing to the Altar. Whereupon the King expressed his resentment and anger, saying if he will not bow to God, let him not bow to me, and this made him the more scruple the next day.

FIFTEEN

THE HOUSES OF CANONS' CLOISTER

John Crook

WITHIN A YEAR OF the foundation of the Order of the Garter, the Black Death was at its height. It is therefore surprising that construction of the domestic buildings required for Edward III's collegiate foundation went ahead so smoothly. Work started in April 1350, and continued for about ten years. The building operations are exceptionally well chronicled in the royal Pipe Rolls and the surviving clerk's accounts, and this documentation formed the basis for the relevant section of William St John Hope's magisterial history of the architecture of Windsor Castle.[1] It must, however, be admitted that Hope's analysis of the development of the Canons' Cloister was fairly perfunctory, occupying no more than three pages;[2] and the first real attempts at getting to grips with the history of the canons' houses were made by Tim Tatton-Brown in articles published in the annual reports of the Friends of St George's and elsewhere.[3]

The area chosen for the College was within the Lower Ward, between the old royal lodgings built by Henry III in the 1240s, much of which had been destroyed by fire in 1295-6, and Henry's chapel of St Edward the Confessor. Edward III had the chapel rededicated to the Blessed Virgin and St George, and it was furnished with stalls for the new fraternity in 1350-53. The builders then turned their attention to accommodation for the secular priests, originally intended to comprise twenty-four 'chaplains', soon defined as a warden and twenty-three 'canons', balanced by twenty-four 'poor knights'.[4] Henry III had ordered in 1240 that a space between the royal lodgings and the chapel should be left as a 'grass plot' (*pratellum*),[5] and around this green court covered walks were then constructed by inserting walls linking the lodgings and the chapel. The pentice roof over these alleys was framed and leaded in 1248.[6] The north, east, and south sides of this irregularly shaped court were remodelled by Edward III in 1354-6 as the cloister that is now known as the 'Dean's Cloister', with an elegant inner arcade incorporating statuary niches and Purbeck marble shafts. First, though, in 1350-1 a vestry, chapter house, and the warden's lodgings were built on the

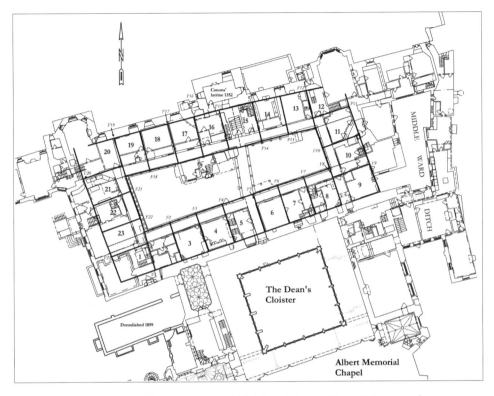

Fig. 31. Plan of Canons' Cloister showing (thick lines) the position of the cross-frames, numbered F1-F23, defining the 23 sets of apartments. The 23 bays, each containing a ground-floor and a first-floor room, are conventionally numbered 1-23, working anti-clockwise round the cloister.

east side of the area. These buildings partially survive within the Deanery. Their fine moulded doorways and traceried windows are a notable feature of the east cloister walk. The warden's principal accommodation comprised chambers over the chapter house, but by 1352 a hall was being built for him, perhaps extending eastwards from the north end of this range over the infilled site of the ditch formerly separating the Middle and Lower Wards.[7]

The north side of the Dean's Cloister incorporated part of the south wall of Henry III's royal lodgings, and it was between this massive wall, 1.55m thick, and the castle's north curtain wall that the canons' accommodation was built in 1352-4. Such were the origins of the group of buildings eventually known as Canons' Cloister that is the subject of this essay. The chambers were grouped around an elongated space 32m long by 9m wide at the west end tapering to

6.6m at the east end, an irregularity resulting from the convergence of the two medieval walls. The only constraint on the eastward extent of the site was the former Middle Ward Ditch and the wall beyond it; while to the west Henry III's 100 ft. long Great Hall, retained for the canons' use, formed the limit of potential development.

The first stage of the construction of the canons' accommodation was the demolition in January-February 1352 of the remains of the royal apartments: 'the throwing down of various walls in the places where the canons' chambers are to be built' and the repair of the thirteenth-century wall that was to be retained. Then a 'great latrine' (*magna latrina*) was formed in the twelfth-century tower on the north side of the site, and the castle's curtain wall on either side of the tower was raised higher to form the rear of the north range of the new chambers; the two other towers at the north-east and north-west corners of the new development were partially rebuilt at the same time. By mid-June 1352 masons were laying the stone footings of the lodgings.

The canons' chambers were built not of stone but wood and are perhaps the earliest timber-framed collegiate accommodation in England. In 1351-2 an entire oak wood was purchased for £66 13s 4d at a place called 'Cagham',[8] and in June 1352 work began on felling 3,004 trees for the royal works. The timber required for the chambers must have used much of this, though some of the timber was used for the lodgings within the Round Tower at Windsor,[9] and also at Westminster.

The three carpenters who assembled the chambers are named in the accounts for 1352-3 as Simon Hurley, John Glemsford, and John Dunstable, who were contracted to build 'twenty-three chambers using the king's timber for the canons of the royal chapel'.[10] In November 1352 a payment was made for 'two acres of land hired for one year upon which the carpenters work at the canons' chambers'.[11] This was presumably the framing yard, possibly at Cagham so that the frames could be constructed there, then disassembled and transported to Windsor. A distinction is made in the accounts between the whole oaks *quercus* and finished timber *mæremium* (a corruption of *materiamentum*), both transported to Windsor 'by land and water', hinting at off-site preparation of the frames. The waste on the other hand, was taken to London where it was sold: the purchase of Cagham Wood was something of a bargain, as after the trees had been converted into building timber the smaller boughs, bark, and twigs were sold on for twice the original cost.

The twenty-three lodgings were arranged on two storeys of unequal height, the ground floor rooms being about 2.7m high, the ones on the first floor rising to 4.80m at the rear. Not only were the upper rooms much taller, they were also deeper, oversailing the cloister walkway that was tucked beneath the front of the building at the expense of the ground-floor rooms. The lodgings were set out in bays that were fifteen feet wide, delimited by cross-frames. Enough of these has survived on three sides of the cloister for the original, quite simple design to be determined, as shown in Figure. 31. The longest timbers were the front posts (5.60m) and the first-floor girding beams (6.30m). The girders were supported at their mid-length by a shorter timber stanchion, and probably rested on corbels set into the rear wall (100 corbels were ordered in April 1353: they were probably of Kentish Ragstone).[12] Additional support would have been provided by the screen walls between the alleys and the ground-floor rooms, though this was a secondary benefit. The frame was more complex at first floor level, with a mid-post over the ground-floor stanchion, and a wall-post planted against the rear wall. The three vertical elements were triangulated at first-floor level by long passing-braces, cross-halved over a mid-rail. Finally the whole assemblage was capped by a principal rafter, sloping down 730mm from apex to eaves.

Linking the transverse frames, longitudinal timbers consisted of (1) a bressumer at the front of each house, tenoned into the principal posts and braced by decorated spandrel brackets, (2) a spine beam supporting the first floor, tenoned and braced into the top of the ground-floor mid-posts, and (3), below the lead roof, front and rear roof plates and a purlin. All these longitudinal elements were braced to the posts supporting them, and the roof plate at the rear was probably additionally supported on corbels.

The internal framing is fairly workaday, but the three carpenters were able to display their decorative skills in the traceried spandrel brackets forming the arcade in front of the recessed walkway. Three bays of the original arcade have actually survived, embedded within the entrance porch to No. 6, Canons' Cloister, an encroachment into the cloister garth; all the other spandrels are modern, such as those adorning the relocated cross-passage. The surviving arcade includes a timber doorway and a corresponding break in the sill-beam, suggesting that the cloister arcade could be entered through an opening in each of the four alleys.

St John Hope was uncharacteristically confused over the construction of the alleys, and one of the drawings published in his *History* shows a jettied structure.[13] One must assume that much less of the primary framing was visible in Hope's day, leading to confusion between original and secondary elements. It must be emphasised that the way the upper rooms oversail the alleys cannot be defined as a jetty in any sense of the term, for the load-bearing timbers of the chambers are those in the plane of the arcade and upper walls; the rear walls are mere screens,

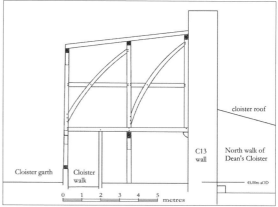

Left Fig. 32. Remains of the probable 14th century fireplace in the rear wall of Bay 4. It had a timber lintel, and an internal feature with a foiled head, which was perhaps a bread oven.

Above Fig. 33. Reconstruction of a cross-frame on the south side of the cloister, typical of all those separating the canons' apartments.

performing a secondary role as regards support. The only stone walls were at the rear of the north and south ranges, and the account rolls mention that in October 1352 the masons were preparing stones for the doors and windows of the canons' chambers. Other payments in 1353-4 were concerned with the important matter of heating: chimneys were inserted into the masonry rear walls of the houses, and in the present choristers' vestry on the ground floor of No. 1 the remains of a blocked fireplace with lateral bread oven are visible in a broom cupboard (Fig. 32). St John Hope thought that this fireplace might in fact have formed part of Henry III's earlier lodgings, which is not impossible on stylistic grounds,[14] and traces of thirteenth-century windows may also be seen on the Dean's cloister side of the south range, together with the scars of buttresses.

By the end of 1353 work on the chambers was coming to an end. Roofing boards had been purchased as early as May of that year, but the lead to cover them was not cast until October and November. Meanwhile the masonry interior walls were being plastered, and the gaps in the cross-frames were being closed. Close studding seems to have been used above the mid-rail of the first-floor rooms, as is still seen in the Catherine Room, and there is some evidence lower down. The infill between the main timbers was the usual wattle and daub: the purchase of laths and clay is recorded in March 1354. The structural timbers appear to have remained visible as a decorative feature, and in the same month Richard Asskeby was paid 100s. for 'painting the woodwork in the canons' chambers according to his own devising, with varnish and ochre.' The completion of the works is indicated by the purchase of twenty-six locks in February 1354 and fifty 'clicket locks' (latches) in March.

The layout of the dwellings may be worked out, for despite much post-medieval reconstruction, many of the partition walls within Canons' Cloister preserve the position of their medieval predecessors, and some still contain medieval timbers. Plotting the position of these walls on the modern plan, as shown in Figure 34, gives precisely twenty-three divisions, regularly spaced at 15ft intervals, and this corresponds with the 'twenty-three chambers' mentioned in those accounts that were drawn up at the start of the work on the cloister; later the number increased. Even though the west side of the cloister was mostly rebuilt in the seventeenth century, it is clear that there must have been five apartments on this side, compared with four on the east side. Within No. 8, at the north-west corner, some fragments of original timber framing survive, including a ground-floor ceiling beam on the line of the inner face of the curtain wall, indicating that Bay 20 was of the same dimensions as the other houses. This beam houses joists running north-south, supporting the surviving counter-chamfered floorboards of the upper storey: a rare survival.[15]

To north and south the rear of the dwellings was defined by solid walls, and a possible survival of twelfth-century masonry within No. 8 suggests that the extent of the house in this direction was determined, as already noted, by the east wall of Henry III's Great Hall. On the east side of the cloister there were no such constraints; nevertheless, a series of aligned walls survive within the houses on that side suggesting that they were originally of exactly the same depth from front to rear as the others.

Despite the regularity of the layout, it is clear that there were significant differences between the sets of chambers. In particular, the floor area of several of the ground-floor chambers must have been reduced by as many as six access passages. The route from the great cloister to the canons' houses was through a timber-framed passage with, at its south end, the stone doorway with Purbeck marble shafts that is a fine fourteenth-century feature of Dean's Cloister; and there was another passage half-way along the north side of Canons' Cloister leading to the latrine and the 'Hundred Steps'. These two passages were linked by a pentice that bisected the cloister, though it must be noted that what one sees today is a nineteenth-century replacement on a different alignment from

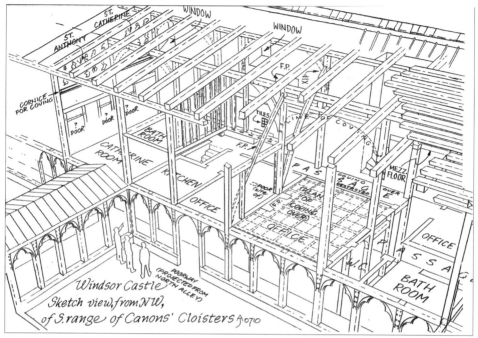

Fig. 34. Surviving medieval framing on the south side of the Canon's Cloister, by Jill Atherton.

the original. Passages would also have been required in order to gain access to the corner bays in the scheme we have proposed; the pair at the west end would have also led to the hall, while that in the south-east corner would have led to the warden's house.

The medieval building accounts refer always to the 'canons' chambers'. Some of the accounts relating to the inception of the works mention that there were twenty-three of them;[16] and given that the Warden had his own house this corresponds to the number of secular priests as originally specified. No provision appears to have been made for the adjustment in the number of priests that Edward III made in 1352, when the definitive composition of his new College was determined and the first statutes issued. It was now to consist of a warden, twelve canons, and thirteen priest-vicars, a total of twenty-six priests balanced by twenty-six Knights of the Garter (the sovereign, Prince of Wales, and twenty-four companion knights). It would seem that by then the layout of the canons' chambers could not be changed, but the fact that twenty-six locks were purchased in February 1354 and a reference to roofing twenty-six canons' chambers probably in October of that year,[17] suggests that two extra sets of chambers were squeezed in somewhere.

Leaving aside the question of the two extra sets, the original design provided for twenty-three large first-floor rooms and twenty-three smaller ground-floor ones of various sizes. St John Hope believed that the canons lived on the first floor, with their vicars in the rooms beneath;[18] but of course this would mean that each of the eleven original canons would occupy two adjacent upper rooms; and each vicar would occupy two ground-floor rooms. But this would have given one too many upper rooms; the arithmetic is uncomfortable, and seems incompatible with clear statements in the accounts that what was actually built was twenty-three residential units. It is surely more likely that (as was long the case in the post-medieval period) the differing status of the canons and their vicars was reflected in the desirability of the available accommodation. As we have seen, some of the ground-floor rooms were small because parts of them had been sacrificed to the passages; and there may furthermore have been a perception that some sets of chambers were better placed than others.

The question of access to the upper rooms is obviously relevant, for if each canon occupied two adjacent first-floor rooms, only eleven (or at the most, twelve) stairs would have been required, though such stairs would have intruded still further into some of the ground-floor rooms. The latter consideration is perhaps the most compelling argument against the pairing up of rooms implied in St John Hope's analysis. There is unfortunately no archaeological evidence for the form and location of the original stairs, or of possible original doors through the main frames. On balance, though, the simpler arrangement of twenty-three/twenty-five sets of chambers seems more likely, each with a simple framed stair to the upper floor. The stairs were perhaps boxed in against draughts, as suggested by the number of locks and latches, which implied that each apartment had two doors: a front door and one internal door. In short, each of the twenty-three (later twenty-five) priests may have enjoyed broadly similar accommodation, comprising a first-floor chamber over a smaller ground-floor room.

One other interesting question needs to be addressed. One of the first buildings to be completed was the great latrine; and it has often been noted that in March 1354 a clicket lock was supplied for the common latrine, with twenty-six keys. As we have already seen, a passage at ground-floor level could easily have been provided, leading out of the north cloister walk. But within the tower great timber beams at first-floor ceiling level suggest that the latrine may have been two-storeyed, and indeed a fourteenth-century doorway once led from a modern lavatory into the north dining room of No. 6, Canons' Cloister. It is unlikely that this can have been a common access for all the canons, and it is surely more probably that at an early date the inhabitant of the adjacent canon's lodgings enjoyed the space within the upper floor of the tower – as indeed did also those canons who inhabited the north-east and north-east houses with access into the other two towers in the curtain wall. This is another example of the way in which the desirability of twenty-three houses of nominally similar design differed owing to practical considerations.

Later Medieval Developments

In the early fifteenth century the vicars were given separate accommodation when in 1409 Henry IV granted the college 'a place called Woodhaw, beside the great hall, to build there houses for the vicars, clerks, and choristers'. This seems to have marked the start of the development of a range of dwellings against the curtain wall, west of Canons' Cloister and beyond the Great Hall. After c. 1480 the vicars would move yet again to their own purpose-built cloister west of the chapel, later called the Horseshoe Cloister. The departure of the vicars meant that the twelve canons could expand into the additional spaces that had become available – a change from mere 'sets' comprising living and sleeping chambers to what one might recognise as individual houses – and henceforth the buildings evolved in a variety of different ways, after the canons acquired greater status and commensurate incomes. The available accommodation was increased still further in 1519 with the construction of Denton's Commons for the thirteen choristers and eight chantry priests.

The height of the tall upper storey meant that it was possible to insert mezzanine floors, as are found in Bays 2-6 on the south side of the cloister. Part of that mezzanine floor was removed during refurbishment works in the 1960s when offices were created for St George's House: the ceilings were presumably felt to be uncomfortably low. Evidence for the mezzanine survives, notably the great tie-beam that crosses the office at the front of No. 2, which must for a time have appeared at ceiling level, below the inserted floor. There was also a mezzanine floor in No. 5, where the first-floor study still shows evidence of what must have been a rather low ceiling, only eight feet above the floor, and still has two tiers of windows, the upper of which lit the mezzanine rooms.

The most obvious enlargement of one of the houses was on the north side, where encroachment occurred into the cloister garth in front of Bays 16 and 17 forming what is now the main façade of No. 6. The addition of a second storey to this house is presumably of the same date, perhaps in the sixteenth century,[19] and the flanking brick chimney stacks are probably contemporary with the first phase of these works. This addition has clearly suffered many changes since it was first built: one can see, for example, that oriel windows both at first- and

Fig. 35. The main façade of No. 6 Canons' Cloister, showing the later bay which encroaches into the cloister garth.

second-floor level on the eastern half of the façade, facing the cloister garth, have been removed (only one survives) (Fig. 35). It is possible that these windows are indicated in Wenceslaus Hollar's birds-eye view of the Castle of around 1670.

The occupant of Bays 4-5 (No. 2) went for a different solution, adding an extension over the Dean's Cloister. As Tim Tatton-Brown has shown, the canon in question was almost certainly Thomas Magnus, who appears to have refurbished and enlarged his house soon after his appointment in 1520.[20] Magnus's arms occurred in a window just above the extension, and the framing of the new first-floor wing (which also has an excellent fireplace and a panelled ceiling with portrait heads that show the first Renaissance influence in any of the houses) has been tree-ring dated to 1511 x 1536.[21] Furthermore, is may be shown that

Canon Magnus was most probably responsible for the fine wall-paintings in the 'Catherine Room', named for the portrait of St Catherine on the east wall (Fig. 36). Until the mid-nineteenth century, indeed, the only way into the rooms that Canon Magnus had added to the rear of his house was via a flight of stairs leading up out of the Catherine Room.

The encroachment into the Canons' Cloister, of which the entrance tower to No. 6 is the most obvious exanple, continued with the placing of chimney stacks within the garth, providing for hearths on the upper floors of the houses. One of these is seen in Bay 13: a big double stack supported on a round-headed arch. It might be late sixteenth/early seventeenth century. Almost certainly of the latter date is the tall stack of Bay 6, which is precariously supported on two Jacobean style timber posts, partly encroaching into what may be an earlier oriel window. This bay forms part of No. 1, Canons' Cloister, and two new stone chimney pieces were installed there between 1738 and 1744, no doubt making use of the much earlier chimney.[22]

The Modern Period

The canon's houses undoubtedly suffered greatly during the civil wars of the 1640s, and those at the west end were irreparably damaged.[23] The lead seems to have been stripped from the roofs of the houses throughout the cloister, and much damage must have been caused by water ingress and general neglect. No. 6, for example, was rebuilt to such an extent that in 1676 it was referred to as the 'new dwelling house on the north wall of the Castle.'[24] Its reconstruction formed part of a major programme of rebuilding and repair at the Restoration of the monarchy, including the complete reconstruction of the west side of the cloister as No. 9 and No. 10.[25] The latter house straddled the footway leading into the north-west corner of the Dean's Cloister, and the southern half, built in the mid-1670s on the site of the canons' chapter house of c.1477, was demolished in 1859. A photograph taken during the demolition shows a stack of wainscoting removed from that part of the house. The northern half of No. 10 was added to No. 9 and now comprises St George's House.

One of the most obvious features of Canons' Cloister to have survived from this period are the front doors, many of which clearly date from the 1660s. Several have retained their original door furniture, as well as later additions such as modern security locks.

It is possible that it was at this time that the opportunity was taken of inserting cellars beneath most of the houses. Originally, only one of the sets of chambers seems to have had a cellar, whose timbers and floor boards are visible beneath

Fig. 36. North-east view in the Catherine Room (Bay 5, now part of No. 2) showing wall paintings and much original framing.

Bay 9, in the south-east corner of the cloister. In 1972 Peter Curnow, an Ancient Monuments Inspector for the Department of the Environment, considered that the basement of No. 1 Canons' Cloister also dated from 1351-3.[26] This is perhaps unlikely given that the walls are of brick, and St John Hope was probably nearer the mark when he thought that the cellar in Bay 7, with its two-light window opening from the Dean's Cloister, was 'Elizabethan'.

From the Restoration onwards the documentary record is more complete, and particular light is shed on the development of the houses by a register in two volumes in the cathedral archives, known as the 'Income Book'. Its purpose was to record the transactions that occurred when a change in occupancy of one of the canonry houses occurred, and the new occupant reimbursed his predecessor for the fittings and fixtures that he inherited. In particular these concerned wainscoting (panelling), for so early as 1607 it had been enacted in chapter that:

> if any of the Canons [...] shall remove from their houses in the Cloister or Depart this lief, havinge bestowed any Charges for Waynscot in the same house or any part thereof, then whosoever shall come unto the same house shall satisfie the Charge thereof to him or his executors as it Cost abatinge only iiijs in the pounde [...] that soe in the ende the same wainscot maie belonge to the house as the goods of the deane and Canons...[27]

The arrangement was further regularised in 1677, and the register dates from this period. As well as providing precious information about successive occupancy of the canons' houses, which otherwise is often unrecorded, the Income Book also gives insight into the way those houses were fitted out.

A similar situation operated in Winchester Cathedral Close from the 1660s, and there the register was called the 'Wainscot Book', showing that it was initially set up to record the transfer of panelling, which was regarded as a semi-movable rather as a fitted carpet might be considered today: an item which in theory could be removed from a house but which in practice was sold on to the next occupant less an allowance for depreciation. This was fixed at 25% at Winchester, compared with Windsor's 20%.

Whereas at Winchester many items mentioned in the Wainscot Book may be identified, it is harder to recognise with certainty many of the fittings mentioned in the Windsor equivalent. A few items, such as the tables of the Garter Knights painted in the Deanery drawing room for Dean Christopher Wren in the 1630s are instantly recognisable, but in many cases the vagueness of the description and the difficulty in working out which rooms are being referred to mean that the fixtures cannot be identified, even if they have survived.

Nevertheless, the canons' houses at Windsor retain some excellent examples of panelling and other decorative woodwork from the late fifteenth to the eighteenth centuries. In this category should be included the excellent coved ceiling in the Warden's office in No. 2, Canons' Cloister (the first floor of Bay 7), perhaps dating from the 1480s. This room was reduced in size in the 1960s with the insertion of a partition at the south end. It contains a bolection moulded marble chimney piece for which Dr Marten paid £6 in 1743 when this was the dining room of the house called 'Shift Guest'.[28]

Panelling in the early seventeenth century was usually of oak, with quite small unpainted panels. Good examples of this kind of wainscot are found in the principal first-floor rooms of No. 1,[29] Canons' Cloister – this is probably too early to fall within the purview of the Income Book. Similar panelling occurs in several other houses – such as the Warden's office where it goes well with the much earlier coved ceiling – but has often been painted. Also in No. 1 is some late seventeenth-century bolection moulded panelling in the rear first-floor bedroom, and this appears to be the wainscot for which Canon Vaughan, occupant of the house since 1695, was reimbursed by his successor in 1714. Wainscot in three rooms is mentioned (two bedrooms including a closet, and the dining room), but the internal layout has been much altered, most recently in 1972 when panelling was moved. All this illustrates the difficulty of identifying work from the Income Book.

Even, so, the volumes provide fascinating insight into changing fashions in interior design, and, together with entries in the chapter minutes, show the extent to which the Canons of Windsor were prepared to invest in dwellings which they occupied only sporadically. No. 4 is a good example. This house has its distant origins in Bay 12 of the canons' chambers, but now sprawls, at first floor level and above, over a large area to the north and east of the cloister, abutting the north end of the Deanery. The interior of the house appears to have undergone a thorough make-over during the tenure of Dr Saumares, who lived there from 1678 until his death in September 1697. Although it was noted in Chapter in 1678 that the repairs of his house had 'been done very well',[30] two years later he was demanding that his kitchen should be repaired. On inspection it was agreed that 'The sinks belonging to his house not only noisome to the inhabitants but pernicious to the foundations; and that the trap door belonging to the cellar being inconvenient and hazardous to be made within the door entering his house'.[31] The hatch to the cellar is now 10ft. away from the front door, so perhaps it was moved northwards. The cellar continued to bother Canon Saumares, and in 1682 damage was caused 'by the breaking in of the common sewer into the said cellar'.[32] All these works were carried out at common expense, but Canon Saumares personally paid for works that fell within the remit of the Income Book. In 1680-81 various workmen received £88 4s 4d for what amounted to a complete refit of panelling, doors, shutters and other joinery work, for all of which he personally paid. Unfortunately very little of this seems to have survived, except in cupboards. The house has evidently had further major interventions since the seventeenth century and much of the wainscoting has been replaced in plaster: as, for example, in the largest room in the house, the 'great parlour' formed within the canted tower.

The most extensive of these was carried out in the early nineteenth century for Dr Keate, the famous headmaster of Eton and a Canon of Windsor from 1820 to 1852. He moved into No. 4 in December 1828. He rebuilt the main stair and first-floor landing lit by an oval oculus in belated Regency style. His most significant contribution to the house was a third-floor study perched on the main roof, which might be likened to a watch-tower, with a view of Eton College to the north. The reeded decoration of the window architraves and bookshelves is typical of the period. Not surprisingly, communication between this eyrie and the servants' quarters four storeys lower down was eventually provided by a speaking tube. Dr Keate appears to have spent about £15,000, and was allowed to claim one-fifth of this as 'income' to the house, as a consequence of 'repairing this house in a very substantial manner & in making very considerable additions thereto.'[33]

This house also demonstrates the way in which the boundaries between the various houses changed over the centuries. A first-floor sitting room in Bay 11, overlooking the cloister, was once part of No. 3 next door, and there is a blocked doorway in the party wall. The divisions between the houses on the north and east side of the cloister are complex in the extreme: No. 4 is predominantly on the first floor and above, as already noted, and oversails the north end of No. 3; but further south No. 3a, subdivided from the parent house, rises through two floors and boasts the most extravagant staircase in the Cloister. On the north side, No. 5 is a compact three-storey unit, but to the west of it No. 6 occupies the upper floors as far as the end of the north cloister range, while No. 7 lies below it at ground-floor and basement level. Things were simpler in the mid-nineteenth century, when Nos. 3-4 were both occupied by Canon Frederick Anson, a canon from 1845-85, and 6 and 7 were in the single occupancy of the William Canning (a cousin of the statesman) (1828-60).

No. 6 contains the best examples of wainscot in the cloister, several of the rooms being clad in the tall, painted deal panelling with simple quadrant mouldings to the panels that became fashionable from around 1700. Also in this house is a fine Jacobean overmantle in the study, part of a nineteenth-century confection that includes an anachronistic Victorian fire surround in the style of Edward Pierce. Good panelling is also to be found on the west side of the cloister, where the building that is now St George's House was formerly No. 9-10 Canons' Cloister, a post-Restoration rebuild. Here a large ground-floor room at the south end may be identified with some confidence as the one in which a joiner called Samuel Wyatt installed 102 square yards of deal panelling in 1682 at a cost of 15 3s. The large panels have bolection moulded surrounds, and the room also contains a good bolection moulded fireplace, typical of its date.

The Income Book also provides insight into developments in plumbing and sanitation. As we have seen, the canons and vicars of the medieval cloister enjoyed a communal facility, the 'great latrine'. There is a reference to a 'pyssing place' in the cloister in 1478-9 which was probably separate from the latrine,[34] and in

1492-3 a window in the latrine tower was repaired,[35] but individual arrangements were probably in place long before the first mention of a flushing lavatory in 1730, when a 'marble water stoole and cisterne' was provided for No. 6.[36] During the same decade a lavatory was provided for the present house No. 2, described in detail in the Income Book: it included 'A Force-pump on leaden pipes, and cistern of the House, and Branch & marble Bason, and brass work with seat and Frame and stink-pot underneath'.[37] Water closets were presumably possible when piped water arrived in the cloister in the eighteenth century, as shown in a proposal plan of 1771,[38] previously the only water supply was from a well house that is shown in Norden's aerial view of the castle of 1607.

From 1833, following the recommendations of the Church Commissioners and the Ecclesiastical Commission Act of 1840, the number of canons was gradually reduced, canonries being suspended at the death of their occupants until the statutory target of four canonries had been reached in 1861.[39] The situation in 1886 is depicted in a fine plan of the College by the Chapter Surveyor A.Y. Nutt,[40] which indicates the names of the occupants: Canon Frederick Anson was in No. 4, Canon William Boyd Carpenter in Nos. 6-7, Canon the Hon. Charles Courtenay in No. 8. Canon Lord Wriothesley Russell lived outside Canons Cloister in the houses now called Nos. 24-5. The number was further reduced to three canonries in 1921, but since 1974 has stood again at four.

This essay can only provide a brief survey of the development of this complex area. It would not have been possible to write it without drawing on Eileen Scarff's painstaking work on the documented history of the houses. I am grateful to her for her support and encouragement.

SIXTEEN

THE DEAN AND CANONS OF ST GEORGE'S IN THE EIGHTEENTH CENTURY

Nigel Aston

IN THE LATER Stuart and Hanoverian periods St George's functioned both as a collegiate foundation and, for much of the time at least, as a *de facto* chapel royal. This unique combination makes it a uniquely rewarding institution to study. Yet the task of reconstructing its history remains to be undertaken systematically despite the recent revival of interest in eighteenth-century Anglicanism. If the cathedral chapters of the period have been understudied notwithstanding the abundance of recent works on the history of particular cathedrals,[1] the investigation of post-Reformation collegiate churches has barely even begun.[2] As a capitular example, Windsor stands comparison with foundations on the scale of Southwell and Ripon and yet, like them, the policies, politics, and personalities of the Chapter, as well as its worship and choral traditions are little known.[3] The powers held by the Dean and Chapter at Windsor eclipsed those of these others : the chapel was exempt from the episcopal jurisdiction of the Bishop of Salisbury and the Dean was not instituted by any bishop for he, in fact, acted as the Ordinary.[4] In part these deficiencies can be considered a problem with the sources. The Chapter Act records at Windsor for this period are intact and yet the survival of personal papers for individual deans and canons is patchy and supplementing these lacunae with a wider trawl would be worthwhile but would probably risk disappointing results. This short essay represents a preliminary step in the direction of understanding with a focus on patronage arrangements for the Dean and major Canons.

The connection with the reigning dynasty is an inseparable part of the history of the chapel in the early modern period. St George's embodied a symbolic alliance of 'throne' and 'altar' in a highly visible and performative manner. This was found particularly in the Chapter's close involvement in the ceremonies, prayers and customary observances of the Order of the Garter. Thus Deans as Registers of the Garter had to be formally introduced in their mantle in a separate ceremony to the monarch by Deputy Garter and Black Rod, sworn, and invested with the ensigns of the Register's office.[5] Because the chapel was a royal peculiar (though one not immune to ministerial interventions), appointments to the Chapter reflected the religious and personal preferences of individual monarchs in a manner that had no parallel elsewhere. And this was notably the case when the sovereign had the castle as his or her place of primary or preferred residence. Monarchs would expect to meet deans and canons in person during their periods in residence so being *persona grata* was indispensable, not least because St George's clergy might be called upon to perform household duties inside the castle and supplement resident chaplains in ordinary. Queen Anne, of course, was as deeply attached to Windsor as she was to the Church of England and constantly resided there in summer (Verrio painted her private oratory on the south side of Brick Court).[6] She gave an exceptional priority to clerical appointments and was always defensive about ministerial intrusion, and the decanal appointments of Thomas Manningham, John Robinson, and the 12th Lord Willoughby de Broke reflected her own moderate Tory preferences (as opposed to firebrands of the Henry Sacheverell kind).[7]

The Queen's immediate successors, George I and George II, did not share her devout and committed Anglicanism – and they certainly lacked her taste for residence at Windsor – but it was there again in full measure under George III. The king's interest in and knowledge of the Church over which he presided as Supreme Governor has no parallel and was reflected both in his sincere piety and his determination to have a personal hand in the exercise of Crown patronage. After the royal family returned to Windsor in the mid-1770s (thanks, in the first instance, to Queen Charlotte),[8] the king became a daily worshipper at St George's Chapel and used all his influence to ensure that the clergy on the staff there were men of his own kidney. Windsor stalls had always been plum appointments but never more so than in the thirty years or so after around 1780 when appointees could comfort themselves with the awareness that, having successfully caught the king's eye once, they stood every chance of gaining his backing again should higher preferment hove into sight. The *locus classicus* is the king's single-minded determination to have his friend the Bishop of Norwich, Dean Charles Manners-Sutton, awarded the archbishopric of Canterbury in January 1805 deliberately thwarting Pitt the Younger's unabashed preference for his former tutor, George Pretyman, Bishop of Lincoln, and bringing Pitt 'to the point of resignation'.[9] This was far from an isolated instance, however: the Hon. Shute Barrington received translation to Salisbury in 1782 and the Hon. William Stuart to Armagh in 1800 as a direct result of the king's high regard for them based upon Windsor encounters.

Had Manners-Sutton not been Dean of Windsor his promotion to the primacy would have been unlikely for it was his amity with the sovereign which made all the difference. He held the deanery *in commendam* with the see of Norwich in an arrangement that became increasingly common in the course of the century, for genteel bishops looked to supplement the income of one of the less lucrative sees.[10] This was seldom the case before the 1760s. When the long-lived Gregory Hascard (appointed 1684 by Charles II) died in 1708, his successor was the moderate Tory, Thomas Manningham (a canon since 1693), and he resigned the deanery in the following year on appointment to the bishopric of Chichester.[11] His successor was the man who had turned down the offer of that see, the priest diplomat John Robinson, Bishop of Bristol from 1710 to 1713, firm favourite of the Harley Tory ministry, and the first and presumably the last Dean of Windsor to hold Cabinet office (as Lord Privy Seal). Significantly, Robinson relinquished the deanery on his translation to London in 1713. In came the sort of well-born Hanoverian Tory who would endear himself to the queen in the shape of George Verney, recently succeeded to the barony of Willoughby de Broke, and a canon since 1701. Though his underlying loyalty to the new dynasty was never in question after 1714, his chances of securing a bishopric were negligible when the newly ascendant Whigs had so many other candidates pressing their claims.[12]

Willoughby de Broke died in harness, as did his successor Peniston Booth (Fig. 37), a Lincolnshire man, who held the deanery for 36 years until his death in 1765, the longest tenure of the eighteenth century.[13] Booth lacked his predecessor's blue blood but he had one key aristocratic connection that made all the difference: his mother's daughter by her first marriage had married Francis, 6th Earl of Lincoln, the kinsman of the Duke of Newcastle, the key ecclesiastical minister of the reign of George II.[14] The duke was not one to neglect his kinsfolk and Booth (vicar of Twickenham from 1724 to 1730) was the beneficiary of this strategy. Even more significant in boosting Booth's career was his marriage in January 1729 to Catherine, the daughter of the senior surviving canon, Edward Jones (1684-1737). Like the majority of Deans, he already held a Windsor stall (in his case since 1722),[15] and the College under his leadership was quietly and constructively led with material improvements made to the Deanery.[16]

Booth's successors as dean over the next forty years reflected the growing dominance of the social elite in the upper reaches of the Church of England with no fewer than four of the six deans being the younger sons of peers, while five of the six were also bishops, another new tendency. The first of these men, the Hon. Frederick Keppel (1765-78), was appointed at the pressing of his brother's political cronies, the Rockingham Whigs. Keppel spent much of his time as a

Fig. 37. Portrait of Peniston Booth (Canon 1722-29, and Dean 1729-65) by an unknown artist.

diligent diocesan in Exeter which was just as well as, despite his suave manners, neither his political sympathies or his consanguinity to the king's sister-in-law, the divorced Duchess of Gloucester, endeared him to George III. The vacancy arising on Keppel's death was filled by the Hon. John Harley, second son of the 3rd Earl of Oxford. The king did get on with him, notwithstanding Harley's blood ties to the 3rd Duke of Portland, Rockingham's lieutenant. He was advanced to a bishopric (Hereford, on the death of Lord James Beauclerk) but died within a few weeks of taking up his see.[17] The next three deans all held Windsor *in commendam*. John Douglas (1788-91) was Bishop of Carlisle and was familiar with the College from having previously held a canonry there between 1762 and 1776. Windsor was something of a consolation prize for his successor, the Hon. James Cornwallis, Bishop of Lichfield and Coventry; he had a been a disappointed candidate for the deanery of St Paul's in 1787 (that went to Pitt's former Cambridge tutor, George Pretyman), and exchanged Windsor for the rather more lucrative deanery of Durham when the latter fell vacant in 1794.[18] That gave the king the chance to install one of his favourite prelates, Charles Manners Sutton (already Bishop of Norwich aged just 35), and he used it as the jumping off position for securing the primacy in 1805. Into his shoes then stepped the Hon. Edward Legge, younger son of the 2nd Earl of Dartmouth, evangelically inclined (and from a family favoured by George III – his brother was Lord Chamberlain) but less obviously 'Methodist' in his sympathies than his father.

Other than the Deanery, there were twelve canonries in the gift of the Crown and these were highly sought after pieces of patronage. As Dorothy Wordsworth found when she came to stay with her uncle, Canon William Cookson, in 1792, the canons were still housed in rambling accommodation in the cloisters behind the chapel,[19] but any discomfort was worth tolerating. In return for a minimum annual monthly residence a canon (at least in the reigns of Anne and George III) would be officiating regularly before the royal family and thereby giving himself a distinctive advantage in gratifying any hopes of ascending further the *cursus honorum*. It was one of the reasons why Swift was so keen to acquire a canonry – or even the Deanery itself in 1711-2 – from the hands of his Tory patron Robert Harley who could never entirely persuade the 'royal prude' Queen Anne of his suitability.[20] The duties were such as one might expect in any comparable Chapter with the addition of canons being 'particularly obliged, humbly to pray for the prosperity of the Sovereign of the most Noble Order of the Garter, from time to time, as also for the happy estate of the Order.'[21] And there was real capitular power collectively. Neither the ministers nor the Dean could intrude preferred candidates into livings held by the chapter of St George's. This was well seen in 1750 when Lord Chancellor Hardwicke was pressuring Dean Booth to get chapter approval for a preferred nominee to the living of Whaddon (Cambs.) in the gift of the 'College'. The assent of all the canons was required whether present in a Chapter or not so the process could take some time. As Dean Booth explained to the Duke: '. . . we have settled rules in cases of this kind to go by in order to prevent all suspicion of partiality, & to preserve peace it was necessary to keep up to 'em otherwise I had sent ye agreement of the Coll: sooner'.[22]

Space precludes a systematic assessment of the backgrounds and career patterns of the major canons but a few main trends can be identified. Family connections are an obvious starting point. Thus Edward Jones, canon for over half a century (1684-1737) saw his son-in-law, Dr Booth, installed as dean while his grandson John Fulham, cousin of Mrs Booth and archdeacon of Llandaff, was a canon (seventh stall) between 1750 and 1777.[23] Senior members of the hierarchy also sought to insert their relatives: the eighth stall being occupied successively between 1730 and 1754 by the son-in-law and two sons of Bishop

Edmund Gibson.[24] Then there was the link with Eton College, one that assumed greater importance in the time of George III, whose affection for Eton began before he came to live at the castle; he paid a visit to the school most years from 1762.[25] One classic instance of a headmaster/canon would be William George (1731-48) who was Headmaster of Eton from 1728 to 1743 and went on to become Provost of King's College, Cambridge, relinquishing his Windsor canonry in 1748 on promotion to the deanery of Lincoln.[26]

Stalls could be used to reward the learned who upheld religion in public controversy, of whom none was more distinguished than Daniel Waterland, the impeccably orthodox theologian and 'the greatest theologian of Gibson's Church-Whig alliance', who was buried in the chapel on his death in 1740.[27] He was run close in reputation by William Derham (1st stall), a Fellow of the Royal Society, and Boyle Lecturer in 1711 and 1712.[28] In a later generation and in a different subject area there was Anthony Shepherd, DD FRS (1777-96), the Plumian Professor of Astronomy and Master of Mechanics to George III from 1768.[29] Derham was a royal chaplain (in his case to George II when Prince of Wales) like Dr Balthasar Regis (first stall, 1751-7), a refugee from the Dauphiné in the 1680s and author of *The Ancientness of the Christian Religion* (London, 1753).[30] The monarch's chief domestic chaplain, moreover, was usually found a stall. One such was the under-noticed Samuel Pratt (fourth stall, 1697-1723) who had entered Queen Anne's household when she was still Princess of Denmark and later acted as sub-preceptor to her only surviving son and heir presumptive, the Duke of Gloucester. Like many eighteenth-century canons – and Dean Booth-Pratt also held the vicarage of Twickenham (1712-23).[31] So too did Philip Duvall, DD., (1772-1808), preceptor to George III's brothers, the dukes of Cumberland and Gloucester, and subsequently chaplain and treasurer to the latter.[32] Duvall was one of the few preceptors in the royal household(s) with a Windsor canonry who did not eventually receive a bishopric.[33] That was certainly not the case for either Henry William Majendie, the Duke of Clarence's preceptor from 1781 and Bishop of Chester (1800), and John Fisher, tutor to the Duke of Kent (178-5) and Bishop of Exeter from 1803. A stall could come an individual's way for political services rendered. This was the case for Thomas Hurdis (1766-84) who had acted as private secretary to the Duke of Newcastle in his later years; Pitt the Younger secured the tenth stall for his former Cambridge tutor, Edward Wilson, in March 1784, one of the politically essential goodwill gestures that attended the controversial and unstable start of his ministry.[34] And just as the Windsor deanery itself could supplement a poorer bishopric, so stalls could act as a similar resource; thus John Ewer held the sixth stall from 1738 to 1774 while being bishop successively of Llandaff and Bangor.[35]

On the basis of our present archival knowledge, St George's, Windsor, was a functional and functioning institution according to eighteenth-century norms. Anglican collegiate churches in the eighteenth century were in a fair state of health and Windsor was no exception. Deans and canons came and went; there were no residence scandals and after Dean Hascard's death in 1708 (he was often in dispute with the Chapter and was even accused of altering the chapter minutes),[36] there was merely the usual range of minor capitular disagreements and spats. The seven minor canons performed their duties unexceptionably, fortified after 1781 by the bequest of Isaac Chapman, minor canon, who bequeathed £10 per annum to each of them, bringing their annual income (including the value of their houses, which some of them let) to approximately £60.[37] Relations between the College and the town were also steady as one writer recalling the 1790s observed: 'The many clergy of the two colleges had somewhat haughty brows under their shovel hats, but were charitable and not very intolerant'.[38] In fact this period might even be considered one of the chapel's most distinguished eras. Windsor re-established itself as a primary royal space from the 1780s with services often lasting up to two and a half hours when the monarch was in attendance.[39] George III made sure that he had a chapel suited to this reinvigorated regalian purpose. It benefited from its proximity to the royal presence in a manner that other foundations could not match, not least in the material improvements and renovations then effected. The restoration beginning in 1785 and supervised by Henry Emlyn cost about £20,000, of which the Chapter paid £5,800 and the king the remainder.[40] And it was all done with an antiquarian sensitivity to its historical character that might not have been the case earlier in the century. Thus Canon John Lockman (1758-1807) (the Master of St Cross Hospital, Winchester) collected all the old glass in the chapel and put it in the west window.[41] All was ready and in good order for the spectacular 1805 Garter installation, a British rejoinder to Napoleonic imperial splendour, one of the grandest state ceremonies of the late Hanoverian monarchy and with St George's, Windsor as its focus. Nothing better highlighted the symbolic unities articulated by this building at a crucial hour in the history of the nation.[42]

SEVENTEEN

THE ROYAL VAULT AT WINDSOR

Julian Litten

THE CHAPEL BENEATH which the Royal Vault lies has had a chequered history. Originally constructed by Henry III in the 1240s, it was dedicated to St Edward the Confessor and served the old royal apartments close by. In 1348 Edward III had it restored for the newly-founded Order of the Garter and rededicated to the Confessor, the Virgin Mary and St George. Attempts from 1483 to use Henry III's building as a Lady chapel for its successor came to nothing and it entered a second period of abandonment. In the 1490s the old building was entirely rebuilt by Henry VII, who anticipated its conversion into a tomb-house for the Tudor dynasty. When the negotiations with the pope for King Henry VI's canonisation failed, however, this project in turn was abandoned, and the king adopted the Lady chapel at Westminster Abbey for his tomb-house instead.

In about 1523 Cardinal Wolsey, a former canon of Windsor, obtained permission from Henry VIII to restore and embellish the abandoned shell for use as his own burial place, commissioning in 1524 an elaborate tomb of marble from Benedetto da Rovezzano, which was in place by 1529. Work was still in progress on the tomb when Wolsey fell from grace in 1530 and Henry VIII took possession of the monument for his own use, though nothing was done to complete the building works. When the king died in 1547 his remains were temporarily deposited in the small vault below the choir (see Fig. 17) for eventual translation to the 'Wolsey' chapel, as the building later became known, on the resumption of the required building works. This, however, was never to be and the chapel again went into a period of abandonment. During the Commonwealth most of its fixtures and fittings were sold and the majority of the remaining items were either destroyed or defaced by parliamentary soldiers.[1] There was every possibility that the chapel might have been demolished and replaced by a circular domed mausoleum to house the remains of Charles I but, though parliament voted a sum of £70,000 in January 1678 'for a solemn funeral for his late Majesty King Charles the First and to erect a Monument for the said Prince of glorious memory', and Christopher

Wren prepared a scheme for a rotunda which would have cost £43,663 2s 0d, the grant was presumably never paid and the scheme came to naught.[2]

James II had the interior of the chapel decorated when it was used for Roman Catholic services by the Queen and her court, but when he was deposed in 1688 it again fell into disuse until 1810, when George III planned to turn it into his own tomb-house. As for Rozavenna's black marble sarcophagus for Cardinal Wolsey, this had been given by George III to St Paul's Cathedral in 1808 to serve as the tomb for Admiral Horatio Nelson (d.1805).

The chapel never became the proposed tomb-house for the Hanoverian dynasty; indeed, apart from the monument by Matthew Cotes Wyatt in the Urswick Chapel in St George's to Princess Charlotte (d.1817), none of the other Hanoverians has a funerary monument, either at Windsor or Westminster. Rather, the Wolsey Chapel remained locked and unused until 1861 when Queen Victoria resolved to have it converted into a memorial chapel to Prince Albert, completed in 1873 under the name of The Albert Memorial Chapel.

A Hanoverian vault, however, was commissioned at Westminster Abbey.[3] Occupying the whole central area of Henry VII's Chapel this was built in 1737 at the behest of George II. Designed by Henry Flitcroft in the manner of William Kent, it was built in three weeks under the supervision of John James, Surveyor of the Fabric to the Abbey.[4] Constructed entirely of ashlar it has a stone floor and roof of groin vaulting. It is three bays long and three bays wide, the stone-shelved arcaded side aisles containing the coffins of George II's children and their spouses. In the eastern apse is a large black and yellow marble sarcophagus with lions' paw feet, carved by Andrew Jelfe, with high-relief white marble crowns, sceptres and crossed palms on the lid sculpted by James Richards, for the coffins of George II (d.1760) and Queen Caroline (d.1737).[5] It is in this vault that George III's parents and most of his siblings rest, but it was not to be the place for him.

After the death of Charles II in 1685, Windsor Castle had fallen out of favour as a royal residence, and though Queen Anne chose to live there, it was in buildings within the precincts rather than in the castle itself. Both George I and George II declined to reside there and the building fell into mild decay, occupied by a host of individuals claiming 'grace and favour' apartments in any part of the castle they could commandeer. George III was attracted to the castle and its neighbourhood, though for many years he merely occupied a lodge beside the south wall as the Royal Apartments required major works before he could consider taking up residence. It was in 1800 that the architect James Wyatt (d.1813) was commissioned to restore the castle's residential apartments, and work was sufficiently advanced by 1804 to allow for their occupation, after which the King began to spend increasing periods of residence there.[6] George III was now sixty-six years old and in the forty-fourth year of his reign. Bouts of illness meant that he was spending less time in London and more at Windsor, so much so that in 1810 he decided that Windsor should now become his main place of residence.

Back in 1804 he had turned his attention to the empty 'Wolsey' chapel, resolving to create a burial vault beneath it as a place of deposit for himself, his wife and their children. The choice of the 'Wolsey' chapel was, however, something of a compromise, for the repaving of St George's Chapel during 1788-90 proved that there was no space beneath the main chapel itself to allow for the construction of any more large vaults.[7] The architect entrusted with creating the new vault was James Wyatt, assisted by his nephew, Jeffry Wyatt. The work took nearly four years to complete, and by the end of it George III was in possession of the largest and most sumptuous private burial vault ever constructed in England.

The creation of a vault of such magnitude beneath an extant medieval chapel was a major engineering feat. The brief was for a vault to occupy the entire foot-print of the chapel, roughly 70 feet long by 28 feet wide, which necessitated the removal of its floor and the excavation of the soil and much natural chalk beneath it to a depth of almost 15 feet. Furthermore, Wyatt had planned an access shaft in the sanctuary of St George's Chapel, connected to the Royal Vault by a subterranean corridor. This was to allow for the funeral liturgy to take place within the chapel itself, after which the coffin would be let down through the shaft by a lift onto the bearers below who would then carry it the short distance to the Royal Vault beneath the 'Wolsey' Tomb House. The mouth of the shaft is covered by a black marble slab 2350mm x 1055mm inscribed:

GR .
III .
ROYAL .
VAULT .

Set into this slab, at its east end, are two lozenge-shaped brasses, each 425mm x 425mm, placed one above the other. The first, relating to Albert, the Prince Consort, reads:

P.C.
FROM
23RD DECEMBER
1861,
TO 18TH DECEMBER,
1862.

The dates refer to the period during which his body rested in the Royal Vault before its removal to Frogmore. The other reads:

BENEATH
THIS . SPOT . WERE
DEPOSITED . THE . REMAINS
OF . H.R.H. THE . DUCHESS . OF . KENT .
FROM . THE . 25TH . DAY . OF . MARCH
UNTIL . THE . 1ST . DAY . OF . AUGUST . 1861,
WHEN . THEY . WERE . REMOVED
TO . THE . MAUSOLEUM . IN
THE . GROUNDS . OF
FROGMORE.

This is not literally true, of course, for the Royal Vault is some distance from the 'spot' indicated.

Shortly after the death of George IV in 1830, Thomas Kelly of Paternoster Row, London, and J. B. Brown of Windsor jointly published a mezzotint of the interior of the Royal Vault, depicting a stone-flagged stone-vaulted chamber of five bays, with octagonal Bath stone columns and four tiers of York stone shelves along its north and south sides and an apsidal east end, all in Wyatt's severe gothic style and redolent of the 1737 Hanoverian Vault at Westminster Abbey; there was also a centrally-placed mortuary table on which the coffin of George IV had been placed (Fig. 38).

The annotated Kelly and Brown mezzotint depicts six coffins, and indicates the position of four others. On the plinth at the east end of the vault were, from north to south, the coffins of Prince Alfred,[8] Queen Charlotte (d.1818), George III (d.1820), Princess Amelia (d.1810),[9] and Prince Octavius.[10] In the easternmost bay on the north side are the coffins of Princess Charlotte (d.1817)[11] and her stillborn son, and that of Princess Augusta, Duchess of Brunswick (d.1813).[12] In the easternmost bay on the south side are the coffins of Edward, Duke of Kent and Strathearn (d.1820),[13] and Prince Frederick, Duke of York (d.1827).[14] On the mortuary table at the west end of the vault rested the coffin of George IV (d.1830).

The perspective of the Kelly and Brown mezzotint is hopelessly inaccurate. A watercolour and a measured drawing of 1873, however, both by Alfred Young Nutt (d.1924), prove more reliable.[15] The measured drawing shows the Vault to be 25m long, 8.54m wide, and 3.96m high, its length and width reflecting the foot-print of the chapel above. It comprises a centre alley 6.4m wide and arcaded north and south aisles, each 1.07m wide; each of the five-bay side aisles are

Fig. 38. View east in the royal vault in 1830 with George's IV's coffin in the centre.

fitted with four tiers of stone shelves, sufficiently long and deep to accommodate adults' coffins. Including the five spaces on the 1.22m plinth in the apse at the east end, and the four spaces afforded by each of the two mortuary plinths in the centre of the Vault, the tomb-house was capable of accommodating ninety-three coffins.[16]

The watercolour of 1873 by Alfred Nutt shows eighteen coffins in place. The additional eight coffins deposited since the issue of the Kelly and Brown mezzotint in 1830 were those of Prince William, Duke of Gloucester (d.1834),[17] William IV (d.1837), Princess Elizabeth (d.1840),[18] Princess Augusta (d.1840),[19] Queen Adelaide (d.1849), Prince Adolphus Frederick, Duke of Cambridge (d.1850),[20] and Princess Mary (d.1857).[21] All the coffins are depicted as being covered in scarlet velvet, with the exception of those containing the remains of George III (d.1820), George IV (d.1830), William IV (d.1837) and that of an unidentified infant, whose outer cases are upholstered in purple velvet.[22]

Writing in June 1876, A.P. Stanley, the Dean of Westminster, said of the Royal Vault at Windsor, 'It is an almost exact copy of his (George III's) grandfather's vault at Westminster – he himself and Queen Charlotte reposing at the east end, and the Princes and Princesses in chambers on each side, leaving the central aisle for sovereigns.'[23]

In the spring of 1873 Queen Victoria expressed her desire for a new access route to the Royal Vault. George Gilbert Scott (d.1878) was commissioned to design this, and the work was carried out under the supervision of the Office of Works at Windsor within an approved government grant of £400. The scheme involved the construction of a flight of steps, covered by a slab, behind the high altar in St George's Chapel. For the Queen's information it was decided that plans and drawings should be made of the Vault. This task was entrusted to Alfred Nutt, who had entered the Windsor Office of Works as a draughtsman some six years earlier; Nutt's highly-detailed watercolour has already been referred to.[24] The large plans of the Vault now in the National Archives, dated 18 April 1873, show the entire ensemble of Royal Vault, connecting passages and corridors. The new access was completed in under a month, being first used by Queen Victoria and Princess Beatrice on 15 May 1873.

Major changes were made to the Vault in 1898. Further work on the access steps was required; the suggestion made known to Nutt was that Scott's slab should be permanently removed and railings with a gate put round the steps to allow access at any time; furthermore, the five pendent oil lamps within the Vault should be replaced by electric light. The spacing of the coffins was also addressed, with those of George III, Princess Amelia, Prince Alfred and Prince Octavius translated to the shelves lining the walls, allowing the high stone dais at the east end to be removed. Attention then turned to the two stone mortuary tables in the centre of the Vault. These were removed once the six coffins they had supported were also translated to the side shelves, so distributed as to ensure that consort shared the same bay and shelf as monarch, a rearrangement which reduced the Vault's capacity to eighty-one coffins. A new stone mortuary table was placed at the west end of the Vault to serve as a place of temporary deposit; it was on this mortuary table that the coffins of subsequent monarchs were placed until their translation to their tombs in St George's Chapel.

The Prince of Wales visited the Royal Vault on 27 October 1898 to see the works in progress. The plans were at that time incomplete for want of money. The Prince accordingly asked Nutt to write to the Secretary to the Office of Works, to the effect that he was pleased with the work so far and wished to see it completed. As a result, the Lord Chamberlain agreed in January 1899 to finance the decoration of the Royal Vault up to £1,500.[25] Later that year Nutt designed grilles to enclose the shelves[26]. This elaborate scheme, however, in gilt-bronze and based on the great west gates of Henry VII's Chapel at Westminster Abbey, proved to be too expensive and the finished design was of simpler bronze grilles in the Perpendicular style, loosely based on the lower section of Tresilian's

Edward IV's gates in St George's Chapel. The dado rails bore the names of those resting on the shelves behind.

The eastern apse was made into a sanctuary approached by two steps of Derbyshire Fossil marble with Hopton Wood polished slabs leading to a third step supporting a stone altar, the front of which was carved with an arcaded gothic motif. Immediately behind the altar is a reredos of glass mosaic, the centre panel depicting 'Christ's Resurrection from the Tomb', flanked by other Biblical subjects, the whole within a carved stone framework. This work effectively elevated the status of the Royal Vault to that of a chapel, though it seems unlikely that the Eucharist was ever intended to be celebrated there. According to a document in the National Archives signed by Nutt, and dated 17 June 1902, expenditure on the Royal Vault between 1899 and 1902 had amounted to £3,017.10s.5d. In 1952 the *Illustrated London News* published an anonymous drawing of the Vault in its commemorative issue on the funeral of George VI (d.1952), clearly depicting Nutt's alterations (Fig. 39).[27]

There have been a number of comings and goings over the years in the Royal Vault. Edward Augustus, Duke of Kent and Strathearn (d.1820), was placed there, as was his wife Victoria, Duchess of Kent and Strathearn (d.1861), until their transfer to the Kent Mausoleum at Frogmore on 1 August 1861. Prince Albert (d.1861) was placed there on 23 December 1861 until his transfer to the Royal Mausoleum at Frogmore on 18 December 1862. Edward VII (d.1910) and Queen Alexandra (d.1925) were in the Vault until 22 April 1927 when they were

Fig. 39. View east in the royal vault in 1952, showing the late-19th century changes.

Fig. 40. The Earl Powlett's burial vault at Hinton St George.

transferred to the sarcophagus supporting their effigies in St George's Chapel. George V (d.1936) and Queen Mary (d.1953) were in the Royal Vault until their own transfer in 1953 to a sarcophagus in St George's Chapel. George VI (d.1952) rested in the Vault until being transferred to a brick grave in the George VI Memorial Chapel in St George's Chapel in 1969, as did the remains of Princess Margaret between February and April 2002. The remains of Princess Andrew of Greece and Denmark (d.1969), the mother of HRH Duke of Edinburgh, rested temporarily in the Royal Vault until 1988 when they were taken to the Convent of St Mary Madgalen, Gethsemane, Jerusalem for burial in the crypt there.

In 1814 John, 4th Earl Poulett, desired to build a transeptal family pew against the north wall of the nave of St George's church at Hinton St George, Somerset, with a two-bay burial vault beneath. Poulett, a friend of both the Prince Regent and his brother, the Duke of Clarence, was a frequent guest at Windsor and may have seen the Royal Vault during its construction; alternatively, he might have heard of it from James Wyatt who had been remodelling Hinton House intermittently since 1794. James Wyatt died in 1813 and Poulett, who was by then fifty-eight, commissioned Wyatt's nephew and pupil, Jeffry, to construct the pew and vault. As Jeffry had recently been assisting his late uncle on the Royal Vault nothing could be simpler than to create a smaller version of it for the Earl Poulett, which explains its similarity to that at Windsor (Fig. 40).

EIGHTEEN

GEORGE III AND QUEEN CHARLOTTE AT WINDSOR

Jane Roberts

WINDSOR was for George III 'the place I love best in the world', where he spent the greater part of his life.[1] It is therefore entirely appropriate that he is today remembered at Windsor by the great equestrian monument at the southern end of the Long Walk – the 'Copper Horse', erected by his son George IV in the 1820s.

George III (1738-1820) had succeeded to the throne in October 1760 at the age of 22, on the death of his grandfather George II. As Prince of Wales he lived chiefly in London and at Kew where his parents had a small estate, in the heart of which was the White House, where his mother (the Dowager Princess of Wales) continued to live following her husband's death in 1751. But through his love of hunting Prince George was also familiar with the Windsor area: the Royal Buckhounds were based at Swinley at this period and there are descriptions of George III's hunting exploits throughout his long life (Fig. 41). He is also known to have been shown the improvements in the Great Park, including Virginia Water, by his uncle William, Duke of Cumberland, during a visit in 1754.

Within a year of his accession, the young king had married Princess Charlotte (1744-1818), from the small north German principality of Mecklenburg-Strelitz. The marriage was magnificently productive, resulting in fifteen children – nine sons and six daughters, born between 1762 and 1783. Soon after their marriage, the king and Queen began to look for a suitable home in which to bring up a young family. A fine early eighteenth-century mansion at the end of the Mall – Buckingham House – was soon purchased. And for weekends and holidays they used Richmond Lodge, George II's country residence. With the death of the Dowager Princess of Wales in 1772, the king inherited the adjoining Kew estate and came to use the White House in preference to Richmond Lodge, which was demolished. Discussions concerning the building of a great new classical palace at Richmond, which would replace both existing houses and might serve as the king's main residence, came to nothing – owing chiefly to financial considerations.

By the mid-1770s the royal family (which now included ten children) therefore used a combination of the White House, the 'Dutch House' (today's Kew Palace), and an assortment of other houses at Kew Green, as their principal rural retreats.

The domestic accommodation at the king's official country residence, Windsor Castle, had not been used by the royal family for several decades. Many parts of the castle were occupied by officers of state, or even by private individuals. Thus today's Queen's Tower, at the south-eastern corner of the castle, was then called the Secretary of State's Tower, after its official occupant. One of the private tenants in the 1760s was the widowed Maria Walpole, Countess Waldegrave, who moved there with her young family after the death of her husband in 1763. When the king and queen visited Windsor in September 1762 – for the former's installation as Sovereign of the Order of the Garter – rooms were found for them in the castle, but for Ascot races in 1767 he stayed elsewhere. The rather informal appearance of the outside of the royal residence at this time is recorded in Paul Sandby's watercolours, the best of which date from the 1760s, before the recommencement of royal occupation. Sandby shows a nursing mother resting on the stone steps inside the Round Tower; a celebratory bonfire in the Middle Ward; beggars inside the castle precincts; and young horses being schooled in the Upper Ward. Meanwhile the State Apartments – similar in extent to those shown to the public today – could be seen by polite society, on application to the housekeeper. Until 1801 this position was held by Lady Mary Churchill, the illegitimate daughter of Sir Robert Walpole (the Prime Minister) and part of a large family with close Windsor connections. Her successor as housekeeper was the Hon. Georgiana Townshend, who had equally strong royal links. The housekeeper's apartment was within the Norman gateway, looking on to the Moat Garden.

During the 1760s three of George III's brothers had residences in the Windsor area: Edward, Duke of York (1739-67) had the use of Cranbourne from 1765 to the time of his death, as warden of Windsor Forest and ranger (or keeper) of Cranbourne Chase. The next brother, William, Duke of Gloucester (1743-1805), was appointed to the same two offices (with the use of Cranbourne) on Prince Edward's death; but as he had secretly married the widowed Maria Waldegrave in September 1766, and soon after purchased a fine estate for her on St Leonard's Hill, Windsor. Prince William effectively had two bases in the Windsor area, the latter of which was now rebuilt and renamed Gloucester Lodge. Meanwhile the next brother – Henry Frederick, Duke of Cumberland (1745-90) – lived at the Great (now Cumberland) Lodge from 1765, when he was appointed ranger of Windsor Great Park on the death of his (and the king's) uncle, William, Duke of Cumberland. Apart from a lengthy period of banishment following

Fig. 41. Matthew Dubourg after James Pollard, *His Majesty King George III returning from hunting*, published 1820. Hand-coloured engraving (The Royal Collection © 2010 Her Majesty Queen Elizabeth II).

his unauthorised marriage in 1771, the Duke and Duchess of Cumberland were often resident in the Great Park.

The governor of Windsor Castle from 1752 was George Brudenell, fourth Earl of Cardigan and first Duke of Montagu (1712-90), who continued in the post until his death, when he was succeeded by his younger brother, James, 5th Earl of Cardigan (1715-1811). Both post-holders held a number of other household appointments and were occasionally at Windsor, where the governor's official residence was the Round Tower.

In broad terms, this was the situation at the time of the king's decision, reached in mid-1776, to return to Windsor and to occupy the small house immediately to the south of the castle that was then occupied by the lord steward. Nearly twenty years later the diarist Joseph Farington reported that the king had originally planned to use the house only occasionally, and that 'if he could have foreseen that Windsor would be their chosen residence He would have prepared the Castle & resided in it.' The Queen's Garden House had been built to house the royal gardener, but in the early eighteenth century it was refurbished for use by Queen Anne as a royal residence. Between late June 1776 and 1781 this modest building was gradually enlarged and in addition a huge crenellated barrack-like block

Above Fig. 43. James Fittler after George Robertson, *South East View of Windsor Castle, with the Royal Family on the Terrace and a view of the Queen's Palace*, published 1783. Engraving (The Royal Collection © 2010 Her Majesty Queen Elizabeth II).

Opposite page Fig. 42. Benjamin West, *Queen Charlotte with her children at Windsor,* 1779. Oil on canvas (The Royal Collection © 2010 Her Majesty Queen Elizabeth II).

was erected to its east. It was estimated that the house now contained more than 100 rooms, following expenditure of around £40,000. The building is shown in the background of West's painting of Queen Charlotte in 1779 (Fig. 42), and also – by now even larger – in the print of the royal family on the South Terrace, published four years later (Fig. 43).

Until George IV's intervention in the early nineteenth century, the Long Walk only extended north as far as Park Street. Between that point and the castle were the gardens and grounds associated with Burford House, built by Charles II for his mistress Nell Gwynn and subsequently occupied by their descendants, the dukes of St Albans. The Queen's Lodge had a quite substantial enclosed area of gardens of its own. But already within a few years, both the residence and the

Fig 44. John Singleton Copley, *The three youngest daughters of George III*, 1785. Oil on canvas (The Royal Collection © 2010 Her Majesty Queen Elizabeth II).

attached grounds were found to be inadequate for the still-growing family, so in 1779 Burford House, with its own more substantial gardens, was purchased by the king and was renamed Lower Lodge. Both houses and gardens are shown in the 1783 print (Fig. 43).

The Queen's Lodge was very close to the southern front of Windsor Castle – with its capacious 'terrace' – but it was separated from the castle by a public pathway, which led from Windsor town up Castle Hill, through the king's Gate, and across the Little (now Home) Park towards Datchet. The lack of privacy would surely have been vexing for the royal family, but this is where they lived while at Windsor, from the mid-1770s until soon after the turn of the century. And it was in the gardens of the Queen's Lodge that Copley set his delightful painting of *The three youngest daughters of George III* (Fig. 44), painted in 1785, two years after the birth of the last of the king and queen's children – the treasured Princess Amelia. No trace of the Queen's Lodge and its gardens survives today for both were swept away in the 1820s. However, Burford House escaped demolition and survives – totally remodelled – as an accommodation block within the Royal Mews.

Although the royal family were at first reluctant to use the castle's domestic accommodation, banquets and celebrations of notable occasions were held there – particularly in 1789, to celebrate the king's recovery and return to Windsor. But redecoration work was under way in the State Apartments almost continuously from the late 1770s. The existence of a steady stream of published guidebooks, from the 1740s on, indicates that these rooms were indeed visited – by the polite public – at this time. And the fact that views of some of the rooms were included (with permission) in Pyne's *History of the Royal Residences* (see Fig. 45) confirms the 'public' (rather than private domestic) nature of this area.² The refurbishment of these rooms was initially entrusted to the king's architect, Sir

Fig. 45. Charles Wild, *Windsor Castle: the King's Audience Chamber*, 1818. Watercolour and bodycolour (The Royal Collection © 2010 Her Majesty Queen Elizabeth II).

William Chambers. Particular attention was lavished on the King's Audience Chamber, which received a new marble chimneypiece while the walls and throne canopy were adorned with blue silk coverings and embroidered borders. In addition, a series of paintings recording the early years of the Order of the Garter were painted for the room by Benjamin West in the late 1780s. After Chambers' death in 1796, James Wyatt was employed to continue the work in this area. He demolished the two seventeenth-century staircases which had once led to the king's and to the queen's apartments, and introduced a single new state entrance staircase – which was itself replaced later in the nineteenth century. Wyatt, like his nephew Jeffrey Wyatville, was happy to work in the gothic as well as the classical style. And it appears that by 1800 George III came to favour that style for Windsor, as being the one that had been used continuously there since the Middle Ages, and which therefore blended most harmoniously with the ancient apartments and chapel. The new state entrance staircase with its vault above were in that style, as were the new windows inserted into the north wall of the upper ward, facing onto the quadrangle.

Meanwhile, the family of George III – like the sovereign's families since the early eighteenth century – continued to sleep, and live, outside the medieval castle walls, and to seek solace in the surrounding area. The lack of privacy at the Queen's Lodge, as well as the lack of mature tree cover within its open garden area, combined with Queen Charlotte's evident love of flowers, gardening, and botany in general, led to the king's purchase – in the early 1790s – of the two estates at Frogmore, to the south-east of the castle and Queen's Lodge, but within easy walking distance. (Although the Frogmore estate is now part of the Home Park, until the mid-nineteenth century it was outside the area of royal parkland.) The smaller of the two houses at Frogmore was demolished and the larger one was remodelled by James Wyatt, with the addition of a colonnaded verandah, and balancing wings at either end of the garden front. The enlarged 35-acre garden onto which the house looked was gradually transformed into an enchanting picturesque setting, with garden buildings (designed by Wyatt, with the help of Princess Elizabeth), covered walks, and a lake. In this work the queen was assisted first by Christopher Alderson, and then by the king's former equerry Major William Price, the younger brother of the writer Uvedale Price.

Frogmore was a place of daily retreat and solace, after the traumatic months of the king's illness in 1788-9. Until its occupation by Princess Augusta (to whom it had been bequeathed) in the 1820s, the royal family never slept at Frogmore. It was instead a place to 'botanise', to paint, and to entertain. In July 1793 the queen wrote of Wyatt's 'many pretty tantalizing proposals about my little paradise', adding 'I am not at all eager to finish at once but can wait with patience' for the completion of work, for 'I mean this place to furnish me with fresh amusements every day'. Four years later Frogmore was the setting for the Princess Royal's marriage to the king of Wurttemberg, when the rooms were adorned with garlands made of cut-paper by the royal ladies and their female friends. It was at Frogmore that Queen Charlotte kept her books, all of which were dispersed – with the principal contents of the house – following her death. In the course of the restoration of Frogmore in the 1980s, a number of the rooms were returned to their early nineteenth-century appearance. Even with planes flying overhead, visitors to Frogmore can today enjoy the peace and tranquillity which gave such pleasure to Queen Charlotte in the late eighteenth century.

Pyne's *History of the Royal Residences*, published in 1819, records a number of the interiors at Frogmore, as well as those at Buckingham House, Windsor Castle and elsewhere. But none of the interiors in the Queen's Lodge were recorded in the work. The reason may well have been that by that late date in the king's reign, the house was virtually abandoned – for in 1804 the family took the momentous decision to move into Windsor Castle itself. Following the move, the queen announced 'I have changed from a very comfortable & warm habitation, to the coldest house, rooms & passages that ever existed, & all idea of comfort is vanished with it'. During the 1790s a Music Room and Drawing Room had been created for the queen's use on the east front, to the designs of John Yenn, Chambers' pupil. These rooms continued to be used by the queen after 1804, when she moved into the Queen's Tower. But the king, whose health was increasingly delicate, instead moved to rooms on the north front, under the State Apartments, and it was there that he was confined from around 1810 to the time of his death ten years later.

Just as the queen's interest in flowers and gardening led to the acquisition of the Frogmore estates, so the king's interest in agriculture and landscape gardening had lain behind his own work in the Windsor estate. On the death of the king's brother, Henry, Duke of Cumberland, in 1790 both the rangership of Windsor Great Park and the use of Cumberland Lodge, reverted to the Crown. James Wyatt was employed to re-case the Lodge in the gothic style, for the occasional use of the king. The state rooms in the Lodge featured in contemporary guidebooks, and could evidently be seen by the polite public. But as the king now took over the day-to-day running of the park, the buildings in the vicinity of the Lodge were used as the main base for that work. The great eighteenth-century kitchen gardens, and the magnificent (surviving) range of stables next to the Lodge, continued to function. And a chapel was established in an outbuilding of the

Lodge, in which the park workers could worship. The king likewise directed his attention to nearby Cranbourne Lodge, to which in the early nineteenth century Wyatt added a gothic tower. Although the tower has survived, the Lodge itself was soon demolished.

The daily life of King George III and Queen Charlotte at Windsor from 1776 to the start of the Regency (1811) is revealed through a combination of textual and visual accounts, including the diaries of Fanny Burney (in waiting on the queen at Windsor from 1786 to 1791), and the account of the king's illness by his equerry Greville. Correspondence between the king and Sir Joseph Banks from 1787, concerning Banks' activity as unofficial (and unpaid) 'shepherd' of the king's merino flock (kept partly in the Little Park at Windsor), and that between the king and Nathaniel Kent, his agent in the Great Park from 1791, demonstrate his hands-on involvement in the daily affairs of the royal estate, and his close personal interest in the labourers employed there. In 1793 a new dwelling was erected for a swineherd at Flemish Farm in the Great Park, to the king's own design.

At Windsor the king and queen soon established a loyal circle of friends and household with whom they were happy to move, and who would attend their occasional entertainments in the castle or at Frogmore. In their early years at Windsor the royal family paid a number of visits to Bulstrode, north of Slough, the home of the scholarly Dowager Duchess of Portland (1715-85). For three years after the Duchess's death the brilliant but aged Mary Delany (1700-88), who had been supported by the Duchess for many years, was accommodated by the king in St Albans Street, Windsor, where she was often visited by members of the royal family. It was there that they first met Fanny Burney, who soon joined the queen's household. Other early acquaintances were the antiquary Jacob Bryant (1715-1804), who lived at Cippenham (near Slough) and presented a magnificent gift of early printed books to the king in 1782.

Meanwhile the royal presence at Windsor may have led to the move – to Windsor, or to Slough – of those more closely associated with the court. Dr James Lind, physician to the royal family, settled at Windsor in the late 1770s and was shown – in August 1783 – at the end of the north terrace, witnessing a meteor. The American artist Benjamin West rented a house in Park Street between around 1780 and 1809, to ensure that he was able to carry out his royal duties promptly and appropriately. And William Herschel, who moved from Hanover to England in 1757, settled in the Windsor area in the early 1780s, at around the time of his appointment as observatory keeper to the king in 1782. The Harcourt family (of Nuneham Courtenay, Oxon.) were also often at Windsor, in attendance on the royal family. The invitation to Windsor for Ascot week in 1793 to the second Earl

Fig. 46. Charles Wild, *Windsor Castle: the Quire of St George's Chapel*, 1818. Watercolour and bodycolour (The Royal Collection © 2010 Her Majesty Queen Elizabeth II).

and his wife was worded by the queen as follows: 'I do assure you, & promise you faithfully, that when we have done Broiling at Ascot, you shall cool yr self at Frogmore, where it looks very *Ruralistic* at present'. The Earl's younger brother and successor, William, third Earl Harcourt, had already purchased Gloucester Lodge at St Leonard's Hill in 1783, a very convenient base during his period as deputy ranger of Windsor Great Park from 1806 to 1830.

Others close to the king were connected more immediately to the castle via their membership of the Chapter of St George, for the royal family worshipped regularly at 'the cathedral' (as they called St George's Chapel), from their first attendance at morning service on 12 August 1776, carefully recorded in the Chapter Archives. All of those associated with St George's therefore became well-known to the royal family, whether canons (such as John Fisher, or Dr Lockman), or deans.

On the arrival of the king and queen at Windsor in 1776 they would have encountered Dean Keppel and his wife Laura, sister of Maria Waldegrave (later Duchess of Gloucester), who had spent part of her childhood at Great Frogmore, the lease of which was held by their father Edward Walpole (son of Sir Robert, and brother of Horace).

Over the following fifteen years the king became closely involved with repair work at St George's, providing the majority of the funding for the 'Great Works' there. This restoration programme commenced under Dean Keppel and continued under his successors John Harley and John Douglas. St George's is the Chapel of the Order of the Garter, of which George III (like his predecessors) was Sovereign, and which he held in particular reverence. The king's appointment of five of his younger sons to the Order in 1786 was closely connected to the 'Great Works', which included the provision of heraldic stained glass in the clerestory windows of the choir (1782); the replacement of the reredos and east wall and window (1785-8); the erection of a new Coade stone choir screen (to 1790); the production of a new tomb for Edward IV (1789-91); and the carving of a number of choir stalls (1786-91), to the same design as those originally produced in the late fifteenth century, to accommodate the princes who had been newly-appointed to the order in 1786. Henry Emlyn, a local carpenter and builder, was the executant architect for this project, working alongside Thomas Sandby – the deputy ranger of Windsor Great Park, Professor of Architecture at the Royal Academy, and the elder brother of Paul Sandby. Apart from the east wall (altered in the early 1860s, as one of many memorials to Prince Albert), these works – executed chiefly between 1785 and 1791 – have largely survived to this day, a clear reminder of the affection in which the chapel was held by George III, who is buried alongside his wife and members of his family, in the Royal Vault, constructed 1804-12 to the designs of his architect James Wyatt, and the subject of a separate article in this volume.

NINETEEN

THE MID NINETEENTH CENTURY RESTORATION
OF ST GEORGE'S CHAPEL

Clare Rider

THE 1840S WERE a significant decade in the field of ecclesiastical restoration. The impact of the Cambridge Camden Society, with its highly influential journal, *The Ecclesiologist*, was widespread. Advocating bold measures in the rebuilding and redecoration of Gothic buildings, the Ecclesiologists attempted to recreate the architecture and ethos of the medieval Church in order to inspire worshippers to new heights of devotion. Whilst Holy Sepulchre Church, Cambridge, underwent a complete make-over between 1841 and 1843 under the direct supervision of the Society and of its architect Anthony Salvin, the Temple Church in London was strikingly refashioned by James Savage, Sydney Smirke and Decimus Burton. Original columns and stone carvings were stripped out and replaced as part of an extensive restoration project; medieval effigies were rebuilt and the interior painted throughout in rich colours and symbolic patterns. It is against this background that the 1840s restoration of St George's Chapel should be viewed.

The Dean and Canons of Windsor employed two leading proponents of 'archaeological Gothic', rather than strict Ecclesiologists, in the works undertaken in the 1840s. Thomas Willement, the pre-eminent stained glass artist of the decade, had already undertaken work for Augustus Pugin and Anthony Salvin before accepting his commission at Windsor in 1840. He was subsequently to be employed by Sydney Smirke and Decimus Burton on the Temple Church in 1842 and by Salvin at Cambridge in 1843. However, whilst popular with the Ecclesiologists, he was primarily an antiquarian and heraldic artist, 'far more interested in coats of arms than in any more spiritual symbolism'.[1] Meanwhile, Sir Edward Blore had been selected by the Office of Works in the 1830s and 1840s to oversee a number of major rebuilding projects, including the restoration of Hampton Court Palace, the improvement of the royal apartments at Windsor Castle, and the reconstruction of the Military Knights' lodgings in the Lower Ward. In addition, he had a large practice restoring colleges and college chapels in

Oxford, including Wadham College, on which he worked with Willement in the 1830s. Appointed Surveyor of Westminster Abbey in 1827, Blore was involved in several other ecclesiastical restorations including Lambeth Palace, Ripon Minster and Norwich and Ely Cathedrals. His appointment at Westminster Abbey was not to the taste of Camdenians, *The Ecclesiologist* condemning him as 'entirely unacquainted with the true spirit of Pointed Architecture'.[2] However, Blore won the respect of the majority of his architectural peers and was employed widely as a designer, project manager and architectural consultant for ecclesiastical and secular restorations. It was in this capacity that he was called in by the Dean and Canons of Windsor on 17 May 1841 to make a survey of the chapel, with particular reference to the condition of the choir Clerestory windows, the west window and the chapel roof. A month later, on 22/23 June 1841, his report was presented to Chapter, who agreed to go ahead with his recommendations, including a 'complete' repair of the west window. This major undertaking, which is described elsewhere in this volume, was prompted by the 'perilous state' of the masonry.[3]

Even before Blore's report had been commissioned, the Dean and Canons had begun to employ stained glass artist Thomas Willement to re-glaze the choir Clerestory. In July 1840 they asked him to design and install four heraldic windows, two to the south and two to the north of the choir, continuing the sequence commenced by Francis Eginton in 1781 in honour of the Garter Knights.[4] The decision to extend the heraldic series seems to have been prompted by aesthetics rather than the need for immediate repairs. Willement, with his antiquarian proclivities and practical experience of stained glass, was an ideal choice for the work, although he made it clear that he wished to design the windows himself in a contemporary (Gothic revival) style, rather than following Eginton's plainer and duller tone. Indeed he made this a condition of his involvement, writing to Canon Cust, the Canon Steward, on 17 July 1840:

> Pray use your powerful interest that the Dean's proposition that the new windows should match the old may not be put into practice, as it would totally prevent me from having anything to do with [the] job – which I am most anxious for, if it can be done by work which will not hurt my reputation.[5]

The Dean and Canons must have agreed to his terms, for Willement was employed by them from 1840 to 1861. During this time he liaised closely with Canon Cust, who was himself an antiquary. Canon Cust had worked previously with Willement on the restoration of the parish church of Cockayne Hatley in Bedfordshire where Cust was rector and lord of the manor and this prior association doubtless lay behind the selection of Willement for the St George's Chapel commission.[6]

On assessing the masonry prior to the installation of the windows, Willement must have become aware of structural problems in the choir Clerestory. Shortly afterwards, when his friend and associate, Sir Edward Blore, was called into survey the chapel, this was one of the three areas on which the Dean and Canons sought information. On Blore's recommendation, Willement was 'instructed to continue the series of Armorial Bearings of the Knights of the Garter for three Windows, in addition to the four Windows he has already executed'.[7] However, the commission for new windows in the choir paled into insignificance beside the major reparation advocated with great urgency by Blore: the complete restoration of the great west window. Because of the magnitude of this project, there has been a tendency to overlook the other works which took place in the 1840s. Thomas Willement's report, *An Account of the Restorations of the Collegiate Chapel of St George, Windsor*, published in 1844, indicates the wide range of tasks undertaken under his supervision to preserve and beautify St George's and its associated chantry chapels.[8]

Much cleaning and repainting took place at this time, some it seems at Willement's own suggestion. On 23 April 1843 the Chapter minutes record that 'Chapter accepts Willement's liberal offer to paint the choir ceiling', making use of the scaffolding which had been erected for the installation of the new clerestory windows. At the same meeting Willement was requested to 'send a specimen of painting for the organ pipes', which he had also agreed to redecorate since they were currently painted a dull dark brown.[9] As a result the largest pipes were gilded and emblazoned with the greyhound, dragon, rose and portcullis, all badges of the House of Tudor. Other fixtures brightened by repainting in 'their proper colours' included the principal lines of bosses in the nave, choir and choir aisles, the centre line in the transepts, the armorials above the organ gallery and the wooden 'royal closet' overlooking the high altar, which had been painted to resemble stone. Willement describes in his 1844 report how the 'royal closet' (the wooden eastern oriel of the Edward IV chantry chapel installed by Henry VIII for Katherine of Aragon) (Fig. 47) was restored to its 'original state', and how the form and carvings had resumed their 'original sharpness and delicacy'. Since all evidence of the original paint had been lost, Willement used his imagination to recreate the Tudor colour scheme:

> The oil painting having so deeply penetrated the grain of the oak that the original tint could not be recovered , it became necessary to add some colour and gilding to relieve

Fig. 47. Timber oriel for Katherine of Aragon of *c.* 1519.

the heaviness of so large a mass of dark colour: this has been effected by emblazoning on the lower panels the rose and portcullis, the badges of king Henry VIII, with his arms and motto 'Dieu et mon droit'; the pomegranate and bundle of arms, with the arms of queen Katherine of Aragon, and her motto, 'Tanta monta'. The heraldic beasts which climb the roof of the closet, the antelope, greyhound, lion and dragon, have been emblazoned, and the smaller ornaments 'parcel-gilt'.[10]

Willement was keen to direct and supervise the repainting himself, writing to Canon Cust on 18 May 1843: 'Hearing by letter from Mr. Canning yesterday morning that he wished while the scaffolding was up in the nave that the painted bosses in the centre should be reinstated, I went to Windsor yesterday afternoon to direct my foreman how they ought to be done'.[11]

Interestingly, on removal of the 'modern' paint work and several layers of lime-wash in the south choir aisle, the decision was taken not to repaint the original ceiling decorations revealed during the cleaning. Willement was excited by these finds, noting in a letter of 18 May 1843 to Canon Cust, then absent from Windsor: 'a very interesting discovery has been made – there are considerable remains of painting to prove that the four piers and the vaulting immediately over the grave stone of King Henry VI had been painted in rich colours, which must have given that part the effect of a royal canopy over the grave'. Surely, he argued, it ought to be restored, particularly since it did not require gilding and was unlikely to cost more than £18. 'And if afterwards', he continued enthusiastically to Canon Cust, 'as you at one time suggested, that window was filled by stained glass referring to the King, the whole of that division would be perfect.'[12] However, although a window in honour of Henry VI was indeed installed in the south choir aisle in 1844, there is no indication that the ceiling decorations were repainted either above or beside the tomb of Henry VI or on the vaulting adjacent to the Oliver King Chapel, where another series of painted 'ornaments' had reappeared during cleaning. This is curious, since there was no hesitation in repainting the bosses in the choir aisles, choir and nave or mimicking the original colour schemes in a number of the chantry chapels.

The Somerset [Beaufort] chantry chapel, and the Somerset tombs within it, underwent an extensive restoration which went far beyond the reparations in the main part of the chapel. Not only were the walls and vaults repainted, but the floor was re-laid with tiles from Tintern Abbey, several of the windows were filled with newly commissioned heraldic stained glass and the effigies and brass screen round the monument were painstakingly restored. In undertaking this work, Willement made every effort to recapture the original ambience of the chantry chapel, a relatively easy task for him since 'so much was evident of the ancient decorations that it became a very easy matter to give every part its original colouring'. Significantly, Willement notes that the whole of the considerable costs were 'defrayed by the Present Duke of Beaufort KG'.[13] As Sarah Brown has commented, Willement was an economic realist and astute fund-raiser, going to 'considerable lengths to interest and involve descendants of those nobles commemorated by or associated with the chapel's medieval chantries'.[14] Consequently, the effigies in the Rutland Chantry chapel were conserved at the expense of the Duke of Rutland KG, and the 'fine monument' in the Lincoln chapel, bearing the recumbent figures of the Earl and Countess of Lincoln, was repaired at the expense of the Duke of Newcastle KG.[15] Subsequently, in 1848, the Lincoln chapel received five new heraldic stained glass windows designed by Willement and a set of new iron bars and railings.[16]

Meanwhile the Bray chantry chapel was cleaned and repaired in 1847, whilst the ceiling, 'ribs' and bosses in the Oliver King chapel were repainted in 1848, reproducing the original colouring discovered during cleaning.[17] The medieval wall paintings within the Hastings and Oxenbridge chantry chapels were cleaned and repaired, but significantly not repainted apart from the inscription. In contrast, the exterior 'heraldic ornaments' on the Oxenbridge chapel were fully emblazoned, including the associated ox, letter N and bridge in the spandrels to the entrance door.[18]

Not all the repairs undertaken in the 1840s were as glamorous as the restoration works in the chantry chapels. More mundane tasks in the main body of the chapel included the stripping and revarnishing of the choir stalls, which necessitated the temporary removal of the stall plates, the cleaning and conservation of the 'elaborate ironwork' by the tomb of Edward IV and the repair, repolishing and reinstatement of the brass lectern in the choir (Fig. 48), at the expense of Canon Cust.[19] Stonework repairs undertaken by local stonemasons and builders, Thomas Bedborough and George Jenner, included the replacement in Bath stone of the pinnacle above Princess Charlotte's cenotaph, the sculpting and fixing of a new canopy 'over the niche in the west entrance', the provision of a new Portland stone step at the nave entrance to the choir, relaying and making good the paving and black ledger stones in the choir and south choir aisle and the repointing and repair of the flashing on the roof of the north and south aisles. It was to Bedborough and Jenner that the major task of cleaning the chapel interior had been assigned, and they were also responsible for the erection and dismantling of scaffolding and other ancillary works during the restoration. The Chapter Bills held in the Chapel Archives indicate the extent of the involvement of Bedborough and Jenner and, from 1847, of Thomas Bedborough alone in the restoration works.[20]

The repainting and building repairs had been undertaken in two main phases, from 1843 to 1844 and 1847 to 1849, with an additional commission for repainting and emblazoning the 'very large bosses' in the north and south choir aisles in 1855.[21] Yet Willement continued to work on the stained glass until May 1861, when the last of his heraldic windows was installed in the north choir clerestory. Between 1840 and 1861, he had designed and completed a total of twenty-five windows in the choir clerestory and choir aisles, all but one of which – the east window in the South Quire Aisle depicting 'The Carrying of the Cross' – remain intact. These were in addition to the five new heraldic windows which he installed in the Lincoln chapel, and the restoration and reglazing of windows in the Oliver King and Beaufort chapels. The nature and significance of Willement's stained glass in St George's Chapel has been assessed in a recent article by Sarah Brown. A visit to the chapel reinforces her enthusiasm for the skilful work of this 'under-rated artist'.[22]

The 1840s restoration of St George's Chapel had been a major and arguably successful project. Sir Edward Blore's involvement seems to have been limited to surveying the Chapel, inspecting progress on the west window and auditing stonemason Samuel Cundy's accounts,[23] whilst the Chapter Surveyor, James Whitman, apparently played little part in the restoration. It was Thomas Willement, with the advice and support of his patron at Windsor, Canon Cust, who had been responsible for the design and colour schemes throughout, based on painstaking antiquarian and pictorial research. True to the spirit of the 'archaeological Gothic', he had transformed a dull and dingy interior into a bright and colourful house of worship, whilst avoiding the excesses that attended the repainting of the Temple Church.

However, even before the installation of Willement's final clerestory window, the baton had passed from him to George Gilbert Scott, who had been commissioned in 1859 to design the architectural framework for the Duchess of Gloucester's tomb in the south choir aisle. It was Ecclesiologists Scott and his former assistants, stained glass artists Clayton and Bell, who were to transform the East End of the Chapel, beginning work on replacing the great east window in the summer of 1862, only one year after Willement had completed his commission.[24] With Willement slipping from favour as representative of an older generation of Gothic revivalists, the late-nineteenth century restoration of St George's Chapel was placed in more fashionable hands.

Fig. 48. The brass lectern in the quire, from an engraving by Henry Shaw.

TWENTY

SIR HAROLD BRAKSPEAR'S RESTORATION OF ST GEORGE'S CHAPEL IN THE 1920s

Martin Ashley

SIR HAROLD BRAKSPEAR, architect, archaeologist and architectural historian, was appointed consulting architect for St George's Chapel in 1906.[1] He had been elected a Fellow of the Society of Antiquaries six years before. He had first come to public attention as an expert in the conservation and repair of medieval buildings as a result of his restoration of Malmesbury Abbey Church in 1899. At the time of his death in 1934, he was recognised as one of the foremost experts on medieval architecture, in particular that of English monastic houses. His successful restoration projects had included those at Nuneaton Priory, Shrewsbury Abbey Tower, and the abbeys of Pershore, Bath, Battle and Lacock. It was, however, for his work on St George's Chapel that he was honoured with a knighthood in 1931, in particular 'the extremely delicate and responsible work of saving the magnificent roof . . . from imminent collapse'.[2]

In 1884 a report from John Thompson of Peterborough, contractor, had recorded successful repairs which had been carried out to the nave stone vault, 'found to be in very dangerous condition', and to the decayed nave roof timbers.[3] Brakspear was nonetheless still very concerned about the remainder of the structure and, in a report to the Dean and canons in June 1918, he quoted Sir Christopher Wren, who in 1682 had criticised the original design of the building, finding the abutments to be 'too nice and tender' and the ceiling vaults to be 'low and flat to ostentation', leaving a very small margin of safety.[4] In this same report Brakspear identified 'two especially urgent and grave matters requiring immediate attention': firstly the roof and vaulting of the choir and aisles and, secondly, the vaulting and upper walls of the south transept. 'In both places are unmistakeable evidence of fresh and alarming movements which, unless attended to promptly, will cause grievous trouble if not ruin of those parts of the building'. Charles Peers, a fellow architect brought in by Brakspear in 1920 to offer a second opinion, reinforced Brakspear's concerns in a letter of 15 April 1920, noting the diminishing strength of the flying buttresses owing to stonework decay; the poor condition of the timber roof; longitudinal cracks in the ceiling vaults; the dangerous state of the parapets and pinnacles, which are so decayed as to be falling; the condition of the Bray and Rutland transepts 'which by their unbuttressed construction offer little support to their vaults'; and the cracking to the vaults of the choir and nave aisles.[5] Peers and Brakspear proposed the erection of an inspection scaffolding and, as a result of subsequent findings, and the breaking of tell-tales which had been placed across cracks in the stone vaults indicating structural movement, massive wooden shoring was installed to the south side of the choir clerestory. One of Robertson's photographs shows large raking shores to every bay of the clerestory wall, demonstrating significant concern for the security of the choir vault.

The invasive programme of works had dramatic implications for worship and the day-to-day life of the chapel. However, the works were undertaken with commitment, and adversity was turned to opportunity by including some 'improvements' in the works programme, such as improvements to the vestry, and a new turret stair to the Song School in the Schorn tower, the reinstatement of the missing leaded roof domes over the Beaufort and Urswick chapels, and reinstatement of the 'king's beasts' which had been missing from the buttress pinnacles since the late seventeenth century.

In 1920 the major repairs contract was again awarded to John Thompson & Sons of Peterborough. Founded as a small firm of stonemasons in the early nineteenth century they had an extensive record of restoration work on cathedrals including Peterborough, Chester, Hereford, Lincoln, Ripon, Salisbury and Winchester, as well as works to institutional buildings in Cambridge, at Glasgow University, Royal Holloway College, and some significant country houses. In January 1921 they erected a construction yard on the south side of the choir, and wooden scaffolding and shoring were constructed with a hoist for lifting materials to high level. In February the cutting of new stone began for the buttresses on the south side of the choir. The decayed stone arches had to be completely renewed, as the flying buttresses resist the thrust of the vault, and Brakspear took no chances in ensuring that they be restored to perfect condition.

For repairs Brakspear chose a limestone from Clipsham in Northamptonshire. Quite different from the Gloucestershire limestone originally used for the chapel and Bath limestones used throughout the nineteenth-century restorations of 'battlements and gargoyles', Clipsham is a durable limestone that remains popular today, and was local and perhaps economic to John Thompson in Peterborough. However, it weathers differently from Taynton stone, which is why a Gloucestershire stone with closer weathering characteristics to the original

Fig. 49. Scaffolding being erected in the choir over the stalls.

stone has recently been chosen by the dean and canons for the present restoration of the external stonework.

During March and April 1921 a huge boarded wall was erected under the crossing arch to screen the choir from the nave, the high altar was relocated and nave choir stalls were installed. Photographs show a curtain behind the altar and dorsal curtains, a tester over one stall presumably indicating the Sovereign's pew, also a pulpit, and a temporary organ. In May wooden scaffolding was erected in the eastern half of the choir bearing directly onto the marble floor, and photographs suggest that the scaffolding posts continued up through the stone vault to carry a temporary roof over the roof carpentry repairs (Fig. 49). Roof repairs began in September and continued through the winter, with all of the principal truss tie beam ends needing extensive repair except for two that had been replaced by Wren in 1682. One tie beam needed completely replacing.

During the carpentry repairs it was noticed that 'tell-tales' placed across cracks in the choir stone vault had fractured. Works were immediately suspended and additional scaffolding and centring installed to support the entire choir vault. Brakspear subsequently noted, 'if this staging had not been fixed with such dispatch there is no question that the quire vaulting would have collapsed.'

The first repairs were made to the flying buttresses of the choir and to the dressings of the choir windows. Messrs. Pearce and Cutler removed the glass to their workshops in Birmingham, where it was conserved. A photograph shows a cross-section through an existing window mullion, 'it being patched four times whereby no strength was left in it'. Plumb-bob and level surveys revealed that the south and north aisle walls were leaning out by six inches and two inches respectively, the centre of the choir vault had dropped by six inches, with a fracture running from end to end. Excavations to investigate why the south wall leaned so much revealed that it was poorly founded on clay overlaying the solid chalk. Throughout the summer and autumn of 1922 the wall was underpinned to as much as thirteen feet below ground level by removing the clay and installing brickwork on a concrete base cast onto the chalk. As repairs to the eastern bays progressed, a temporary roof was erected for carpentry repairs to the western half of the choir roof. Repairs to the choir roof structure, clerestory windows, parapets and pinnacles continued until March 1923, following which the choir stone vaults were reconstructed, one bay at a time. Brakspear had reported that 'the whole (vault) was in such a condition it was impossible to make it secure without resetting the vault' (Fig. 50). The pendants and carved bosses were retained in position and jacked up to their correct level whilst the remainder of

Fig. 50. Resetting the vaults on the new centring.

Fig. 51. Cutting stone in the construction yard on the south side of the Chapel.

the vaulting was re-set around them.

Throughout 1923 and much of 1924 newly carved 'king's beasts' were installed on the buttress pinnacles of the choir and the Bray and Rutland chapels. The beasts had been removed after Wren's survey of 1682 had recommended that the original beasts, being 'decayed and [might] by falling break the lead', should be removed and replaced by more fashionable Renaissance pineapples; this latter recommendation was not implemented. The beasts served no structural purpose. However, it was essential that they be installed prior to the choir vault being reset so as to minimise any potential for disturbance after its reconstruction. The new beasts were carved in Clipsham stone as a gift from Mr F.G. Minter of the Suffolk construction firm F.G. Minter Ltd.

The wooden scaffolding was extended into the Bray and Rutland transept chapels, and in September 1924 repairs were commenced to the roof structure and the stone vaulting of the crossing above the organ loft. The roof structure was reconstructed in fir rather than oak to minimise weight bearing onto the crossing arches. In January 1925 the construction of new transept buttresses in Clipsham stone was begun. The south transept buttresses were complete by the end of that year and the north transept buttresses by August 1926. The buttresses were a dramatic intervention, radically altering the external appearance of the transepts, incurring loss of historic fabric, necessitating the reconstruction of the chapel south porch on a new diagonal orientation, and blocking of one of the stained glass windows to the Oliver King chapel. Brakspear noted, 'no-one can regret more than I the necessity of their erection'. The fan vaulted parts of the Bray transept vaulting were reconstructed, although the tierceron-vaulted centre section only required re-pointing. The timber roof structures were repaired and strengthened and the stone wall-tops were reinforced with concrete ring beams to restrain the outward thrust of the roof and vault structures. Unfortunately, inadequate provision was made to prevent wet cement from dripping down the inner wall faces during the work, and recent stone cleaning has revealed quite serious disfigurement from cement runs. Throughout 1925 and much of 1926 the windows of the Bray and Rutland chapels were repaired and re-leaded, and those in the choir aisles had their iron stanchions and saddle-bars reinstated.

It seems that timber roof structures over the north and south choir aisles and ambulatory were so damaged as to require substantially replacing in steel. In the Edward IV chantry above the north aisle, a new oak floor was constructed on steel channels, and oak panelling to the north wall was reordered around the stone arch-braces of the flying buttresses Brakspear had re-introduced as a structural improvement. In October 1926 repair works were commenced to the Schorn Tower, and by July 1927 the choir was completed, the wooden scaffolding removed and relocated to the nave, and the choir and transepts were re-opened for use. Scaffolding and centring were installed to support the nave vault, on the choir side apparently projecting through the stone vault to carry a temporary roof over the roof carpentry repairs.

Brakspear reported that cracking and settlement in the south aisle and Beaufort chapel had been concealed by re-facing works in 1877. Settlement still evident in the western bays of the nave clerestory illustrates the cause of Brakspear's concerns in this area of the chapel. Excavations revealed that parts of the Beaufort chapel were built over what seemed to be a former chalk pit some nine feet deep and fourteen feet wide. The pit was filled with rubble, and a bridge of un-keyed course stones was all that supported the south and west walls of the Beaufort chapel and nave aisle including the weight of the westernmost flying buttress. Underpinning proved to be a considerable undertaking, requiring concrete piers to be built down onto solid chalk spanned by steel beams to carry the slender walls of the chapel. A high-level concrete ring beam was installed to resist the thrust of the roof. The stonework was repaired, dislodged stones of the ceiling vault reset, and a new leaded cupola roof was constructed in the style of cupola domes that had survived over the Beaufort and Urswick chapels until the eighteenth century. The underpinning and other repairs to the Beaufort chapel took until late 1929 to complete.

In September 1927 the renewal of the flying buttresses on the north side of the nave began, commencing from the east. By March 1928 the pierced parapet to the north aisle and all of the flying buttresses and pinnacles on the north side of the nave were completed, the westernmost pair of buttresses being founded on a new concrete wallplate, the better to resist thrust. The leaded windows of the south clerestory and most of the north were repaired by July 1928. However, at the beginning of August the works were closed down and the workmen dismissed because of a shortage of funds. Happily, works re-commenced in October as a result of a donation from Lord Woolavington, and repairs were then undertaken to the south parapets and pinnacles and the remaining clerestory windows of the north clerestory. In November 1928 six new 'king's beasts' in Clipsham stone were erected on the north aisle pinnacles.

At the end of October carpentry repairs to the principal nave roof timbers began, continuing until April 1929. Two tie beams were completely renewed, involving hoisting enormous 42ft long oak beams up to roof level and manhandling them into place. As the carpentry repairs progressed, the remedial brick piers installed by John Thompson in 1884 to support the rotted ends of the nave tie beams from the tops of the walls were removed. In May 1929 the temporary steel girder that had been used since 1921 for slinging up the principal roof tie beams for repairs to their beam-ends was finally removed from site. Re-boarding and re-leading of the nave and nave aisle roofs was carried out between July 1929 and April 1930, and concurrently repairs to the nave vault were undertaken, starting from the east end. Because John Thompson had already undertaken repairs to the nave vault in the 1840s, work proceeded speedily, and by November 1929 it was complete and the heraldic bosses were re-polychromed. Structural repairs to the Urswick chapel were completed by October 1930 in similar manner to those for the Beaufort chapel, and a new leaded cupola roof constructed as for the Beaufort chapel.

In April 1929 Brakspear commenced repair works to Henry Emlyn's 1780s Coade stone organ gallery. The central organ case had been divided into two using some material from the old organ case, much of the work being in new oak, to Brakspear's designs. Brakspear was concerned about the ability of the 'iron rods covered with a thin layer of patent stone' to bear the thirty ton weight of the new organ. The western Coade stone arcade piers were rebuilt in limestone from Brakspear's own village of Corsham (Wilts.), and underpinned with new concrete and brick foundations built down to the natural chalk. The weight of

Fig. 52. The Chapel from the south-west with the nave covered in scaffolding.

the organ cases was distributed by a new steel frame in the floor of the organ loft, and steel stanchions were inserted between the Coade stone choir screen and the choir stalls to carry the load. New 'wind trunking' of stoneware pipes laid under the south aisle floor connected the organ to the blower chamber in the western undercroft. This was re-discovered in 2007 when the chapel floors were lifted for installation of a new sound amplification system.

Works to the west wall of the chapel began in early 1929 when the west window glass was removed by Pearce and Cutler, both for conservation and to allow re-ordering of the 76 figures of sovereigns, popes, bishops, and knights to a scheme proposed by M.R. James, the provost of Eton. The window was re-installed in November 1929, although repairs to stonework continued until October 1930 to allow casting a new reinforced concrete beam over the window-head. The window is the third largest in Britain, and recent restoration of the external stonework has demonstrated just how distorted the window arch had become, prompting Brakspear's repairs. Coade stone statues of the Madonna and Child, St Edward, and St George dating from 1789 were refixed into substantially renewed Clipsham stone niches to the west gable. Brakspear noted that two of the niches were themselves of Coade stone, no doubt fixed with iron cramps that had rusted and fractured the cast stone. Interestingly, stone cleaning inside the chapel has recently revealed a niche in the north choir aisle also discovered to be in Coade stone, perhaps a companion piece to Henry Emlyn's west front Coade niches. Brakspear replaced the pierced stone parapets of the stair turret roofs on either side of the great west window in Clipsham stone, and renewed the carpentry and leadwork of their cupola roofs. Finally in 1930 Brakspear replaced the Bath stone parapets to Sir George Gilbert Scott's processional west steps of 1870, using Clipsham stone to a less decorative design than Scott's original. Externally, paths were reformed to suit the altered orientation of the south entrance porch; ground was lowered against the south side of the chapel to show the wall plinths to their original level, and new pavings and channels were laid between the buttresses to carry away rainwater from the roofs.

A ceremony formally re-opening the restored chapel took place on 4 November 1930 in the presence of King George V and Queen Mary, and in December 1930 the builders finally left the site, exactly ten years after commencement of the work.

When we look back on Brakspear's massive restoration, and Robertson's photographic record of it, we might reflect on how attitudes to restoration have changed in the eighty years since that time. Approaches to such work today would probably be more sensitive, involving the repair of decayed stonework rather than its wholesale replacement. Yet, whatever the view that is taken of Brakspear's general approach, and that of his contemporaries, there can be little doubt that what he accomplished was an admirably thorough piece of work. It resolved significant structural issues and confirmed the structural safety of the chapel for a long time to come. For that reason alone we owe Sir Harold Brakspear a considerable debt of gratitude.

TWENTY-ONE

THE ORGANS IN ST GEORGE'S CHAPEL

Roger Judd

FROM THE BUILDING of the present chapel in the fifteenth century to the early seventeenth century references to organs are tantalisingly brief and vague. In 1496-7, for example, an entry in the Treasurer's accounts records 'the moving of the little organs to the new Quire' and then bringing them back.[1] The Precentor's accounts in the sixteenth century record payments to the maker of the organs and money for repairing the organ in the choir. It is not until 1609 that clear information about the organ appears, when the Dean and canons entered into an agreement with Thomas Dallam of London, 'organmaker'. Dallam was instructed to 'take downe and remove the greate Organs wth all that belonges thereto And the same to set over the Quire Doore repayringe amendinge and perfecting the said Whole Instrument'.[2] Dallam was to be paid £60 for this work, and the Chapter also paid £35 for gilding the casework. From this agreement it would appear that Dallam brought together several small instruments which were in the choir, probably actually on the floor, and amalgamated them into an instrument on the organ gallery. The existing case was to be enlarged to make this possible.[3]

After 1609, the next significant date is 1637, when an organ builder from the Midlands was engaged to work on the instrument. This contractor was Emmanuell Creswell, who was working at St Peter's, Wolverhampton, where the Dean of Windsor, Dr Christopher Wren, was also Dean, holding the two positions in plurality. Creswell was charged by the Chapter to make an 'unblameable' organ for £110; painting and gilding this instrument were set at a further £120. From later in the same year there comes an intriguing letter from the Lord Chancellor, written on behalf of the King, to the Chapter, which says '. . . his Majestie therefore and his most noble knightes having observed the care and seen the cost you have bestowed in adorning his Chappell with a new and curious Organ, to sound aloud the praise of the Almighty: . . . soe you have offered an instrument of praise to fill upp the melody of voyces which praise the Lord:

Fig. 53. Hollar's view of the west end of the quire, looking west with the chair organ.

Another decency you have kept in the workmanshipp That as your Chappell is cornized and frized with Angells as Tutelars, soe you have beautified your organ in a melodious methode with Angells blowing and sounding ...'.[4] It may be the case that the 'new and curious organ' with its 'angels blowing and sounding' had some form of automata on top. But whether or not it did, we will never know for certain. Seven years later, in 1644, Canon George Evans reports that the organ had been taken down.[5]

On Charles II's Restoration in 1660, the canons of St George's moved quickly to re-instate the organ. In October that year the Chapter Acts record that Mr Dallame (sic) is 'to make an organ for the Church and to have 600£ for it'.[6] This Dallam is Robert, who was the son of the maker of the instrument of 1609. As in 1637, the organ and the case were to be gilded at a cost of £120. The Dallams were a Catholic family and they had had to flee England during the Commonwealth. So they crossed to Brittany and started up their trade there, where a number of their instruments survive to this day, a few in remarkably original condition. When we look at the instruments at Pleyben and Ergué-Gabéric, it is possible to understand how such a relatively large sum as £120 could be spent on decorating the organ at Windsor. Not only are the instruments richly gilded, they are also decorated in vibrant colours; the visual aspect of the casework, therefore, was

Fig. 54. Hollar's view, looking south to the Bray Chapel, of the front of the screen with the great organ above.

conceived as reflecting the sounds that emanated from within.

What did the organ in St George's look like? By remarkable good fortune the instrument stands out clearly in a number of the engravings which Wenceslas Hollar (d. 1677) provided for Elias Ashmole's great work *The Institution, Laws and Ceremonies of the Order of the Garter*, published in 1672. Hollar's drawings of the interior of the Chapel show the organ case from a variety of different angles. It is important, however, to be cautious in making use of this evidence, because there are indications that Hollar exercised a fair degree of artistic licence. This is a point which will emerge clearly as we go along.

Many books on the history of English organs have carried illustrations of the two best known of Hollar's engravings (Figs. 53 & 54). These two engravings are annotated in Ashmole's book. The organ reproduced in Fig. 53 is described as the

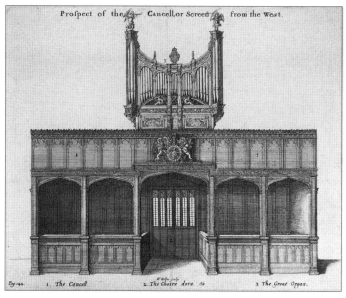

Fig. 55. The great organ on the screen, looking east.

Chair Organ – in other words, the part of the instrument that is at the back of the organist's seat, or chair. The instrument reproduced in Fig. 54 is described as the Great Organ. When Hollar's other engravings are examined, however, a degree of confusion becomes apparent. Inspection of the originals of Hollar's drawings and engravings, now in the Print Room of the Royal Collection, highlights the problem. Alongside Hollar's signature on one of the engravings is the date 1663, which suggests that Hollar was drawing the organ case as it existed after the Restoration and not, as many organ historians have supposed, the instrument of 1609. Perusal of Richard Pennington's *Descriptive Catalogue* of Hollar's etchings points the way to a resolution of the problem.[7] Pennington notes that a very different view of the organ is to be found in Ashmole's hand-written draft of *The Institution* . . . now in the Bodleian Library at Oxford.[8] Examination of this manuscript indicates that Hollar's engraving in the book was in fact taken from the precise opposite side of the organ. If the picture is looked at carefully, it is clear from shading on the two side towers that light is coming in from the left of the drawing. For this to happen, the case would have to be on the eastern side of the screen, and not where Hollar places it, on the west, as shown in Fig. 54. This in turn leads to the conclusion that Hollar omitted this case from Fig. 53, where to have included it behind the Chair case would have confused the composition of his engraving.

The second Hollar drawing to which Pennington draws attention is in the British Museum.[9] Pennington's description of this reads 'Above screen is a balustrade and above that the organ with the tall pipes at the left and right, and the smallest in the middle forming a semi-circle. On the tallest pipes are angels blowing trumpets.' This again is important information. As can be seen from Fig. 55, Hollar has omitted the Chair organ from the picture (compare Fig. 53).

From other views of the nave which either show the complete west face of the case or show an oblique view, it is clear that the west facing case was a different composition from that seen in Fig. 54. In Fig. 57. a detail from a larger engraving that looks across from the Rutland to the Bray chantries shows the back of the organ case facing into the nave. Even allowing for a degree of simplification on Hollar's part, the two cases do not share the same outline, even remotely.

The natural conclusion to draw is that Hollar realised that he could not have the Great Organ case (Fig. 55) in the same drawing as the Chair case (Fig. 53) without having a thoroughly muddled engraving. Accordingly, with considerable artistic licence, he reversed the position of the Great case and had it facing west (as in Fig. 54). Judging from the pen and ink drawing of the Great organ case, this was a most handsome organ case, and Hollar, having made this detailed close-up drawing, would have wanted to make use of it in the engraving for Ashmole. It is difficult, however, to account for the completely different composition of the case as depicted in Fig. 56. It may be that it never existed in that form. Alternatively, it

Fig. 56. Drawing of the great organ case, seen from the west.

could have been a preliminary design which was never brought to realisation.

So far we have considered only the external aspect of the organ. Do we have any idea what its specifications might have been? The direct answer is unfortunately in the negative. However, by looking at what is known of the organ of Worcester Cathedral we can discover what a similar instrument of this date contained. Thomas Dallam built an organ for the cathedral in 1613, four years after he had provided St George's Chapel with one, and a full contract exists there between him and the Dean and Chapter. Exactly as the Windsor instrument had, it had two keyboards, with eight stops on the Great Organ, and five stops in the Chair Organ. Again as at Windsor, in the Civil War the organ was removed (in 1646), and at the Restoration it was brought back.

In this latter connection, in 1666 Worcester engaged the services of Thomas Harris, who had married into the Dallam family. Harris's contract, dated 5 July that year, calls for an instrument almost identical with the 1609 one, and it has some interesting references to the organ at Windsor. 'The great organ case to be designed after the manner of Windsor Church before the wars, a double perspective, the great pipes on the north and the south ranging with the middle columns of the stone arch, and the so next great declining towards the east continually till the smallest in the middle meet within 2ft or 3ft resembling the diminution of pillars in a prospect, and rising by degrees to that end . . . '.[10] The contract also says that the Chair Organ should be like the design at Windsor before the wars; the description is rather flowery: 'a cherub expanding its wings so as to return downe (sic) perpendicular, and the great pipes shall be in the place of the first and second quill, as on the north and south sides, and the rest proportionately less and less towards the cheeks of the cherub . . . '. The cases containing this instrument remained in place on the Quire screen at Worcester until around 1850.

Just as Charles Wild had created some excellently detailed paintings of St George's Chapel in 1816, so too did he at Worcester in 1823. Accordingly, we are given a very good likeness of the organ from both choir and nave. The Great Organ case there seems to have been destroyed sometime after about 1850, but the Chair case found a new home in the church of St Mary and St Michael, Mistley in Essex where it can be seen to this day. This makes it possible for the Windsor historian to make a direct comparison between the physical reality of a surviving part of the Worcester case and the artistic survival of the Hollar engraving at Windsor. It becomes immediately clear that the old Worcester Chair case does not in any way resemble the Windsor Chair case as engraved in 1663 by Hollar. If the Worcester contract of 1666 was carried out to the letter, the

Fig. 57. Pen and ink drawing of the great organ case.

Windsor case of 1609 must have resembled that now at Mistley. From this it would seem that the Restoration case at Windsor was indeed new in 1660, and not the 1609 case restored, as earlier historians have suggested. Hollar's pen and ink drawing (Fig. 57.) speaks of 'the New Organ'. Accordingly it seems safe to assume that the organ built by Robert Dallam in 1660 was new in every aspect.

Further research at the National Archives at Kew has brought to light a remarkable collection of drawings by Henry Emlyn, which he made when entrusted with the restoration of the chapel in the 1780s. King George III gave money for the provision of a new organ, by Samuel Green, housed inside a new case designed and built by Emlyn. According to legend, the pipework of the old organ was disposed of to the local parish church in Windsor; we say 'according to legend', because there are no documents which actually bear this story out; however a number of nineteenth century writers allude to it happening. Because the cases would have been too big to fit into the parish church, we must presume that both the Dallam Great and Chair cases were destroyed. Amongst Emlyn's beautifully drawn and detailed plans for his new organ cases, there is a fine drawing of the Dallam Chair case, which would seem to indicate that at least that part of the 1660 organ survived until the late eighteenth century (Fig. 58). It is very difficult to guess why Emlyn was moved to draw the old case – after all, the design of his own Chair case owes nothing to the previous one. As with so

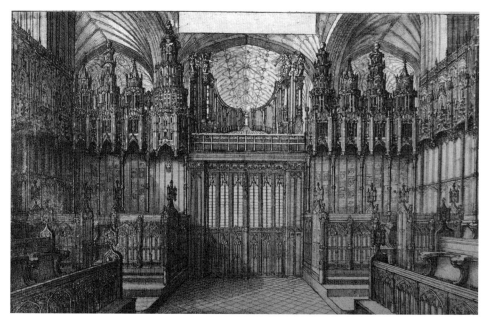

Fig. 58. Hollar's view of the west end of the quire, looking west, with the drawing modified with a new chair organ.

much about the early history of the organ in St George's Chapel, we will almost certainly never know.

Visually the organ remained unchanged from 1789 to the 1920s great restoration of the chapel. Internally, however, it went through many alterations during this time. After the work to the fabric of the chapel, in 1928/9 Emlyn's case was cut in two, and each half was moved to the sides of the gallery, so that the vault could be seen from one end of the chapel to the other. At the same time the instrument was substantially enlarged, and uniquely provided with two consoles, placed at ninety degrees to each other on the organ gallery. This instrument lasted until the early 1960s when a major rebuild became necessary as the complex mechanism inherent in the dual console arrangement failed. The present organ dates from 1965, and is by Harrison and Harrison of Durham, still housed in Henry Emlyn's albeit altered cases; it is widely recognised as one of the finest British organs to have been built in the second half of the twentieth century. Sadly, no part of the Dallam instrument today remains.[11]

TWENTY-TWO

THE GEORGE VI MEMORIAL CHAPEL

Hugo Vickers

THE FIRST STRUCTURAL ADDITION to the exterior of St George's Chapel since the chapel was completed in 1528 was the George VI Memorial Chapel, which was built between a buttress of the north choir aisle and the Rutland chantry during the winter months of 1968-69. The chapel was built to house the body of George VI, a king who had been called unexpectedly to the throne, who had reigned over Britain during the difficult years of the Second World War, and the no less difficult period of peace that followed it, and who had been so particularly devoted to St George's Chapel. He is one of the benefactors of St George's Chapel, whose name is read out at the quarterly obits, in particular for reviving in 1948 'the annual solemnity of the Order of the Garter.'[1]

Originally the plan had been that George VI would have a tomb similar to those of George V and Queen Mary in the north nave aisle, and Edward VII and Queen Alexandra to the right of the high altar in the choir. Discussions took place between the Queen Mother, the Dean of Windsor (Rt Rev Eric Hamilton) and others between 1954 and 1960. The sculptor, Sir Jacob Epstein was approached to undertake an effigy of the King and assured the Queen Mother that he could create something which would be appropriate and not too bold for St George's Chapel. But the Queen Mother was concerned that his work might be too 'bold' and finally her advisors decided not to commission him. The Queen Mother then considered an effigy by Henry Moore, but this idea was also dropped.[2]

Eventually the idea of a new chapel was agreed. The Duke of Edinburgh was one of those who had reservations about the idea, and there were delays while the Fine Arts Commission discussed the effect of such a modern addition to St George's Chapel, the chapel being a medieval masterpiece in the Perpendicular style. The new Dean of Windsor, Rt Rev Robin Woods, took the line that as long as it was the very best that a contemporary architect could create, it would pass the test of time.[3]

All the problems were resolved and the chapel was duly built under the guidance of the architects, George Pace of York and Messrs Seely and Paget. A black marble stone was placed in the floor, under which the King's body would lie. This was similar to those of Henry VI, Henry VIII and Charles I. The inscription gave the King's name – simply GEORGE VI and his dates 1895-1952. On the wall to the left of the altar was a bas-relief sculpture of the King's head, looking to the left, and his shoulders. He is depicted in the robes of the Order of the Garter.

Originally the chapel was to contain eight lancet windows with plain glass. But the Knights of the Garter (including Royal and Stranger Knights such as the Duke of Windsor and Prince Paul of Yugoslavia) responded to a plea from the then Chancellor of the Order, the 5th Marquess of Salisbury, to contribute donations of £2,500 in order that John Piper might be commissioned to design stained glass to enhance these windows. The sum was easily achieved and Patrick Reyntiens made the windows. In thanking the Knights, Lord Salisbury wrote of George VI: 'He was, I feel, though so humble, – and perhaps in a way because he was so humble – a really great man.'4

Wrought iron gates were built at the entrance to the chapel, these being designed in a modern Gothic style. They were not dissimilar to the gates on the tomb of Edward IV to the left of the high altar.

Two panels were created either side of these gates. The one to the left gave the style and titles of George VI, and the one to the right, bore the words that the King had used in his first wartime Christmas broadcast. These had been written by M. Louise Haskins and read:

> I said to the man who stood at the Gate of the Year, 'Give me a light that I may tread safely into the unknown'. And he replied 'Go out into the darkness, and put your hand into the Hand of God. That shall be to you better than a light, and safer than a known way'.

The original intention had been that this right-hand panel would eventually be replaced by the styles and titles of Queen Elizabeth, but this has not happened.

In March 1969 the coffin of George VI, still covered by the Royal Standard which had been used at his funeral in 1952, was brought from the Royal Vault, and buried in the new chapel. A service of dedication was held a few days later, on 31 March, described as an Evensong, in the presence of The Queen, The Queen Mother, most members of the Royal Family and the Knights of the Garter, including Prince Paul of Yugoslavia. The service included 'The Dedication' which took place in the north cuire aisle, the Royal Family, the Knights of the Garter and others, standing outside the small chapel as the Dean of Windsor said:

We incorporate this memorial chapel into the Queen's Free Chapel of Saint George, dedicating it to the glory of God in memory of King George VI whose body lies therein; in the name of the Father, and of the Son, and of the Holy Ghost. *Amen.*[5]

At the time the new chapel was hailed as 'a new addition to the Chapel that happily blends into it both artistically and functionally'.[6] The Queen Mother was pleased with the result. She judged the chapel 'a truly peaceful & holy place.'[7] Following her death at the age of 101, on 30 March 2002, her coffin was laid to rest in the chapel. At the same time the ashes of Princess Margaret, who had died on 9 February the same year, were brought from the Royal Vault and placed in the chapel.

Queen Elizabeth's name, simply ELIZABETH, was added to the black marble, with her dates 1900-2002. Her bas-relief, again a head and shoulders in Garter robes, was placed facing that of the King. A while later a memorial slab was placed at a slight angle to the wall, commemorating Princess Margaret, the inscription surrounded by her favourite prayer, and above that a bas-relief showing her features.

Thus the George VI Memorial Chapel became the latest structural addition to St George's Chapel. Over the years it has blended in well with the architecture of St George's. It is a fitting memorial to a much loved King and Queen.

TWENTY-THREE

MAPS, BUILDINGS AND TREE-RINGS: THE 1729 GREAT HASELEY ESTATE MAP AT WINDSOR

Julian Munby & Dan Miles

A MONG THE ARCHIVAL treasures returned to Windsor in 1963 by the Church Commissioners was a splendid estate map of Great Haseley (Oxon.) made by William Burgess in 1729[1] (Fig. 59). This is a classic survey of an open field parish, with individual strips of arable identified with their owners and acreage, and pictorial representations of individual buildings, which gives the map a very special quality. Indeed, it is one of the finest of the couple of hundred estate maps at Windsor, and is of special importance for the history of Great Haseley, its topography and historic buildings. This prompts speculation about the built history of the village, and gives an opportunity to report a recent discovery in one of the College properties.

The interest of the Dean and Chapter went back to March 1478 when Queen Elizabeth Woodville granted them the manor, and lasted until the estate passed to the Ecclesiastical Commissioners in 1867. Although Great Haseley (in Ewelme Hundred) has not yet been covered in a volume of the Oxfordshire *Victoria County History* it does have an unusual historical asset, a three volume manuscript history of the parish written by Thomas Delafield in the 1730s.[2] Moreover, it also has another early estate map, surveyed by a notable early surveyor, Joel Gascoyne,[3] in 1701 which has previously been better known than the Windsor map, and from which the open fields have been ably plotted and discussed.[4]

It will be for others to reconstruct the village fields and pattern of landholding. The sources are rich. As a result of the fields being enclosed in 1822 following a private act of 1820, there is an enclosure map and award.[5] The parish was also mapped for the Tithe Redemption survey in 1838, the first edition OS (Ordnance Survey) 25 and 6-inch maps date from the 1870s, and there are of course the comprehensive maps and data of the 1910 Valuation Survey.[6] At Windsor there are

Fig. 59. William Burgess's 1729 map of Great Haseley.

leases, rentals and court rolls dating from the fifteenth century to the nineteenth, and other materials survive in the County Record Office. The intention here is to look at what the 1729 map can tell us about the buildings of Great Haseley.

The shape of the village has not greatly changed since the early eighteenth century, although the disposition of the houses has evolved over the centuries. The village plan is linear, with a singularity at each end: a twist past the church and manor house at the east end (Church Hill), and a winding inner lane (Mill Lane) at the west end, linking the main street (Rectory Road) and the back lane. One loss has been the southern lane joining the ends of the village by sweeping round the parkland then known as the Grove, and traversed by an avenue where the footpath now runs. The OS maps show an earthwork where the former road followed the south side of the Grove. As always, it is tempting to engage in speculation on the origins of the village as expressed by its topography: a manorial core at the east end, a 'planned' addition in the centre, and another core (or area of expansion) at the west end. Such a reconstruction may be true, but hard to prove without some archaeological evidence. One significant pointer must always be the tenurial topography, and it will be noted immediately from this map that the Windsor copyhold tenants are spread across the full extent of the village, suggesting that the present arrangement is of some antiquity.

The buildings are shown in an attractive manner with little drawings of red-roofed buildings at each site (Fig. 60). Dwellings are shown with one or two chimneys, barns and outhouses with a plain roof. The parish church is shown as an elevation of the south side, and likewise the manor house, of two storeys with attics, and a central cupola. Gardens, just as the houses, have not been individually depicted, but have rows of orchard-style trees to indicate distinct land use. Not surprisingly, the principal historic houses in the village can be identified as being present in 1729, and several buildings that are not listed as being of architectural or historic interest were also in existence, though these may have been rebuilt since.

It is perhaps more surprising that a dozen or so buildings present in 1729 have vanished, and their sites remain open. Some may have been outhouses and barns, but others do seem to be entire habitations that have disappeared. Two, at the west end of the village on Rectory Road, seem (like most of the houses around them) to have originated as encroachments on small parcels of land added to an existing close. They are both shown as single-chimney cottages. At the east end of the main street, just before the junction with the Thame Road, one cottage or structure built forward into the road exists no more, though the road frontage now includes the extension, which also comprises the adjacent smithy at the corner. Behind the manor house, along the north side of the courtyard was a long two-storey range, most likely domestic offices or farm buildings. There was an open space fronting the manor and church at Church Hill, with an irregular rounded island on which were about four cottages and outbuildings. No trace of these remains above ground, though some may lie buried under the western edge of the island, and parts of others may have survived the recent landscaping of the area. Across the road to the west, below the church on Latchford Lane, there were three cottages where there is now a nineteenth-century house and more recent building. Further down, on the Thame Road an entire smallholding has disappeared into an arable field, where in 1729 there was a house and barn in its own close.

Less surprising is the addition of buildings to the village since 1729. Their appearance can be traced by comparison with the Tithe Map and others on the late nineteenth-century OS plans of the village. Many more have of course appeared in the twentieth century, but nearly all of them remained within the traditional envelope of village plots and closes. One exception was a further piece of encroachment on the main street, where an open triangle of land where

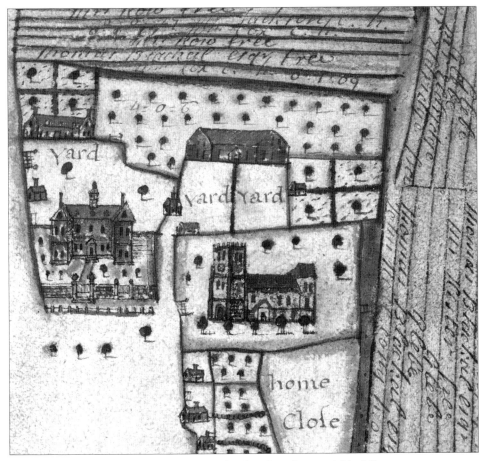

Fig. 60. Detail of Burgess's map showing the church and manorial buildings.

the school stands has gradually been infilled in the nineteenth and twentieth centuries.

All these matters are perhaps unexceptional, and typical of the ebb and flow of village settlement. What is less usual is to have such a graphic demonstration of the appearance of the village at a relatively early date, in a map with links to other documentation. This allows the possibility of linking buildings to people, and to further documentation (such as probate inventories) which can illuminate the development of the village. It is from the dialogue between place, structures and documentation that the village history must be written, and it is the existence of rich administrative archives like those at Windsor that will make this possible. For the earliest history of the village, the 1729 'time-slice' is of great value in allowing an insight into one layer in the long history of development. It underlines an important point that is now increasingly understood: in thinking of 'deserted', moving and shrunken villages, it is important to remember the role of settlement change within the existing village plan. The archaeology of the village is likely to lie beneath the garden or village green, and the thousands of villagers buried in the churchyard may never have lived very far from it.

The second part of this paper turns to a remarkable building, the manorial or tithe barn at Church Farm, and the results of recent investigation of the dating of its truncated principal trussed roof by dendrochronology, which has provided a date and raised interesting questions about an unusual feature (see appendix for dating results). The Great Haseley barn forms part of a farmyard complex adjacent to the church and the manor house. As originally constructed in 1313, it consisted of a nine-bayed stone barn with two porches on the south and buttressed on all four sides. It measured 30 feet wide by 125 feet long internally, and would have had ten trusses which were of an unusual combination of arch-braced and truncated principal-rafter.

The technical description of the roof is as follows. The principals are mortised into the tops of solepieces, which were themselves mortised into extended ashlar pieces which were used to hook the truss on the inside of the stone wall. The principals are surmounted by collars on which arcade plates sit. The truss is restrained entirely by slightly curving arch-braces with spandrel struts. Above the collar is a superstructure with a principal notched over the arcade plate and clasped by a short strut, with an upper collar above, but with no ridge. Below the arcade plate is a twin-tenoned butt-purlin, and above the purlins are clasped. All windbraces are straight, rectangular in section and rise steeply to the horizontal members, with that to the arcade plate rising from the top of the lower purlin. The rafters were jointed over the arcade plate, and there do not seem to have been any wallplates originally.

Evidently this was the last in an increasingly ambitious genre of barns such as those at Great Coxwell (Berks.), Little Middleton (Worcs.) and Stanway (Gloucs.), but all of the former were different and 'safer' in having arcaded construction and/ or well anchored crucks. Great Haseley had tried to go one better and dispense with the crucks. However, as is now apparent, the experiment had proved to be unsuccessful as early as the 1480s.

In 1482 the manor of Great Haseley was granted by Edward IV to the Dean and Canons of St George's Chapel, and there are references in the one extant early account roll to the bailiff expending a significant sum on repairs to 'the great barn of the manor' in 1485-6.[7] This possibly referred to attempts to repair the existing fourteenth-century roof, but it may have been found to be beyond repair and the 1494/5 dendro-date presented here may relate to a decision to replace the roof structure from bays seven to ten. The new section takes the shape of an arcaded structure within the fourteenth-century stone walls, with long substantial arcade posts, ties, queen struts and collars with curved plank windbraces. Several of the posts have been extended with a bridled scarf and a sample taken from one of these proves that some of the posts were extended originally owing to their being too short.

In the early nineteenth century the three western bays, including trusses 1-4, had evidently collapsed and these bays were demolished up to truss 4. The only surviving phase 1 trusses, nos. 5 and 6, had broken and nearly slipped off the walls during the same catastrophe, but it was possible to prop them with inserted arcade posts and to cleat the broken collars, on one the date and initials 'T M 1811' was found.

An interesting feature of the original barn is the sequence of assembly marks which are mainly in Arabic numerals, starting with '1' for the western truss and running eastwards. As each truss is composed of handed members, there was no need to 'tag' the marks to differentiate between right and left. A problem did exist with the longitudinal timbers as there were two identically handed arcade plates, windbraces, etc. in each bay. This was solved by using Arabic numerals on the north side, and Roman numerals on the south. Assembly began with truss 1 adjacent to the stone gable end, then truss 2 was assembled and set into position, then the longitudinal timbers between the first two trusses were inserted and numbered, the first bay starting with the number '2'. The marks were cut with a 9mm gouge and measure about 100mm overall.

The barn at Great Haseley is not unique in the use of Arabic numbers in its construction; however it is very rare. Investigations over the last decade have revealed a select corpus of buildings from the first quarter of the fourteenth century in which the assembly or carpenter's marks consisted of Arabic numbers, sometimes in conjunction with the more traditional Roman numbering system. Although occasionally seen in late sixteenth- and seventeenth-century buildings, such as Mapledurham House (Oxon.) of c.1610-12, when the use of Arabic-based numbers was common in most other aspects of life, the use of Arabic numbers so early shows a much higher degree of sophistication in the work of the master carpenter.

Great Haseley's barn, dating from 1313, is the earliest of this group, and the only one of its kind in Oxfordshire. The next example chronologically is that at the priory of St John in Wells, dating from 1314, a domestic building thought to have been a guest house to the now lost priory. This is probably the most complete set of Arabic numbers found *in situ* in a medieval timber roof. As at

Great Haseley, Arabic numbers were used on one side of the roof, whilst Roman numbers were used on the other. This building is followed by the Bishop's Palace at Salisbury. This had been commenced in the early 1220s at the same time as the eastern chapels of the cathedral. There are remains of the primary build in the bishop's drawing room and the inner chamber and, although the roofs have been rebuilt, about twenty reused timbers have been found with both Arabic and Roman gouged numbers which have been dated to 1315/16. Presumably, as at Haseley both kinds of numbers were used to indicate different sides of the roof.

These examples were followed by the King's Head inn at Wells, built in 1318/19. This is an exceptionally early example of fully developed moulded and sunk cusping to the open hall roof. Again it has the same arrangement as the others with Roman on one side and Arabic on the other. The latest example of Arabic numbers is found at West Court Farm, Shalbourne (Wilts), constructed in 1319/20: a high-status aisled hall with base cruck and crown-post roof. The hall was originally of two bays with cross-wings at each end, but only one and a half bays of the hall survive reasonably intact. There are other fragmentary stragglers such as the Court House in Long Sutton (Somerset), dating to 1328 where some Arabic numbers were noted, and one or two others in the Somerset and Wiltshire region.

What is really significant about this extraordinary collection of five buildings built within a seven-year period between 1313 and 1320, is that all use a combination of both Arabic and Roman assembly marks to differentiate orientation. Some of the buildings, such as the Great Haseley and Wells examples, use the numbers strictly in sequence, but this can only be surmised in case of the Bishop's Palace at Salisbury owing to the timbers having been reconstructed on at least more than one occasion. Conversely, the numbers at Shalbourne were clearly *not* used in sequence, and employed the conventional tag to differentiate the hands of the roof on the main trusses.

So why have these five been found to have been built within the space of seven years? It might be suggested that they are all the work of the same master craftsman; indeed, the fact that each roof was completed about one year after another might lend weight to such a possibility, were it not for the fact that the numbers are significantly different in style between each building. This suggests that a different hand had carved the numbers in each case. Most likely this person would have been the master carpenter who would have placed the numbers on the frame components; however, it is just possible he delegated this to an assistant. One of the Wells examples shows that the marking out of the numbers was not entirely straightforward. Other possible explanations are that the buildings were supervised by master carpenters, all of whom were apprenticed from the same source. The fact that they are all from Oxfordshire, Wiltshire, and Somerset would suggest some sort of geographical connection. Certainly, the buildings were not constructed for the same person. Although documentary research has not been done on some of the buildings, they were not all owned by the Church. We do know that Shalbourne was owned by a William de Harden in 1320.

One can, of course, continue to speculate – the use of Arabic numbers was not so unusual in the academic circles from which churchmen would have come, but what kind of dialogue did such people have with craftsmen? Likewise it is hard to envisage that a group of carpenters had just come back enthused from a timber-framing conference where a paper had been given on a new and improved method of numbering! What is significant is that, of the medieval examples which have been identified and dated, five should come from within so short a period. For the moment the puzzle must remain. Clearly, however, we have here, as with the village map, the matter for further research and investigation into the history of Great Haseley.

TWENTY-FOUR

THE ARCHIVES OF ST GEORGE'S CHAPEL, WINDSOR CASTLE

Eleanor Cracknell

ST GEORGE'S CHAPEL is the only collegiate church in England which has maintained a continuous existence from its mediaeval foundation to the present day. This, coupled with the close connection with the Royal family and the Order of the Garter, means that it holds a unique place in the nation's history. The archives of the chapel trace the history of the College and its extensive properties over six centuries. Of national and international significance, the collection includes some of the country's most remarkable medieval seals and charters.

With the founding of the College in 1348, it was realised that provision would need to be made for the many important documents generated by the daily administrative needs of the College. This is mentioned explicitly in the Statutes of 1352:

> We do order and enact that the said Warden and College shall have a common seal, and a coffer or chest in which the said seal, the instruments, the charters and the letters, the privileges and other writings shall be deposited: we do enact moreover that the said coffer or chest for the same be secured with three different locks and keys.[1]

During the years 1353-1355, the Aerary was built in the juncture between the Dean's Cloister and the western part of the chapel, to serve as a treasury in which to keep the jewels, money and, in addition, the charters of the College. Early records show the care and attention that was spent on the records, with the existing chest for muniments receiving new keys in 1367 as well as a new cupboard being provided at the same time. In 1378, four boxes were also purchased to house the growing number of documents.[2]

Despite the provision of suitable accommodation, it would seem that little care was spent in properly filing the documents for ease of use. Adam de Houghton, Bishop of St David's and chancellor of England, visited the chapel in 1378, and in his injunctions following this visitation he wrote that:

Fig. 61. Maurice Bond working in the Aerary, surrounded by the document boxes.

Moreover it is found that the Privileges, Charters, and Letters concerning the state and Foundation of the said College are kept too remissely and negligently; Whereupon We will and ordain, that henceforth the said muniments, Privileges, Charters and Letters be without delay deposited in the Treasury of the said Chapel in one Chest or Coffer under two or three locks, of which Keys let the Dean of the same place carry one, and let others whom our Lord the King by his Council will ordain, carry others.[3]

Perhaps this was the reason for the purchase of the additional boxes, and in 1422-23 a John Horsted was paid 6d a day for 2 days' work building a cupboard with drawers for the rolls and evidences of the College.[4] However, attitudes towards the keeping of the records do not seem to have altered much because a second visitor in 1432, John Kemp, archbishop of York and a later chancellor of England, had to expressly forbid members of the College from taking records away from the Aerary:

Henceforth they shall by no means retain in their own hands privately any common muniments, letters or instruments, or other property of the College, except so far as on the ground of their office, or in virtue of the Statutes, or by express consent of the Chapter, it shall be granted to them so to do. And if any one of them shall now or in the future have in his possession, otherwise than is here provided, such muniments, letters or instruments or other property of the College, then within 15 days after notice of this our injunction, or after that hereafter they shall have come into his hands, he shall deliver them in the presence of Chapter, to be placed in safe custody as the Chapter shall decree. And he shall not do this, but shall retain them or any of them in his possession contrary to the order aforegiven, he shall ipso facto lose his daily allowances for so long as he shall thus act.[5]

With the building of the new chapel in the 1480s, the money holdings began to move out of the Aerary into the newly built counting house in the tower on the south-east corner of the chapel. The documents still had to share the Aerary with the treasures but they benefited from improved security including new stout doors and strong iron grating to the windows.[6] However, over the years these relics and jewels were sold off so that by 1552, according to a letter by the Royal Commissioners of Edward VI, 'there is now but a small porcion of things remayneng in the Colledge, in comparison to that w[ch] there was at the taking of the said Inventory in the Kings Mat[yes] dayes that dead is.'[7] By 1560, the Aerary was completely a record repository, and it is around this time that we see the first real evidence that the records were being kept systematically. The drawers of the 1422 press have written in a mid- to late sixteenth-century hand details of the contents, with individual drawers for Royal Grants and Charters, fifteen drawers for the different accounts of the steward, treasurer, precentor and other officers, and drawers for the different properties.

Even with this improvement in space and organisation, by 1612/13 the records were again in disorder, with the Chapter Acts recording that they were to be viewed and ordered.[8] This order was repeated in 1638, and again in 1640 'The Aerary to bee reduc'd into order when the weather shall grow warme & the dayes longer the 1st week of March.'[9] In 1663 a Mr Anthropos was paid £3 for sorting the papers,[10] and a second press was built to house the increasing numbers of property records. In 1714 the Chapter Clerk was again paid to put the Aerary into order.[11]

Despite this seeming lack of attention to order, there is evidence that trouble was still being taken over the proper housing and preserving of the documents. Mr Dugdale was paid £5 for preserving the papers in 1667;[12] in 1672 the Canons were ordered to gather up all the counterparts of leases and house them in the Chapter House or Aerary;[13] a catalogue of the books kept in the Chapter House was created;[14] and in 1789 these Chapter Acts and other books were moved to the Aerary as the cupboards they were being kept in suffered from damp.[15] In 1822, the books and papers were removed to the Deanery so that the Aerary could be cleaned and repaired.[16] In 1862, urgent work to the fabric of the Aerary

Fig. 62. The archivist's office in the Schorn tower, with 'overflow documents'.

was carried out under Anthony Salvin and the records were once again taken out, this time going to the Chapter Room. On their return, they were rearranged with, for the first time, assistance of a professional archivist, Mr Burt, the Assistant Keeper of the Public Record Office.[17]

This growing concern for the building and classification of the records may have arisen from increasing requests from external researchers for access to the muniments. Over the years, there had been periodic requests from people such as Elias Ashmole and William Dugdale, but in 1861 the Society of Antiquaries requested permission for its members to view the documents. Permission was granted on 11 May 1861 and the Chapter Clerk was instructed to admit named individuals to the Muniment Room.[18] Although this increased access does not appear to have led to the production of any calendar or catalogue at that time, events six years later would make this essential.

On the 26 June 1867, an Order in Council of the Ecclesiastical Commissioners ordered the College of St George to surrender its landed property to the Commissioners. The Chapter Clerk was instructed to 'select & schedule muniments, books, papers, plans & surveys in the Aerary, Chapter Room & Chapter Clerk's office related to management of the estates' and to begin his list in 1750.[19] This marked the removal of a vast number of documents from the Aerary. These selected items were handed over on 1st September 1867 and numbered between three and four thousand.

With the removal of so many documents, attention turned to the surviving ones. The appointment of Canon John Neale Dalton in 1885 marked a turning point in the life of the records as he was the first member of Chapter to show any real interest in them. In 1891, Canon Dalton was requested to see to the 'systematic rearrangement' of the contents of the Aerary.[20] This he did, with money granted to alter the presses in accordance with his scheme. Work began on numbering each document with a shelf reference with a view to producing a complete calendar. In addition, some transcription work also took place, with Mr Hope Scott (better known as Sir William St John Hope) paid £10 for copying ancient Chapter documents.[21] Finally, on 2 February 1900, permission was granted to seek estimates for printing the Aerary calendar. This printing of the first part of the calendar eventually took place in 1908, with Messrs Sonnenschien chosen as printers, and £150 granted towards the cost. Each volume was to be sold at £1 1s.[22] The second part was printed in 1933, and also in that year permission was granted to 'genuine students' to carry out research on the documents.[23] By 1940, Chapter was able to say that certain documents were in 'daily use for research'.[24]

Even though it no longer housed the property records, with the growth in the administrative records of the College the Aerary was once again soon full. In 1954, the second floor of the Schorn tower was fitted up to accommodate the overflow documents.[25] The number of researchers applying to use the records continued to rise as awareness of the importance of the archives was improved through the Historical Monographs series, launched in 1938, and with the publication of the full catalogue in 1957. The return of the Church Commissioners records in 1967, coupled with the rise in the use of the documents, led to permission being given for the first floor of the Schorn tower also to be used for the accommodation of documents, the archives staff and researchers.[26]

There the records continued to grow in number. In 1996 the first application was made to the Heritage Lottery Fund for the building of a new archive house

Fig. 63. Her Majesty the Queen opening the new archives repository in the Vicars' Hall undercroft on June 18th 1999. The Dean of Windsor is on the left with Dr. Eileen Scarff on the right.

on the site of the former Chapter House, abutting the Vestry. In the application, conditions in the Schorn tower were described as being completely unsuitable.

> There is no further storage capacity for records in the Aerary and Schorne tower Rooms...The Schorne does not have a proper controlled environment...The approaches to it [Lower Schorne room] (via the roof or spiral staircase) are hazardous for both archivist and readers and risk damage to records. During winter it is much too cold to work in, with temperatures frequently falling below those prescribed in the Health and Safety at Work Act 1974. The available space for readers is insufficient... there is no area under direct control of the Archivist large enough to accommodate parties of visitors or to enable small exhibitions of documents.[27]

The initial application was rejected on the grounds that there were existing buildings available. Eventually, the former residence of a minor canon in the undercroft of the Vicars' Hall was selected, another application made, and this time £234,000 was granted.

Work began on converting the building. Two strongrooms were created for the archives, and a further two for the collection of rare books which joined the archives for the first time. A search room with accommodation for 5 researchers was provided, office accommodation for staff, and a permanent exhibition area to display highlights from the collections. The new repository was opened on 18 June 1999 by Her Majesty Queen Elizabeth II (Fig. 63).

For any institution, a major question is what records to produce and keep. The daily running of St George's led to the creation of records documenting decisions, monitoring expenditure and receipt, recording correspondence with interested parties and representing the formal acknowledgement of transactions and grants. In addition, some records were created to meet the requirements of external auditors, and these form some of the most insightful into the daily life of the College. These start with Chapter appointments and the formal registration of the oaths sworn by new members, with the Statutes of 1352 requiring that:

> 53. Item. We do enact that of such oath there be made a public enrolment containing the date and form of the same, and the name of the person so swearing, which shall remain for evermore in the possession of the Warden and chapter under careful custody.

The Injunctions of February 1550 required that attendance of the choral staff be noted in a book dedicated to that purpose:

> yearly one of the Priests of the Choir shall be chosen Chantor, who shall set the Choir, and see all things therein done therein seemly under the Dean, and shall diligently note the absence and other defaults of the said Prebendaries, Preachers, Priests and Clerks, and shall write all their perditions, and keep a book thereof with himself, and present the copy of the same in writing every Saturday in the Chapter house to the Dean and Canons present.

A second set of requirements over record keeping related to the detailed recording of decisions and activities over property holding, enabling the long history of property ownership to be accurately traced. The Injunctions of October 1550 required a copy of every lease to be written up in the Great Register:

> 5. And moreover we enjoin that none Indenture nor grant shall be sealed with the common seal before the same Indenture or Grant be Registered either word for word, Or else the effect of the Covenants and Grants in a great book called the Register prepared for that purpose which shall evermore remain in the College, and never more be taken out of the same, but for the more part kept with the common seal in the chapter house.

The Injunctions of 1572 took this further, ordering that in addition to writing up the basic covenants of the leases in the Register, the decision to grant the lease in the first place was to be recorded in the Register of Chapter Acts:

> 7. Moreover that from henceforth, when and as often as leases or other grants

whatsoever are to be made and passed by the said Dean and Chapter or the more part of them, that it be done distinctly particularly in any sort as that an Act be forthwith entered thereupon by the Chapter Clerk or his deputy in the book or Register of their Acts purposely to be prepared and appointed therefore and that every of those who gave their voices or consent unto such Act or Acts do forthwith before their departure and breaking up of their chapter subscribe their names to the said Act or Acts, being so entered.

As the records grew in volume, so decisions had to be made about their management. The first person to be given responsibility was the Chapter Clerk. Although not mentioned in the Statutes, the office of Clerk soon became one of great administrative importance. According to the 1550 Injunctions, he was to be learned in Latin and able to write well, and a principal role would be 'to write all the Chapter-Acts, Letters missive, and to write such other muniments and escripts'.[28] With the role of creating the records and documenting the activities of the College came the responsibility of keeping them safe and accessible. However, this was not the only task of the officer, who was also often sent to inspect properties, hold courts, assist in the receipt of monies, represent Chapter as the executive officer and on occasion represent them in the law courts in times of litigation.

Some early Canons took an interest in the records from an antiquarian's point of view, notably Thomas Frith (Canon 1610-1631) and Dr George Evans (Canon 1660-1702), both of whom copied numerous documents into notebooks, memoranda volumes and on individual sheets of parchment. For many records, these extracts are the only copies that survive and scholars have much to thank them for, but it was not until the engagement of Maurice Bond as Honorary Custodian of the Chapter Muniments on 2 April 1949 that the records saw the first person specifically appointed solely for their care and management.

Maurice Bond was Honorary Custodian from 1949 until 1975. His wife Shelagh worked alongside him from the time of their marriage in 1954 until her untimely death in 1973, acting as Honorary Assistant Archivist. Together they oversaw the introduction of air conditioning to the Aerary, instituted a complete programme of document restoration leading to the repair of thousands of papers and parchments according to national standards, curated exhibitions of the material, provided proper access to researchers and contributed enormously to the knowledge and understanding of the history of the College.

On Maurice Bond's retirement in 1975, Canon Fisher was appointed as Keeper of the Muniments and Archivist[29], and on 1 January 1976 Grace Holmes was appointed as Temporary Assistant Archivist.[30] In 1977 she was granted permission to be titled Archivist and she continued in her office for twelve years.[31] Eileen Scarff was appointed to succeed her in 1989.[32] Within a year of her appointment she was able to report to Chapter that the number of historical searches and enquiries had increased four-fold, the number of researchers had doubled and the number of group visits from local and national societies had increased considerably.[33]

Dr Scarff continued as Archivist for almost 20 years, adding the post of Chapter Librarian to her role in 1994. Under her administration the profile of the archives was raised dramatically both within the College and outside. The records have never had such care and attention spent on them, and they owe much of this to the hard work and dedication of Dr Scarff.

TWENTY-FIVE

PUTTING ST GEORGE'S ARCHIVES ON THE MAP

Christopher Kitching

S<small>T GEORGE'S CHAPEL</small> H<small>AS</small> been fortunate over the generations in attracting a succession of dedicated honorary librarians and archivists. A new phase of development was initiated in 1989 with the appointment of Dr Eileen Scarff on a paid, initially part-time, basis, as Archivist (and later as Librarian and Archivist) to the Dean and Canons. She was to stay in post for two decades, bringing about a major transformation in the fortunes and standing of the Archives and Library. Over time, her post grew to become a full-time one, underpinned by volunteer staff, and eventually with some paid assistance.

The move to Windsor was a perfectly logical step in a career that had begun with detailed scholarly research for her PhD on the medieval fenland abbeys. Her first paid appointment had come in an editorial post on the Middlesex section of the *Victoria County History*, under its formidable General Editor, Ralph Pugh, who prided himself on being able to spot a rising talent. Then, as now, work on the *VCH* required not just an instinct for a good primary or secondary source to build up an authentic picture, but also fastidious discipline in meeting strict research and editorial standards. This played to Eileen's existing strengths in local history, and her respect for the multiplicity of sources, archival, printed and personal, from which alone it can be constructed.

There then came a brief sojourn in Scotland from 1974 to 1976, when family circumstances took her north of the border. She secured a Research Assistantship with the Scottish Record Office, and in 1975 was to become a Fellow of the Society of Antiquaries of Scotland. In 1976 she returned to England, and to a Research Assistantship with the Historical Manuscripts Commission (HMC) in London, under its Secretary, Godfrey Davis who, like Ralph Pugh, was a shrewd judge of talent and potential. She was rapidly promoted to fill a vacant Assistant Keepership, by open competition in November 1976.

From the time of my own appointment as HMC's Assistant Secretary in 1982 until Eileen's move to Windsor in 1989, we were colleagues. The Commission's editorial work had recently been freshly channelled by Godfrey Davis into the production of a series of Guides to Sources for British History, in at least three of which Eileen had a hand.[1] Those who worked for and alongside her in these years remember her capacity for hard work, her patient and kindly approach to colleagues, the high standards of consistency she both set and expected, and the speed with which she assimilated information. All of these attributes she was to need in spades at Windsor.

The investigative work for the HMC Guides called for a growing number of visits to private and institutional owners of archives. At the same time, the Commission's increasing case-load of advisory work for grant-awarding bodies and government – in which all the curatorial staff played a part and pooled ideas – widened all our horizons. It made us acutely aware of the inter-woven nature of public and private archival evidence for telling the story of individuals, communities, and the nation as a whole. Collectively, we had a close knowledge of the evolving national standards for the care and conservation of archives. We needed to look critically at applications for advice and support. And we used that experience to ensure that if we ourselves had to make a case in support of an archival project, whether to a private owner or a minister of the crown, it was as robust and unassailable as possible. Of course the other key focus of HMC's work was the gathering-in and indexing of finding-aids for the National Register of Archives: not as an end in itself, but in order to disseminate this information freely to researchers. It might not have been so apparent at the time, but in retrospect every one of these accumulated experiences would be seminal in the success of Eileen's work at Windsor.

In parallel with this official work, in 1977 the Buckinghamshire Record Society was looking for an honorary Assistant General Editor. Godfrey Davis put them in touch with Eileen, who was now living in the Thames Valley. She was given an assurance that the work (which of course had to be undertaken entirely in her own time) would not be onerous, as the Society at that time had insufficient funds to publish anything for at least a year. But after rising to become honorary General Editor in 1979, Eileen, who is not one to settle for half-measures, vigorously fostered the Society's work and encouraged the editors of its individual volumes first to come forward and then to deliver. A colleague has characterised her work as 'insistent but never demanding, steering successive volumes through to publication with patient tact'. She remained the Society's General Editor for 28 years. In that time she saw through the press no fewer than fourteen volumes, of an impressive diversity, ranging from the thirteenth century to the nineteenth. She saw too that some sources, such as private memoirs and diaries, could have an appeal wider than the Society's regular membership, so for these she introduced a paperback version (alongside the hard-back library edition) so that they might reach a wider readership and generate extra sales. In recognition of her achievements she was elected a Vice-President of the Society in 2007 upon her retirement from the General Editorship. This work continued throughout most of her time at Windsor, providing useful external contacts and maintaining sharp editorial skills that would prove useful in her paid employment.

So it might be said that when Windsor was ready for Eileen, Eileen was well-prepared for Windsor. She knew a great deal about archives and their care. She had a sure instinct for the kind of evidence that was important to scholars, and brought with her the well-honed research and editorial skills already alluded to. Underpinning all was a conviction that archives have a story to tell, but that the process can only begin when their owner accepts that they are of interest and value to a wider constituency. And it can only continue to fruition when they are not only well ordered but also well catalogued and well housed, with provision for consultation as well as storage.

When Eileen arrived at Windsor, to face the new day-to-day demands of responsibility for an historic archive, she was a part-time, singleton appointee. The archives were housed in premises – the Schorn and the Aerary – that were fittingly historic, and had served this purpose for centuries. But the storage areas were unheated, and whilst the archives had mostly survived to tell the tale, the premises fell far short of the best current standards, not only for archives but also for the staff tending them! In winter – and for a good part of the rest of the year too – the archivist, however warmly dressed, came close to suffering hypothermia in the cause of duty. Physical access to the stored archives was either by means of a spiral staircase – the last thing one wants when carrying bulky documents – or across the roof leads. There was no running water nearby for washing, WC or drinking facilities. And there was no space in which to accommodate readers, so any research on behalf of enquirers could only be undertaken by the archivist. Against this background, it was not surprising that the archives were little known to, or used by, the outside world. They could not be conveniently worked on, arranged, described and conserved in their existing accommodation, let alone made available for research. And yet they were clearly significant to a heritage well beyond the confines of St George's Chapel. Eileen's persistence and persuasiveness was, over time, rewarded with official blessing on her initiatives. One after another – despite inevitable problems along the way – these bore fruit which will be a lasting legacy of her term of office.

The archivist is not a member of the Chapter, and it is probably fair to say that up to that point the Chapter had tended to see the archives and library as a little world of its own, quietly ticking over in capable hands and requiring little attention. But since almost everything that needed to be done required additional funds and additional staff, paid or voluntary, Eileen saw from the start that no progress would be made without strong commitment from the Dean and Canons. She had a vision of what the archives and library could be, and she had to set about communicating it to the governing body: in modern parlance to 'raise their game'. Although the scale of the challenge appeared daunting to all concerned, and its priority in the scheme of things was an issue to some, she carefully argued her case. It was Eileen's great good fortune that the incoming Dean, Patrick Mitchell, was a man with strong antiquarian interests. He quickly recognised how unsatisfactory things were and determined to support her in bringing about improvements. Crucial support in Chapter would come also from the Canon Librarian, Canon John White, himself a medievalist.

Working for any small organisation has its peculiar challenges. The institution will have its own ways and traditions, and there may be complicated cross-currents within a small community. Eileen took all this in her stride. She had the vision and commitment to set realistic goals and to work steadily towards them, single-handedly if necessary. She was good at making friends and allies; she knew when to defer and when to stand firm, and she would learn to keep short-term challenges and setbacks in perspective, by focusing on the achievement of longer-term objectives. In all this she was helped by a lively sense of humour and by a busy and fulfilling life outside the Castle walls.

Chief among her successes was the conversion of the lower range of the Vicar's Hall into new accommodation of the highest standard for the archives and books.

This required planning and commitment over a long period but was completed in 1999, at roughly the mid-point of Eileen's time at Windsor. Adjacent space was included for staff offices, a public reading room and an exhibition area, all under one roof.[2] All this was achieved thanks to a generous grant from the Heritage Lottery Fund, and smaller contributions from other benefactors. To put it succinctly like this is to under-play the complexity of the negotiations to secure the accommodation for this particular purpose rather than for the other uses to which it could have been put on so constrained a site. The devil, of course, was in the detail: arguing issues with the architect or the Chapter, persuading all involved of the need to work to the best standards for the care of archives and books, and to pay attention to minutiae, both in grant applications and in the actual building and finishing processes.

The new building formally brought under Eileen's management the historic

Chapter library – attenuated by sale in a previous generation of anti-historicism, but still comprising 6,000 volumes from the late fifteenth century to about 1715. Finding the right finish for the shelves, to meet both aesthetic and preservation requirements and ensure that there was no adverse effect upon the ancient books, was a major challenge. But, worse still, many of the books were in poor condition, and there was no budget for their repair, so Eileen set about raising the money for an expert condition survey to be undertaken. Armed with this, she was able to make successful applications for more substantial grants to restore the collection.

Much had already been achieved by Eileen and her staff even before the development of the new building, but once that was in place Eileen and the assistants she trained (both paid and volunteer) redoubled their efforts to arrange and publicise the archives. The archives have proved invaluable in informing archaeological and restoration work on the chapel and the other buildings of the precinct, down to such details as the route of sewers and water courses. Eileen worked particularly closely with the consultant archaeologist, Tim Tatton-Brown, most recently on 'Marbeck', the song school and organist's house since the nineteenth century which, as she was able to show, was probably first built in the reign of Edward IV, about 1480, for the College's chantry priests. Reference files were initiated to give pointers to the archival sources for each building or part of a building, including the chapel itself, and also to the history of the many Chapter livings.

The biggest transformation has been in terms of public access to the archives. Cataloguing proceeded apace, and although Eileen was no computer expert herself, she saw that Windsor must keep pace with the national trend (and readers' expectations) to computerise archive catalogues and make them available for remote access via the Internet. The CALM system of computer cataloguing was purchased and implemented, and after years of patient staff work, a great part of the finding aids may now be consulted online. An excellent website has also been developed for the archives and library, and this too moved with the times by introducing in 2008 a 'blog' of regular news and comment. Historic plans in the archives have been digitised in association with Cambridge University Library, and with the help of external grants a number of the archives, particularly those concerning the fabric, have been conserved to modern standards.

Eileen continually strove to open up the source materials and make external scholars aware of their potential, as is attested by many acknowledgements in citations. Particular links were forged with Royal Holloway University of London, Reading University, a number of Oxford colleges and the History of Parliament. Eileen was a lynch-pin of three historical conferences on Windsor

Fig. 64. Dr Eileen Scarff (centre) with her staff in 2007, with from left to right, Mrs Enid Davies, Mr Thomas Kennett, Mr Richard Wragg and Miss Eleanor Cracknell.

and the chapel, and joint editor of the proceedings for two of these.[3] Group visits were welcomed, for example from national and international professional bodies, from local history groups, and from a number of consultations held in St George's House. Exhibitions were arranged, both inside the Undercroft and in the display area in the south choir aisle, for which Eileen had a personal hand in sourcing the exhibition cases; and small exhibitions were also laid on for school parties and visiting groups from Chapter livings. She personally financed the launch of a very successful 'Adopt a Book' scheme, whose benefactors were invited to Open Days to look round the new premises and learn more about the work undertaken. In the wider world, she was elected a Fellow of the Society of Antiquaries of London in 1990 and a Fellow of the Royal Historical Society in 2001. She maintained wider contacts through a number of outside bodies including particularly the Cathedral Libraries and Archives Association.

The pleasant task of compiling this short appreciation has been made easier by the absolute consistency of the picture of Eileen that has emerged from the friends and colleagues who have helped along the way. Throughout her career she has shown a remarkable degree of friendship, loyalty and respect to all those with whom she has worked, as well as to a wide range of colleagues and members of the general public, and as a result has earned widespread esteem and affection. This book is itself a living testimonial of admiration for a great archivist, the person who more than anyone else has had the vision to put the Archives of St George's Chapel Windsor on the map.[4]

REFERENCES

CHAPTER ONE

1. T. Tatton-Brown, 'Windsor Castle before 1344', in J. Munby, R.Barber and R.Brown, *Edward III's Round Table at Windsor*, (Woodbridge 2007), 27.

2. S. Brindle and B. Kerr, *Windsor Revealed: New Light on the History of the Castle* (London 1997).

3. T. Tatton-Brown, in Munby et al., *Edward III's Round Table*, 56.

4. R. Sanderson and K. Gardner, 'Conservation of Reigate stone at Hampton Court Palace and HM Tower of London', *Journal of Architectural Conservation*, 3 (2001), 7-23.

5. T. Tatton-Brown, 'The quarrying and distribution of Reigate stone in the Middle Ages', *Medieval Archaeology*, 45 (2001), 189-201.

6. G. Tyack, S. Bradley and N. Pevsner, *Berkshire* (New Haven and London, 2010), 670.

7. T. Tatton-Brown, in Munby et al. *Edward III's Round Table*, 55.

8. K. Blockley, 'The Vicars' Hall, St George's Chapel, Windsor Castle', *Archaeological Journal,* 157 (2000), 354-74.

9. Hope, *Windsor Castle*.

10. W. J. Arkell, *Oxford Stone* (London 1947), 72.

11. Ibid., 110.

12. T. Tatton-Brown, 'The paving of St George's Chapel, Windsor', *Annual Report of the Friends of St George's,* 2004-05, viii, 6 (2005), 293-401.

13. I. Freestone, 'Forgotten but not lost: the secret of Coade stone', *Proceedings of the Geological Association,* 102 (1991), 135-38.

14. M. Ashley, 'The restoration of the West Front', *Annual Review of the Friends of St George's,* 2006-07, viii, 8 (2007), 414-17.

15. Hope, *Windsor Castle*, 259-61.

CHAPTER TWO

1. *Flores Historiarum*, ed. H.R. Luard (3 vols., Rolls Series, 1890), ii, 481.

2. Hope, *Windsor Castle*. There are subsequent accounts of the castle under Henry III in *The History of the King's Works. The Middle Ages*, ed. R.A. Brown, H.M. Colvin and A.J. Taylor (2 vols., London 1963), ii, 866-9 and V. Jansen, 'Henry III's Windsor: castle building and residences', in Keen and Scarff, 95-109. The most detailed recent account of Henry III's Windsor (finished in 1999) was researched by Stephen Priestley and written by Steven Brindle in connection with English Heritage's work at the castle: 'Windsor Castle.

Draft Historical text, Part Two: The Reign of Henry III', together with an English calendar of the primary record sources in a separate Appendix: 'Windsor Castle: Payments and Supply of Materials in the Reign of Henry III', both privately printed by English Heritage.

3. See J. Geddes, 'Who was Gilebertus?', *Annual Report of the Friends of St George's, Windsor*, vii, 9 (1997-8), 376-9; and ch. 7 below.

4. For this period in general see J.R. Maddicott, *Simon de Montfort* (Cambridge, 1994), chapters 5-8.

5. *Documents of the Baronial Movement of Reform and Rebellion 1258-1267*, ed. R.F. Treharne and I. J. Sanders (Oxford, 1973), no.35.

6. E.F. Jacob, *Studies in the Period of Baronial Reform and Rebellion 1258-1265* (Oxford, 1925), 234-5.

7. TNA, Just 1/ 59, m.1d (http://aalt.law.uh.edu/AALT4/JUST1/JUST1no.59/ bJust1no59dorses/IMG-1511.htm), accessed 04/02/2010. For this reference see G. A. Williams, *Medieval London: from Commune to Capital* (London, 1963), 234 where the episode is cited slightly out of context. The Latin reads: 'vero predictus burgensis [Richard de Walbrook] *propter timorem castri de Wyndes' cuius terra predicta est vicina ad predictam terram quem ad firmam acceperat accedere non audebat et ita iacuit inculta et sine custodia.*'

8. *Cronica Maiorum et Vicecomitum Londoniarum*, ed. T. Stapleton (Camden Society, 1840), 78-9.

9. Brindle and Priestley, 'Windsor Castle: the Reign of Henry III', 31-2. Brindle and Priestley also, as part of their work, edited, annotated and reprinted Craib's Itinerary as 'The Itinerary of King Henry III'. Brindle's introduction to this (2-7) provides the first proper analysis of Henry's itinerary.

10. See further the analysis in Brindle and Priestley, 'The Itinerary of King Henry III', pp.2-7.

11. What follows develops the remarks in Brindle and Priestley, 'Windsor Castle: the reign of Henry III', 33.

12. These figures include examples from 1255-57. The architectural history of all the royal places and castles mentioned in this paragraph can, of course, be found in Colvin's *History of the King's Works*.

13. John Maddicott has kindly provided a copy of this analysis, which is included as an Appendix to the recently published version of his Ford lectures, *The Origins of the English Parliament 900-1327* (Oxford 2010). We have assumed that parliaments which are said in the sources to be in 'London' in fact met at Westminster.

14. There were large areas for stables in the middle and lower wards.

15. TNA,E101/349/27. In general see D. Carpenter, 'The Household Rolls of King Henry III of England', *Historical Research*, 80 (2007), 22-26. It should be said that in 1260 Henry was still under the control of a baronial council which may have made his time at Windsor unusually quiet. The contrast is less marked in 1266 (TNA, E 101/ 667/ 50), the only other occasion when it can be made. Then the average of four weeks at

Westminster was £21 a day. This was followed by Easter week when the costs jumped to an average £30, Easter day and its vigil costing around £150. In the following week at Windsor (including one day on the way at Kempton), the average cost per day was £18. This, however, was another unusual period since Henry was preparing for the siege of Kenilworth which may have made Windsor particularly busy. Brindle and Priestley mention that an advantage of Windsor was that it could be supplied from neighbouring manors. The surviving household rolls do not indicate this.

16. For Eleanor and Windsor, see M. Howell, *Eleanor of Provence: Queenship in Thirteenth Century England* (Oxford, 1998), 32, 76, 99-100.

17. TNA, E 101/ 349/ 16 and E 101/ 349/ 22; see Carpenter, 'Household Rolls of King Henry III', 44-5; and Katherine Meissert, 'The Household Rolls of Eleanor of Provence' (unpublished MA dissertation, King's College London, 2005), which includes in an Appendix a transcription of the rolls.

18. For what follows see D. A. Carpenter, 'An Unrecognised Chronicle of the Period of Reform and Rebellion in England 1256-1265: the Pershore Flores Historiarum', forthcoming.

19. *Flores Historiarum*, ii, 489.

20. It is possible that the Clewer (Curfew) Tower was built to hold a great 'machine' above the vaulted basement, c. 1230, since there are slots in the walls to hold vertical timbers. We owe this point to Tim Tatton-Brown.

21. *The Royal Charter Witness Lists of Henry III*, ed. M. Morris (2 vols., List and Index Society, 291-2, 2001), ii, 51.

22. *Close Rolls 1247-51*, 8.

23. Brindle and Priestley, 'Windsor Castle: the Reign of Henry III', 37. And for the chapel, see below, ch. 3.

24. TNA, E101/349/27.

25. For this aspect of Henry's piety, see S. A. Dixon-Smith, 'The Image and Reality of Alms Giving in the Great Halls of Henry III', *Journal of the British Archaeological Association,* 152 (1999).

26. TNA, JUST 1/ 52, m.15. See D. Carpenter, *The Reign of Henry III* (London, 1996), 323.

27. *Documents of the Baronial Movement*, no.35.

28. Carpenter, 'The Household Rolls of King Henry III', 44-5.

29. Brindle and Priestley, 'Windsor Castle: the Reign of Henry III', p.37. Margaret Howell's analysis of a roll recording payments to Eleanor's messengers shows that while she had links with many of the king's ministers, and with friars, the noble women she was close to (apart from Eleanor de Montfort and Joan de Valence) were either Savoyards or connected by marriage with Savoyards. Howell commented that 'one must conclude that Eleanor had made no attempt to cultivate a wider range of English aristocratic contacts'.

30. *Matthaei Parisiensis Chronica Majora*, ed. H.R. Luard (7 vols., Rolls Series, 1872-83), v, 264.

31. For the significance of the window, see Howell, *Eleanor of Provence*, 20.

CHAPTER THREE

1. The dating of the Lower Ward at Windsor is problematic, as is the original date of the Great Hall in the Lower Ward, the first documentary reference to which only comes in 1196. The ward and the hall could have been laid out by Henry I when he moved the royal residence from Old Windsor, c. 1110; alternatively, they may date from the reign of Henry II. The author would like to thank Tim Tatton-Brown for reading and commenting on the draft and advising on various points.

2. *Calendar of Liberate Rolls* 1240-45, 205.

3. *Roles Gascons*, I. ed. F. Michel, 1242-54, (1885) No. 1484.

4. *Calendar of Liberate Rolls* 1245-51, 13. *Close Rolls* 1242-7, 442.

5. *Calendar of Liberate Rolls* 1245-51, 172, 187, 203, 255. *Close Rolls* 1247-51, 54.

6. Hope, *Windsor Castle*, i, 58-9.

7. *Calendar of Liberate Rolls* 1245-51, 215.

8. The books included a missal, a breviary with collects, chapter and hymns, two antiphons, two psalters, and two graduals. *Close Rolls,* 1247-51, 447, 505.

9. P. Tudor-Craig, 'The Fonts of St George's Chapel', in *St George's Chapel, Windsor, in the Fourteenth Century,* ed. N.E. Saul (Woodbridge, 2003), 151-63.

10. TNA, E372/97. Pipe Roll 37 Henry III, m. 10. This confirms that there were four chaplains paid 50 shillings per annum, and refers to scaffolding for painting the chapel.

11. *Calendar of Liberate Rolls* 1251-60, 514.

12. TNA, E101/492/27. 28, 29 and 30 are the accounts for the work, for 1350-1, 1351-2, 1352-3, and 1353-4.

13. J. Harvey. *English Mediaeval Architects. A Biographical Dictionary down to 1550* (2nd edn., Gloucester, 1984), 242-5.

14. TNA, E101/492/27, m. 8 has the wages for the principal craftsmen for the first year, 1350-1.

15. Ibid., mm 2, 4. TNA, E101/492/30.

16. Ibid. Robert Burwell is variously described as carving the seats of the stalls, and 'working' them. By August 1351, he and his collaborator, John Gurdon, were carving the 'pomelia', or end finials, in late 1351 he is referred to as carving the 'sedilia', and by January 1352 he was carving the Queen's pew.

17. TNA, E101/492/28, m. 10. For 24 'gumphis', 'pro glad. pend. super. stall. in. chor. capell.'

18. TNA, E101/492/28, mm. 10, 14, 15.

19. T. Tatton-Brown, 'The Deanery, Windsor Castle', *Antiquaries' Journal,* 78 (1998), 347 ff.

20. TNA, E101/492/27, m. 6. E101/492/28, m. 5.

21. TNA, E101/492/28. m. 6.

22. Ibid., m. 9.

23. Ibid., mm. 9ff have regular references to payments to these 15 or so glaziers under

John Lincoln and John Athelard for the rest of the year.

24. TNA, E101/492/30. mm. 3. 9. On 30. ix. 1353 John Talwyth was paid for transporting eight cases in his 'shout', with glass for the windows at Windsor, from Westminster'.

25. TNA, E101/492/28, m. 14. June 1352.

26. TNA, E101/492/30, mm. 7-11. John Lyndes was working on the 'lettron' for three months.

27. Ibid., m. 11. To Stephen West for one piece of timber bought for 1 cross to be made, 7s. William at Pemere for two pieces of timber bought or two images to be made, viz., of Mary and John, 5s. No references have been found to the images actually being carved.

28. Hope, *Windsor Castle*, i, 201. The Pipe Roll for 41 Edward III records charges made by Sampson, sheriff of Derby and Nottingham, for the cost of transporting 'a certain table of alabaster' to Windsor in 10 carts, each with 8 horses and 2 men, for 17 days.

29. J. Geddes. *Medieval Decorative Ironwork in England* (London, 1999), 151, 156-7.

30. Hope, *Windsor Castle*, i, 374-5.

31. TNA, E492/11, quoted in St John Hope, *Windsor Castle*, i. 87.

32. Christopher Wilson, in C. Wilson, P. Tudor-Craig, J. Physick and R. Gem, *Westminster Abbey*. (London, 1986). 27.

33. W.R. Lethaby, *Westminster Abbey and the King's Craftsmen* (London, 1906), 150ff.

W.R. Lethaby. *Westminster Abbey Re-examined*, (London, 1925), 90-95.

34. *Calendar of Close Roll*, 1242-7, 141. Harvey, *English Mediaeval Architects*, 251-3.

35. The best discussions of Master Henry's career and origins are those in Harvey, *English Mediaeval Architects*, 251-3. P. Binski, *Westminster Abbey and the Plantagenets* (New Haven and London, 1995), 15, 42-3. C. Wilson in *Westminster Abbey*, 25-6.

36. Binski, *Westminster Abbey and the Plantagenets*, 35.

37. Lethaby, *Westminster Abbey*, 140-3. Wilson, *Westminster Abbey*. 22, 37; B. Harvey, 'The Monks of Westminster and the Old Lady Chapel', and T. Tatton-Brown, 'The Building History of the Lady Chapels', in *Westminster Abbey, the Lady Chapel of Henry VII*, ed. T. Tatton-Brown and R. Mortimer (Woodbridge, 2003), 23-5, 189-192, fig. 5.

38. Harvey. *English Mediaeval Architects, 253*.

39. The chapel appears in the earliest known view of Windsor Castle, in the background of a view of Henry VI founding Eton College, in a manuscript copy of Ranulf Higden, 'Polychronicon' of *c.* 1450, in Eton College Library. This is illustrated in Hope, *Windsor Castle*, i, plate xix.

40. I am grateful to Tim Tatton-Brown for pointing out to me the probable link to the Lichfield Lady Chapel. And see Tatton-Brown, 'The Building History of the Lady Chapels', 190, 1.

CHAPTER FOUR

1. TNA, E101/391/15, printed in N.H. Nicolas, 'Observations on the Institution of the Most Noble Order of the Garter', *Archaeologia*, 31 (1846), 1-163.

2. J. Vale, *Edward III and Chivalry* (Woodbridge, 1982), 79-81.

3. W.M. Ormrod, 'For Arthur and St George: Edward III, Windsor Castle and the Order of the Garter', in *St George's Chapel, Windsor, in the Fourteenth Century*, ed. N.E. Saul (Woodbridge, 2005), 13-34 at 19-20.

4. For these comments, see J. Munby, R. Barber, R. Brown, *Edward III's Round Table at Windsor* (Woodbridge, 2007), 41, 180.

5. M. Biddle and others, *King Arthur's Round Table. An Archaeological Investigation* (Woodbridge, 2000), 415.

6. H.E.L. Collins, *The Order of the Garter, 1348-1461. Chivalry and Politics in Late Medieval England* (Oxford, 2000), 242-54.

7. Ibid., 255-8.

8. For full references to the examples in this paragraph, see N.E. Saul, *English Church Monuments in the Middle Ages. History and Representation* (Oxford, 2009), 225-7.

CHAPTER FIVE

1. D'A. J. D. Boulton, *The Knights of the Crown. The Monarchical Orders of Knighthood in Later Medieval Europe* 1325-1520 (Woodbridge, 1987), in the most thorough recent account of the Order of the Garter (pp. 96-166), comments that the reason for the annexation of the office of prelate to the see of Winchester is unknown, but adds that 'the historic importance of the see and its associations with the Arthurian tradition probably played a part in its selection for the honour' (p. 148).

2. *Calendar of Close Rolls 1346-9*, 396-7; T. Rymer, *Foedera*, ed. J. Caley and F. Holbrooke (London, 1825), III. i, 139. I am grateful to W.M. Ormrod (whose book, *The Reign of Edward III, Crown and Political Society in England* 1327-1377 (London, 1990), appeared while this article was being written) for these references, which show that the story that Edward proceeded along the south coast from Sandwich via Portsmouth and Southampton to Winchester, retailed by Martin and followed by Moberly, cannot be corroborated from the contemporary sources (G. H. Moberly, *Life of William of Wykeham*, 2nd edn. (Winchester and London, 1893), 12, quoting (inaccurately) Thomas Martin, *Historica Descriptio Complectens Vitam... Guillielmi Wicami* (London, 1597), Bk. 1, Cap. 2 (Sig. B4v)). The point is of some interest in demolishing the tale that it was on this occasion in Winchester that Edward chanced to meet and at once recruited the young William of Wykeham to his service. If Wykeham was then, as Martin alleges, Edington's secretary *('Edintonio Episcopo turn erat a consiliis et epistolis')*, Edward could as well have met him in London during the Michaelmas legal term of 1347, when both Edward and Edington were present with few interruptions, as Ormrod has demonstrated (letter of 25 Feb. 1991).

3. J. Vale, *Edward III and Chivalry* (Woodbridge, 1982), 77-9; the quotation is

taken from p. 77.

4. Ibid., 83-4; Boulton, *Knights of the Crown*, 116.

5. For St Stephen's, see *The Victoria History of the Counties of England, London*, (London, 1909), 566; *Calendar of Entries in the Papal Registers Relating to Great Britain and Ireland. Petitions to the Pope*, i, 1342-1419 ,186-7; ibid., *Papal Letters*, iii, 1342-62, 330. For St George's, see below.

6. *Calendar of Patent Rolls* 1348-50, 144.

7. For Edward Ill's works in creating the college, see R.A. Brown, H. M. Colvin, A.J. Taylor, *History of the King's Works*, ii (London, 1963), 872-5.

8. *Calendar of Papal Registers. Petitions to the Pope*, i, 1342-1419, 187-8.

9. *Calendar of Papal Registers. Papal Letters*, iii, 1342-62, 395.

10. Ibid., 383-4, 399. For the texts of these and other relevant letters, see now *Original Papal Letters in England 1305-1415*, ed. P.N.R. Zutshi (Vatican City, 1990), nos. 227, 229-30, 232-3,241. I owe this reference to the kindness of Professor C. N. L. Brooke.

11. A. K. B. Roberts, *St George's Chapel, Windsor Castle, 1348-1416. A Study in Early Collegiate Administration* (Windsor, 1947), 107, cf. pp. 17-18, 143, 145, 238.

12. For the status of the existing chapel, see J. H. Denton, *English Royal Free Chapels 1100-1300: A Constitutional Study* (Manchester, 1970), 129-30, and for that of the new foundation, ibid., 116-17. Edington's role in the foundation of the college at St Stephen's seems to have been equally deliberate, for St Stephen's lay also outside his diocese. W.M. Ormrod has suggested in his thesis ('Edward III's Government of England, 1346-1356' [Oxford D.Phil., 1984], 222-61, esp. 232-3) that Edington's attempts as treasurer (an office he held from 1344-56. to produce greater cohesion between the various departments of finance in the later 1340s were related to the use of the canonries of St Stephen's for officials of the Exchequer of Receipt, or Lower Exchequer.

13. Roberts, *St George's Chapel*, 107, took the view, without quoting further evidence, that the statutes were drawn up by William Edington at the king's request, but the matter falls short of proof.

14. E. Ashmole, *The Institution, Laws & Ceremonies of the Most Noble Order of the Garter* (London, 1672), unpaginated appendix, and cf. pp. 190-3.

15. A fifteenth-century French version among Ashmole's manuscripts in the Bodleian Library (MS Ashmole 764, ff. 123r-136v) includes these additions. It was used by Juliet Vale *(Edward III and Chivalry*, 84, 148 (n. 14), 151 (n. 72)), who discussed the dating of this version and of the statutes in general. For the most recent discussion of the surviving texts of the statutes, see Boulton, *The Knights of the Crown*, 118-22.

16. Cf. MS Ashmole 764, fos. 123r-v; and see Vale, *Edward III and Chivalry*, 184.

17. Cf. MS Ashmole 764, fos. 123v-124v (Art. 3), 124v (Art. 4), etc.

18. As Boulton points out, however, the other titles used in this list show that the prologue did not reach its present form before the spring of 1354: *Knights of the Crown*, 121.

19. Cf. MS Ashmole 764, fo. 129v: 'Lesquelles denominations escripra le chief prelat dudit ordre, c'est assavoir l'evesque de Winchestre pour le temps estant ou en son absence

le dean, ou registreur, ou le plus ancien residencier dudit college . . .'. The language of the surviving French versions differs much less than does the language of the Latin versions. Since the French and Latin versions both refer to the founders as if still alive, the French of the 15th-century manuscripts, such as Ashmole 764, quoted here, may be essentially that of the original version of the statutes, while the Latin versions may be independent translations from the French original, even if (as seems to be the case) the earliest version of the text now surviving is in Latin: Boulton, *Knights of the Crown*, 118-19, 122.

20. *The Register of William Edington, Bishop of Winchester*, 1346-1366, ed.S.F. Hockey (Hampshire Record Series, 7, 1986), xxiii-xxvi, at p. xxiv. The itinerary provided by Dom Hockey omits all reference to the bishop's periods of residence in Southwark: these can easily be established by noting the place and date printed to the right below each entry throughout the register. The itinerary only records, of course, those places where Edington carried out episcopal functions of the kind normally entered in an espicopal register. It cannot therefore provide a complete personal itinerary.

21. Public Record Office, *List of Foreign Accounts*, Lists and Indexes 11 (1900), 104.

22. Vale, *Edward III and Chivalry*, 77-8, 82; Ashmole, *Institution*, 236; J. Anstis, *The Register of the Most Noble Order of the Carter*, 2 vols. (London, 1724), i, 11-15, 171, 310; G. F. Beltz, *Memorials of the Order of the Garter* (London, 1841), 7; N. H. Nicolas, *History of the Orders of Knighthood of the British Empire*, 4 vols. (London, 1842), i, Appendix, xv-xviii, xix*- xlviii*; N. H. Nicolas, 'Observations on the Institution of the Most Noble Order of the Garter', *Archaeologia* 31 (1846), 1-163, esp. pp. 134-40.

23. Roberts, *St George's Chapel*, 45, cf. pp. 65, 149.

24. *Chronicon Galfridi le Baker de Swynebroke*, ed. E.M. Thompson (Oxford, 1889), 108-9; translated by Boulton, *Knights of the Crown*, 116-17.

25. *Calendar of Fine Roll 1347-56*, 231 *(bis)*. I owe this reference to Prof. Ormrod.

26. *Register of William Edington*, i, nos. 747-9.1 am grateful to Professor Brooke for his advice on the significance of these entries in the register.

27. See, for example, the words of Froissart and Jean Le Bel quoted by Boulton, *Knights of the Crown*, 102, 105.

28. See Martin Biddle *et al.*, *King Arthur's Round Table* (Woodbridge, 2000), 349-57, fo. discussion of the Arthurian status of Winchester in the thirteenth and fourteenth centuries. The present article emerged from the need to establish the conditions under which the Round Table ceased to be an actual table and was hung on the wall of Winchester Castle Hall in the mid fourteenth century, dealt with in Chapter 11 of that book. I am grateful to the late Dr A.J. Taylor for his comments on drafts of Chapter 11, and on an earlier version of this article, and for his initial suggestion that one should explore the role of William of Wykeham in the changes through which the table went at this time. I am also much indebted to Prof. W.M. Ormrod, who read this article in an earlier draft and made several important corrections and suggestions which I have followed. The responsibility for any errors which remain is my own.

CHAPTER SIX

1. The size of Windsor's first guildhall and gaol can be judged from a *c.*1820 map of the town; it took up a good third of Church Street: TNA, MR 1455.

2. SGC, 1.G.15.

3. A full account of the case of the Windsor martyrs is reproduced in R. R. Tighe and J. E. Davis, *Annals of Windsor* (2 vols., London, 1857), i, 527-51.

4. Bodleian Library Oxford, MSS Ash. 1126, f.30b.

5. SGC, 1.G.14.

6. See for example, Berkshire Record Office, Wi/FA1/2/19.

7. SGC, XV.44.125.

8. See for example, TNA, E 101/492/28.

9. There are a series of articles dealing with late medieval pilgrimage to Windsor and particularly the popular cult of Henry VI. See for example R. Marks, 'Images of Henry VI', in *The Lancastrian Court*, ed. J. Stratford (Donington, 2003), 95-110.

CHAPTER SEVEN

1. J. Geddes, *Medieval Decorative Ironwork in England* (London: Society of Antiquaries, 1999), 153-7, 385. This book provides a full discussion of the St George's ironwork, with a bibliography.

2. Ibid., 260-72, 385-7.

3. Ibid., 265.

4. Ibid., 237.

5. Ibid., 250-3.

6. Ibid., 224.

CHAPTER EIGHT

1. Quoted in C. Ross, *Edward IV* (London, 1974), 182.

2. Hope, *Windsor Castle*, i, 238.

3. *History of the King's Works,* ed. R.A. Brown, H.M. Colvin, A.J. Taylor (2 vols., London, 1963), i, 291.

4. *Oxford Dictionary of National Biography*, ed. H.C.G. Matthew and B. Harrison (60 vols., Oxford, 2004), iv, 595-6.

5. J.M.J. Fletcher, 'Bishop Richard Beauchamp, 1450-81', *Wiltshire Archaeological Magazine*, 48 (1938), 161-173 and *Royal Commission for Historical Monuments: Salisbury, the Houses of the Close* (1993), 53-72.

6. Hope, *Windsor Castle*, ii, 375.

7. Documentary evidence suggests that many of the senior artists, at least, were foreigners.

8. Ross, *Edward IV*, 226.

9. Hope, *Windsor Castle*, ii, 376.

10. T. Tatton-Brown, 'Windsor Castle before 1344', in *Edward III's Round Table at Windsor*, ed. J. Munby, R. Barber and R. Brown (Woodbridge, 2007), 13-28.

11. It was actually only a peace treaty, but the meeting between the two kings was considered of such importance that Edward IV had it elaborately depicted on the misericord of his own 'Sovereign's Stall' in the choir a few years later. See M. Bond, *St George's Chapel, Windsor* (Windsor, 1975), 35.

12. J. Harvey, *English Medieval Architects* (2nd edn., Gloucester, 1987), 159.

13. Ibid.; and Hope, *Windsor Castle*, i, 398-406.

14. The polygonal chapel on the north-east corner was probably demolished in *c.* 1650, but it is shown on John Norden's 1607 bird's eye view of the chapel: British Library, Harleian MS 3749, fo. 3.

15. T. Tatton-Brown, 'The building history of the Lady chapels', in *Westminster Abbey. The Lady Chapel of Henry VII*, ed. T. Tatton-Brown and R. Mortimer (Woodbridge, 2003), 191.

16. T. Tatton-Brown, 'The paving of St George's Chapel'. *Annual Report of the Friends of St George's*, 2004/05, viii, 6, 293- 301.

17. W.C. Tennant, 'Croes Naid', in *Annual Report of the Friends of St George's* (1943), 5-14.

18. R. Marks, 'A late Medieval pilgrimage cult: Master John Schorn of North Marston and Windsor', in Keen and Scarff, 192-207.

19. This pope is also famous for building his own magnificent private chapel at the Vatican, the Sistine Chapel, and it is recorded that on 23 September 1483, a mass for the soul of Edward IV was sung in the new Sistine Chapel'. See A.F. Sutton and L. Visser-Fuchs, *The Royal Funerals of the House of York at Windsor* (Donington, 2005), 31.

20. Transcribed in Hope, *Windsor Castle*, ii, 412.

21. Fletcher, 'Bishop Richard Beauchamp', 164.

22. Hope, *Windsor Castle*, ii, 376.

23. Later, in 1519, the arch was filled with a wooden bay window for Katherine of Aragon. This doubled the viewing area in the closet within Edward's chantry chapel.

24. For details, see Sutton and Visser-Fuchs, *Royal Funerals of the House of York at Windsor*, 111-124.

25. See Chapter 7 above.

26. Emlyn's infilling of the arch abuts the original lining of the arch in Tournai marble. A similar lining of Tournai marble was, perhaps, originally intended in the arch above, around the proposed 'tomb' of Edward IV.

27. They were published in E. Ashmole, *The Institution, Laws and Ceremonies of the most Noble Order of the Garter* (London, 1672), and F. Sandford, *Genealogical History of the Kings and Queens of England* (London, 1673).

28. For the vaulting sequence, see T. Tatton-Brown, 'The constructional sequence and topography of the chapel and college buildings of St George's' in *St George's Chapel in*

the late Middle Ages, ed. C. Richmond and E. Scarff (Windsor, 2001), 3-38, and 13.

29. There is another carved string course of Caen stone (above Reigate stone ashlar) in the side aisles below the windows. This is mainly of elaborately carved vine leaves and grapes, but it also includes other motifs, including garden snails, the personal motif of Bishop Beauchamp.

30. This is fully documented and transcribed in Hope, *Windsor Castle*.

31. *History of the King's Works*, ii, 884.

32. The final accounts run from 11 January 1483 to the same date in 1484. They record ironwork for the windows and stallwork being finished.

33. Hope, *Windsor Castle*, ii, 429-46, and C. Tracy, *English Gothic Choir Stalls*, 1400-1540 (Woodbridge, 1990), 48-51.

34. It was perhaps already intended for the old chapel to be converted to a new Lady Chapel.

35. This event was ordered by Richard III, who must have witnessed the end of the translation in the chapel. Henry VI's burial vault was examined in 1910, see W. H. St John Hope, 'The discovery of the remains of King Henry VI in St George's Chapel, Windsor Castle', *Archaeologia*, 62 (1911), 533-542.

36. For the cult, see B. Spencer, 'King Henry of Windsor and the London pilgrim' in *Collectanea Londiniensia, Studies in London archaeology and history presented to Ralph Merrifield*, ed. J. Bird, H. Chapman, J. Clark (London, 1978), 235-264; and see chapter 11, below.

37. Hope, *Windsor Castle*, ii, 383.

38. *History of the King's Works*, iii, i (1975), 308.

39. *Ibid*, 306.

40. For the story of the long struggle for possession of Henry VI's body, see below chapter 11.

41. For a transcription of the depositions, see A.P. Stanley, *Historical Memorials of Westminster Abbey* (3rd edn., London 1867), 600-16.

42. For Oliver King, see below, ch. 12. Cardinal Wolsey had a monumental tomb made for himself in 1524-9, probably in a workshop at Westminster Abbey, and his partly completed monument was acquired by Henry VIII in 1530. This was never completed, but it was put in the Lady Chapel at Windsor in 1565. The most valuable parts of it were removed, and sold, on the orders of Parliament between 1643 and 1646: Hope, *Windsor Castle*, ii, 478-485. The rest was finally destroyed in *c.* 1808, when George III's vault was started.

43. This vault, uncovered in 1869, is shown in the frontispiece of Stanley, *Historical Memorials*.

44. Anon. *Memoirs of the Last Two Years of the Reign of King Charles I* (1815), 195.

45. His gravestone in the north choir aisle records that 'he paved the body of the choir'.

46. As also recorded on the 1837 slab.

47. Sir Henry Halford, *An Account of what appeared on opening the coffin of King*

Charles the First in the vault of King Henry the Eight in St George's Chapel at Windsor (1813).

48. A.Y. Nutt, *Replacing of Relics in The Grave of Charles I*, a hand written manuscript in St George's Chapel Archives.

CHAPTER NINE

1. Hope, *Windsor Castle*, passim, and especially 398-406 where accounts of 1478-84 are printed. See also J. Harvey, 'The architects of St George's Chapel', pt 2, *Report of the Friends of St George's Chapel* (1962), 85-95, G. Tyack, S Bradley, N. Pevsner, *Berkshire* (New Haven and London, 2010), 652-68, and T. Tatton-Brown, 'The construction sequence and topography of the chapel and college buildings at St George's', in *St George's Chapel, Windsor in the late Middle Ages,* ed. C. Richmond and E. Scarff (Windsor, 2001), 3-38.

2. Notably William, Lord Hastings, who in his will of 27 June 1481 referred to the place assigned for his tomb by the express wish of Edward IV (Hope, *Windsor Castle*, 420).

3. J. Harvey, *The Perpendicular Style*, 1330-1485 (London, 1975), 213.

4. W.R. Lethaby, *Westminster Abbey Re-examined* (London, 1925), 38-9.

5. See T. Tatton-Brown in *Westminster Abbey: the Lady Chapel of Henry VII*, ed. T. Tatton-Brown and R. Mortimer (Woodbridge, 2003), 189-92, and the plan of the old Lady Chapel at Westminster Abbey by Tatton-Brown on p. 24.

6. M. Hastings, *St Stephen's Chapel and its Place in the Development of Perpendicular Style in England* (Cambridge, 1955), 63.

7. R. Willis, 'On the construction of the vaults of the Middle Ages', *Transactions of the Royal Institute of British Architects* (1842), 50, pl. IV.

8. A.W. Clapham and W.H Godfrey, *Some Famous Buildings and their Story* (London, 1912), 121-38; J. Schofield, *Medieval London Houses* (New Haven and London, 1994), 160-3, fig. 39.

9. Harvey, *Perpendicular Style*, 210.

10. M. Turner, *Eltham Palace* (London: English Heritage, 1999),10.

11. P. Tannery, *Memoires Scientifiques*, V (Paris 1922), 87-8.

CHAPTER TEN

1. A.F. Sutton and L. Visser-Fuchs, "Chevalerie . . . in som partie is worthi forto be comendid, and in some part to ben amendid': Chivalry and the Yorkist Kings', in *St George's Chapel, Windsor, in the Late Middle Ages*, ed. C. Richmond and E. Scarff (Windsor, 2001), 107-33; D. Schneider, *Der englische Hosenbardorden. Beitrage zur Enstehung und Entwicklung des 'The Most Noble Order of the Garter' (1348-1702) mit einem Ausblick bis* 1983 (2 vols. in 4 parts, Bonn 1988).

2. College of Arms, MS M 15, fo. 12v, and British Library, MS Cotton Julius C vi, fo.

253v, printed in C.L. Kingsford, *English Historical Literature in the Fifteenth Century* (Oxford, 1913), 380-1.

3. J. Stow, *Annales or A General Chronicle of England continued unto* 1631 (London, 1632), 429-30; J. Anstis, *The Register of the Most Noble Order of the Garter . . . usually called The Black Book* (2 vols., London, 1724), i, 196-8.

4. The accounts of the great wardrobe for this period are found in TNA, Exchequer of Receipt: Miscellaneous Books, E36; Exchequer Accounts Various, E101; Enrolled Accounts: Wardrobe and Household, E361; and Princeton University Library, MS 101.

5. S. Mitchell, 'Late Medieval Ladies of the Garter, 1348-1509: Fact or Fiction', in *Textiles and Text. Re-establishing the Links between Archival and Object-based Research*, ed. M. Hayward and E. Kramer, (London, 2006).

CHAPTER ELEVEN

1. M. Condon, "God Save the King': Piety, propaganda and the perpetual memorial', in *Westminster Abbey: The Lady Chapel of Henry VII*, ed. T. Tatton-Brown and R. Mortimer (Woodbridge, 2003), 59-61.

2. R.R. Sharpe, *London and the Kingdom*, 3 vols. (London, 1894-5), iii, 385-6.

3. R. Fabyan, *The New Chronicles of England and France*, ed. H. Ellis (London, 1811), 660.

4. A.P. Stanley, *Historical Memorials of Westminster Abbey* (2nd edn, London, 1868), 571.

5. T. Tatton-Brown, 'The pavement in the chapel of St Edward the Confessor, Westminster', *Journal of the British Archaeological Association*, 153 (2000), 73, 76.

6. N.E. Saul, 'The growth of a mausoleum: the pre-1600 tombs and brasses of St George's Chapel, Windsor', *Antiquaries Journal*, 87 (2007), 220-58.

7. D. Starkey, 'Henry VI's old blue gown', *The Court Historian*, 4, 1 (1999), 1-28; and P. Strohm, 'Interpreting a chronicle text; Henry VI's blue gown', in *London and the Kingdom: Essays in honour of C.M. Barron*, ed. M. Davies and A. Prescott (Donington, 2008), 335-45.

8. 'A Brief Latin chronicle', in *Three Fifteenth-Century Chronicles*, ed. J. Gairdner (Camden Society, 1880), 184.

9. *A Chronicle of the first thirteen years of the reign of King Edward the Fourth by John Warkworth*, ed. J.O. Halliwell (Camden Society, 1839), 21, with a new edition in *Death and dissent: Two fifteenth-century chronicles*, ed. L. Matheson (Woodbridge, 1999), 61-124. Other Yorkist accounts and newsletters include *Historie of the Arrivall of Edward IV in England and the finall recouerye of his kingdoms from Henry VI A.D. MCCCCLXXI*, ed. J. Bruce (Camden Society, 1838); L. Visser-Fuchs, 'Edward IV's 'memoir on paper' to Charles, Duke of Burgundy: the so-called 'Short Version of the Arrivall'', *Nottingham Medieval Studies*, 36 (1992); and 'Yorkist notes, 1471', in C.L.Kingsford, *English Historical Literature in the Fifteenth Century* (Oxford, 1913), 374-5. Reports abroad are in *Calendar of State Papers, Milan, 1385-1618* (London,

1912), 156-7; Phillippe de Commynes, *Memoirs*, transl. Michael Jones (London, 1972); Thomas Basin, *Histoire de Louis XI*, ed. C. Samaran and M.- C. Garand (Paris, 1966); and J. de Waurin, *Recueil des croniques et anchiennes istories de la Graunt Bretagne*, ed. W. and E.C.L.P. Hardy (5 vols., Rolls Series, 1864-91), v, 675.

10. Soon afterwards, *The Crowland Chronicle Continuations, 1459-1486*, ed. N. Pronay and J. Cox (London, 1986), had no doubt that the king had been murdered, and neither did Henry's former chaplain, John Blacman, *Henry the Sixth* , ed. M. R. James (Cambridge, 1919), 40. John Rous's 'History of the Kings of England', transl. A. Hanham, *Richard III and his Early Historians, 1483-1535* (Oxford, 1975), pointed the finger at Richard III, while early sixteenth-century accounts are *Chronicles of London*, ed. C.L. Kingsford (Oxford, 1905); *The Great Chronicle of London*, ed. A.H. Thomas and I.D. Thornley (London, 1938); Fabyan, *New Chronicles; Three Books of Polydore Vergil's English History*, ed. H. Ellis (Camden Society, 1844), and John Stow, *The Annales or Generall Chronicle of England* (London, 1615).

11. C.F. Richmond, 'Fauconberg's Kentish rising of May 1471', *English Historical Review*, 95 (1970), 673-92; Sharpe, *London and the Kingdom*, 1, 314-16.

12. W. J. White, 'The death and burial of Henry VI, a review of the facts and theories, Part I', *The Ricardian*, 6, no. 78 (September 1982), 70-80.

13. TNA, E403/ 844 (24 June), partly printed in *Foedera*, V, ii, 4. See J. Röhrkasten, 'Londoners and London mendicants in the later middle ages', *Journal of Ecclesiastical History*, 47 (1996), 446-77.

14. T. F. Reddaway, *The Early History of the Goldsmiths' Company, 1327-1509* (London, 1975), 139-40, 285-8.

15. B.P. Wolffe, *Henry VI*, 2nd edn (New Haven and London, 2001), 361-71; V. Davis, *William Waynflete: Bishop and Educationalist* (Woodbridge, 1993), 43. See C.L. Scofield, *The Life and Reign of Edward the Fourth* (2 vols., London, 1923), i, 576, for the bishops of Lincoln, Chichester, Llandaff and St Davids.

16. Westminster Abbey, MS 12183 f. 19-23; M. K. Jones and M.G. Underwood, *The King's Mother* (Cambridge, 1992), 52. These discussions included Margaret's young son, Henry, Earl of Richmond.

17. N.E. Saul, *Richard II* (New Haven and London, 1997), 428, 469-74.

18. *Calendar of State Papers, Milan*, 156-7.

19. *Henrici VI Angliae Regis miracula postuma*, ed. P. Grosjean (Brussels, 1935), summarized in *The Miracles of Henry VI*, ed. R. Knox and S. Leslie (Cambridge, 1923). The veneration and miracles have been much discussed.

20. SGC, XV. 34. 60; W. J. White, 'The death and burial of Henry VI, Part II', *The Ricardian*, 6, no. 79 (December 1982), 106-17; Hanham, *Richard III and his Early Historians*, 123 (for John Rous); R. Edwards, *The Itinerary of King Richard III, 1483-1485* (London, 1983), 23.

21. Ibid., 1-39; A. Sutton and L. Visser-Fuchs, with R.A. Griffiths, *The Royal Funerals of the House of York at Windsor* (London, 2005), 50, 64-5.

22. M.A. Hicks, *Anne Neville* (Stroud, 2006), 212-13.

23. W. St John Hope, 'The Discovery of the Remains of King Henry VI in St George's Chapel, Windsor Castle', *Archaeologia*, 2ⁿᵈ series 12 (1911), 533-42; C.R. Beard, *The Tomb and Achievements of King Henry VI at Windsor* (Frome, 1936), and J. Geddes, 'John Tresilian and the gates of Edward IV's chantry', in Keen and Scarff,168-9. Also above Chapter 7.

24. TNA, DL29/526/8391.

25. BL, Add. MS. 6298 f.148, reproduced (e.g.) in Beard, *Tomb and Achievements*, Fig. 4. Stow, *Annales*, 424, records that the tomb had been removed by James I's reign.

26. P. Lindley, "The singuler mediacons and praiers of al the holie companie of Heven': Sculptural functions and forms in Henry VII's chapel', in Tatton-Brown and Mortimer, *Westminster Abbey*, 266.

27. L.A. Craig, 'Royalty, Virtue and Adversity: The Cult of King Henry VI', *Albion*, 35 (2003), 187-209.

CHAPTER TWELVE

1. J. Britton, *The History and Antiquities of Bath Abbey Church*, with continuation by R.E.M. Peach (Bath and London, 1887). I am most grateful to Dr Lucy Rutherford, Bath Abbey Archivist, for her help with this study.

2. Bath, City Library, Irvine Papers, boxes 5 and 6. In box 5 is a drawing dated 1871 of the north choir arcade marking the 'floor of what may have been the vault prepared by Bishop Oliver King' together with a slab on edge forming part of the west wall of the vault.

3. E.M. Hick, *Bath Abbey: an architectural and historical guide* (London 1913).

4. P. Mitchell, *Bishop Oliver King and the Present Abbey (Priory) Church* (Bath Abbey 2000 Lectures, Friends of Bath Abbey, 1996).

5. *Calendar of entries in the Papal Registers relating to Great Britain and Ireland: Papal Letters*, 16, ed. A.P. Fuller (Dublin, Irish MSS. Commission, 1986), 325-6.

6. *The Registers of Oliver King and Hadrian de Castello*, ed. H. Maxwell-Lyte (Somerset Record Society, 54, 1939), *passim*.

7. 'The Historia Minor and the Historia Major', ed. J.A. Robinson in *Collectanea*, I (Somerset Record Society, 39, 1924), 66.

8. Personal visits are recorded to Bristol, Glastonbury, Athelney, Cleeve and Bridgwater: *Registers of King and Castello*, nos. 226, 288, 299, 441-3.

9. Ibid., xii.

10. *Victoria County History of Somerset*, ii, ed. W. Page (London, 1911), 77.

11. J.A. Robinson, 'Correspondence of Bishop Oliver King and Sir Reginald Bray', *Proceedings of the Somersetshire Archaeological and Natural History Society*, 60 (1914), 1-10.

12. *Somerset Medieval Wills*, 1501-30, ed. F.W. Weaver (Somerset Record Society, 19,

1903), 44-7.

13. Irvine papers, box 5.

14. *Calendar of the Manuscripts of the Dean and Chapter of Wells*, ed. W.P. Baildon (Historical MSS. Commission) (hereafter *Wells MSS.*), 2 (1914), 172, 241.

15. *Wells MSS.* 2, 157, 159.

16. Robinson, 'Correspondence', 6.

17. *Calendar of Close Rolls 1500-09*, 51.

18 *Wells MSS.* 2, 163.

19. Ibid., 176.

20. *Calendar of Patent Rolls 1494-1509*, 338.

21. *Somerset Medieval Wills, 1501-30*, 111-13.

22. Ibid., 167-70.

23. *Somerset Medieval Wills, 1531-58*, ed. F.W. Weaver (Somerset Record Society, 21, 1905), 3.

24. I am grateful to Tim Tatton-Brown for this information.

25. *Dean Cosyn and Wells Cathedral Miscellanea*, ed. A. Watkin (Somerset Record Society, 56 (1943 for 1941), 10.

26. W.J. Rodwell, *Wells Cathedral: Excavations and Structural Studies, 1978-93* (2 vols., English Heritage 2001), 199-244, especially 242-4.

CHAPTER THIRTEEN

1. A. Smith, 'Henry VII and the appointment of the King's Glazier', *Journal of Stained Glass*, XVIII: 3 (1988), 259-61. For Flower's subsequent career, see A. Oswald, 'Barnard Flower, the King's Glazier', *Journal of the British Society of Master Glass-Painters* XI:1 (1952), 8-21.

2. J.A. Knowles, 'Disputes between English and Foreign Glass-Painters in the Sixteenth Century', *Antiquaries Journal* v (1925), 148-57.

3. R. Marks, *Stained Glass in England during the Middle Ages* (London, 1993), 205-228.

4. R. Marks, 'The Glazing of Henry VII's Chapel' in *The Reign of Henry VII*, ed. B. Thompson (Stamford, 1995), 157-174; H. Wayment, 'The Medieval Stained Glass' in *A History of the Stained Glass of St George's Chapel, Windsor Castle*, ed. S. Brown (Windsor, 2005), 1-64.

5. H. Wayment, *The Windows of King's College, Cambridge* (Oxford 1972) and in *History of the Stained Glass of St George's Chapel*, ed. Brown, especially pages 18-19.

6. T. Tatton-Brown, 'The constructional sequence and topography of the chapel and college buildings at St George's', in *St George's Chapel, Windsor in the Late Middle Ages*, ed.C. Richmond and E. Scarff (Windsor 2001), 3-38.

7. W.H. St John Hope, *Windsor Castle. An Architectural History* (London 1913), ii, 384.

8. Wayment in *History of the Stained Glass of St George's Chapel*, ed. Brown, 2-7.

9. S. Strobl, 'Report on the Condition of the West Window of St George's Chapel at Windsor Castle' (August 2000), unpublished report in the chapel archive; I am also grateful to colleagues Martin Ashley, Chapel Surveyor, Steve Clare of Holy Well Glass, Wells and Tobit Curteis of Tobit Curteis Associates for recent discussion of the window's current condition and its causes.

10. T. Tatton-Brown 'St George's Chapel, Windsor – The West Window', *Report of the Friends of St George's*, viii, 1 (1999-2000), 18.

11. SGC, VI.B.5, 6 May 1692.12. SGC, XVII.61.10 (e).

13. Published in J Britton's *Architectural Antiquities of Great Britain* (London, 1822).

14. SGC, VI.B.8, 25 August 1777.

15. Emlyn's annotations of a drawing of 1790, SGC, E.13.

16. Wayment in *History of the Stained Glass of St George's Chapel*, ed. Brown, 6.

17. S. Baylis 'The Eighteenth-century Windows – and Where are they Now?' in *History of the Stained Glass of St George's Chapel*, ed. Brown, 93-95.

18. St John Hope, *Windsor Castle*, 394; SGC, XVII.9.9.

19. S. Brown 'So Perfectly Satisfactory': The Stained Glass of Thomas Willement in St George's Chapel' in *History of the Stained Glass of St George's Chapel*, ed. Brown, 109-146, especially 123.

20. SGC, M.166/11.

21. SGC, M.166/12.

22. SGC, XVII.61.21.

23. Presumably those repaired by Kimberley and either not used by him, or removed c1777.

24. The arms of Edward IV, Henry VIII (rather than those of Henry VII), Edward VI and George III.

25. Wayment in *History of the Stained Glass of St George's Chapel*, ed. Brown, 6-7.

26. W. Drake 'The Stained Glass of St George's Chapel, Windsor Castle', *Journal of the British Society of Master Glass Painters*, viii, 4 (1943), 149-51.

27. SGC, XVII.61.21.

28. SGC, M.166/12.

29. SGC, XIV.1880/36.

30. Tatton-Brown, 'The West Window', 21-2.

31. Rushforth advised on the restoration of medieval glazing at Tewkesbury Abbey and Great Malvern Priory, the subject of his renowned study of medieval glass and iconography, *Medieval English Imagery* (Oxford, 1936).

32. SGC, CL.17/1(6), letter from M.R. James to H. Brakspear, 29 March 1929

33. See above, note 26.

34. I am grateful to Stephen Clare and Tobit Curteis for sharing information and opinion with me on these technical issues.

35. J.A. Knowles 'Historical sketch of the stained glass of St George's Chapel', *Journal of the British Society of Master Glass Painters*, x, 3 (1949-50), 133.

36. One of the figures described thus by Wayment (panel 3n) is probably a composite figure of a knight with a pope's head.

37. J. G. Clark, 'The St Albans monks and the cult of St Alban: The late medieval texts', *Alban and St Albans: Roman and Medieval Architecture, Art and Archaeology,* ed. M. Henig and P. Lindley (Leeds, 2001), 218-230.

38. R. Marks and P. Williamson (eds), *Gothic: Art for England 1400-1547* (London, 2003), 429.

39. Clark op. cit. and G.F. Reinicke (ed), *John Lydgate. Life of Saint Alban and Saint Amphibalus* (New York and London, 1985).

40. Nigel Ramsay and Margaret Sparks, 'The cult of St Dunstan at Christ Church, Canterbury' in Nigel Ramsay, Margaret Sparks and Tim Tatton-Brown (eds.), *St Dunstan: His Life, Times and Cult* (Woodbridge, 1992), 311-24.

41. At Canterbury, the display is of kings. M H Caviness, *The Windows of Christ Church Cathedral Canterbury* (London, 1981),232-3; At York the theme is one of apostolic and episcopal succession and legitimacy. Thomas French and David O'Connor *York Minster: The West Windows of the Nave* (London,1987), 15-18.

CHAPTER FOURTEEN

1.T. Tatton-Brown, 'The Deanery, Windsor Castle', *Antiquaries Journal*, 78 (1998), 345-90, at 357; idem, 'Destruction at St George's Chapel in the 1640s', *Annual Report of the Friends of St George's* (1995-6), 295-8.

2. For general observations on Windsor Castle during the civil war, interregnum and Restoration, see O. Morshead, *Windsor Castle* (2nd edn., London, 1957).

3. On the restoration of the cathedrals and collegiate churches, see I.M. Green, *The Re-establishment of the Church of England, 1660-1663* (Oxford, 1978), ch. 3; S.E. Lehmberg, *Cathedrals under Siege. Cathedrals in English Society, 1600-1700* (Exeter, 1996); K. Fincham and N. Tyacke, *Altars Restored. The Changing Face of English Religious Worship, 1547-c.1700* (Oxford, 2007), ch. 8.

4. Biographical details of the deans and canons of these years have been assembled from: S.L. Ollard, *Fasti Wyndesorienses: the Deans and Canons of Windsor* (Windsor, 1950); E.H. Fellowes, *The Vicars or Minor Canons of His Majesty's Free Chapel of St George in Windsor Castle* (Windsor, 1945); 'Extracts from the papers of Thomas Woodcock (ob. 1698)', *Camden Miscellany, XI* (Camden, 3rd series, 13, 1907); *Oxford Dictionary of National Biography*, ed. H.C.G. Matthew and B. Harrison (60 vols., Oxford, 2004); *Clergy of the Church of England Database*, 1540-1660 (www.theclergydatabase.org.uk).

5. A.G. Matthews, *Walker revised. Being a Revision of John Walker's* Sufferings of the Clergy during the Grand Rebellion, 1642-60 (Oxford, 1948).

6. His monument, by William Byrd of Oxford, survives: S.M. Bond, *The Monuments of St George's Chapel, Windsor Castle* (Windsor, 1958), no. 43 [see Fig. 30].

7. On the experiences of Episcopalians in the 1640s and 1650s, see K. Fincham and

S. Taylor, 'Episcopalian Conformity and Nonconformity, 1646-1660', in *Royalists and Royalism during the Interregnum*, ed. J. McElligott and E.M. Smith (Manchester, 2010), 18-43, and 'Vital Statistics: Episcopal Ordinations and Ordinands in England, 1646-1660', *English Historical Review*, forthcoming.

CHAPTER FIFTEEN

1. Hope, *Windsor Castle*.

2. Ibid., ii. 501-4.

3. T. Tatton-Brown, 'Destruction at St George's Chapel in the 1640s', *Report of the Society of the Friends of St George's* (hereafter *Report*), vii, No. 7 (1995-6), 295-8 and pl. V; 'The Deanery, Windsor Castle', *Antiquaries Journal* 78 (1998), 345-90; 'The Constructional sequence and topography of the Chapel and College buildings at St George's', in *St George's Chapel, Windsor in the Late Middle Ages*, Historical Monographs relating to St George's Chapel, Windsor, vol. 17, ed. C. Richmond and E. Scarff (Windsor, 2001), 3-38; 'The Canons' Houses and Cloister at Windsor', *Report*, vol. VIII, No. 3 (2001-2), 121-25 and pls. 9-12; 'The Accounts Office, No. 2 The Cloisters', ibid., vol. VIII, No. 5 (2003-4), 231-7.

4. A. K. Roberts (*St George's Chapel, Windsor Castle 1348-1416* (1947) 6-7. The chapel of St Edward the Confessor was staffed by eight chaplains, to which Edward III initially added a warden and fifteen more chaplains.

5. *Liberate Roll* 24 Hen III, m. 22.

6. Hope, ii. 496.

7. Tatton-Brown, 'The Deanery', 347, see note 3 above.

8. The location of 'Cagham' is uncertain. Julian Munby, 'Carpentry works for Edward III at Windsor Castle', in *St George's Chapel, Windsor in the Fourteenth Century*, ed. N. Saul (Woodbridge, 2005), 225-37, at 232, argues that 'Cagham' is Cakeham near Selsey in Sussex, but there are no indications on the ground for an oak forest in the area and the place-name, attested in the 13th century, appears always to have had an unvoiced middle consonant, 'k' rather than 'g'.

9. Ibid., 234.

10. Hope, *Windsor Castle*, i. 171, citing Pipe Roll 28 Edward III, within which are accounts provided by Robert de Bernham, master of the works: *Et Simoni Hurle Johanni Glymesforde et Johanni Dunstaple carpentariis pro carpentria .xxiij. camerarum de meremio regis pro canonicis collegii capelle regis ibidem ...*

11. Hope, *Windsor Castle*, i. 165, n. 156.

12. Ibid., i. 170 (accounts for 1352-3).

13. Ibid., i. 148. The drawing was by J. C. Buckler.

14. Ibid., ii. 503.

15. Simon Underdown et al. *No. 8 Canons' Cloister, Windsor Castle, Historic Building Investigation and Recording*, Report by Oxford Archaeology, March 2010.

16. e.g. Hope i. 172: twenty-three pairs of hinges purchased for the canons' chambers.

17. Ibid., i. 174.

18. Ibid., ii. 501.

19. Hope, ibid., ii. 503, considered the encroachment dated from the 'end of the seventeenth century', which is surely too late.

20. Tatton-Brown, 'Accounts Office', see note 3 above.

21. A. J. Arnold, R. E. Howard, and C. D. Litton, 'Tree-ring analysis of timbers from the roof of the Accounts Office, Dean's Cloister, Windsor Castle, Windsor, Berkshire', *English Heritage Centre for Archaeology*, 2/2005.

22. SGC, *Income Book*, i. 107.

23. Tatton-Brown, 'Destruction', see note 3 above.

24. SGC, Chapter Acts, 10 July 1676.

25. For the reconstruction, see in particular S. Bond (ed.) *The Chapter Acts of the Deans and Canons of Windsor, 1523-1672* (Windsor? 1966), 212-3.

26. SGC, '1 Canon's [sic] Cloister ; A note on the discovery of the concealed early Tudor? work', unpubl. report dated 26th July 1972.

27. SGC, Chapter Acts, 12 June 1607, printed in ibid., 66. The minute was rather inaccurately transcribed into the front paste-down of vol. i of the Income Book.

28. *Income Book*, i. 113.

29. Known in the Income Book as No. 2: another example of the difficulties of analysing the houses of Canons' Cloister.

30. SGC, Chapter Acts, 26 Dec 1678.

31. SGC, Chapter Acts, 1 Nov 1680.

32. SGC, Chapter Acts, 19 Aug 1682.

33. SGC *Income Book*, ii. 62.

34. Hope, *Windsor Castle*, ii. 501.

35. Ibid.

36. SGC, *Income Book*, i. 72.

37. Ibid., i. 113.

38. 'A Plan & Description of Water Pipes for the Better Serving of the Revd Dean, Cannons [sic] and Singing Men of Windsor', SGC XVII.61.43.

39. S. L. Ollard, *Fasti Wyndsorienses : The Deans and Canons of Windsor* (Windsor, 1950, reprinted 1999), *passim*.

40. SGC, P.108/6.

CHAPTER SIXTEEN

1. S.E. Lehmberg, *Cathedrals under siege: cathedrals in English society, 1600-1700* (Exeter, 1996). There is some coverage in idem., *English cathedrals: a history* (London, 2005). And see generally G.Cobb, *English cathedrals, the forgotten centuries: restoration and change from 1530 to the present day* (London, 1980).

2. A. Rogers, *Southwell Minster after the Civil Wars* (Nottingham, 1974) is a rare example of a relatively recent look at the functioning of a non-episcopal Chapter.

3. But see O. Hedley, 'Court and Chapel, 1760 to 1873, Part I', *Annual Report of the Friends of St George's*, 1960, 20-6, and the superb study by D. Burrows, *Handel and the English Chapel Royal* (Oxford, 2005).

4. J. Pote, *The History and Antiquities of Windsor Castle, and the Royal College, and Chapel of St George* (London, 1749), 118-9.

5. For details of one such ceremony see *Morning Post and Daily Advertiser*, Monday, June 8, 1778; issue 1759.

6. O. Hedley, *Windsor Castle* (London, 1967), 131, 134.

7. G. Holmes, *British Politics in the Age of Anne* (London, 1967), 277.

8. J. Brooke, *King George III* (London, 1972), 285. Charlotte acquired Queen's Lodge in 1776; her whole family was housed there by 1778: Hedley, *Windsor Castle*, 145.

9. G.M. Ditchfield, *George III: An Essay in Monarchy* (Basingstoke, 2002), 94; J. Ehrman, *The Younger Pitt. The Consuming Struggle* (London, 1996), 749-52.

10. Of course, Deans of Windsor were also Deans of Wolverhampton (another royal peculiar) though residence requirements for that latter post were not onerous. The subject remains to be fully studied. Minor decanal duties included lobbying for appointments such as Governor of the Poor Knights, see Booth to Newcastle, 30 Nov 1750, British Library, Add. MS. 32723, fo. 326.

11. S. L. Ollard, *Fasti Wyndesorienses: the Deans and Canons of Windsor* (Windsor, 1950), 49.

12. He was still the first of the Lent Preachers to preach before George I in 1715 after the Bishop of London, Dean of the Chapel Royal. *British Weekly Mercury*, Saturday, February 5, 1715, issue 502.

13. *Gentleman's Magazine*, 1st ser., 35 (1765), 443.

14. S. Taylor,'The Fac Totum in Ecclesiastic Affairs? The Duke of Newcastle and the Crown's Ecclesiastical Patronage', *Albion*, 24 (1992).

15. He was collated Chancellor of St Paul's cathedral on 22 July 1733 succeeding his father-in-law Canon Edward Jones.

16. Two of the plates in Pote's *History and Antiquities of Windsor* were inscribed to him and the canons.

17. *World and Fashionable Advertiser* (London, England), Wednesday, October 24, 1787; issue 243. He successfully predicted that he would succeed to the vacant see of Hereford on the death of Lord James Beauclerk. He held the deanery of Windsor *in commendam* in the few weeks he passed as Bishop of Hereford. As one obituarist stylishly put it: ' . . . in little more than two months from the date of the King's appointment, he had his final translation from the King of kings': *Gentleman's Magazine* , 57 (1787), 1130; 58 (1788), 84.

18. Mrs Cornwallis reported 'the Bishop found his house at Windsor better than he expected, and his first residence there went off very well. I went with them to Court the

day Miss Cornwallis was presented, but they are now so well acquainted with their royal neighbours that a Drawing-Room appears no longer formidable to them'. Quoted in A.L. Rowse, *Windsor Castle in the History of the Nation* (London, 1974), 168.

19. Ernest de Selincourt, *Dorothy Wordsworth: a biography* (Oxford, 1933), 33. For the Canon's Cloister. see above, Chapter 15.

20. A. Tindal Hart, *The Life and Times of John Sharp ArchBishop of York* (London, 1949), 103-4.

21. Pote, *History and Antiquities*, 80.

22. Booth to Hardwicke, 27 April 1752. See also same to same 15 April: Hardwicke Papers, British Library, Add. MS. 35591, fos. 323, 5.

23. Ollard, *Fasti Wyndesorienses*, 78, 113.

24. Ibid., 123.

25. Brooke, *George III*, 287. For Eton's good relations with the early Hanoverian regime see H. Smith, *Georgian Monarchy, Politics and Culture*, 1714-1760 (Cambridge, 2006), 178. Eton was not the only school to have some of its staff as canons. Thus Robert Friend (second stall, 1729-37) was Headmaster of Westminster from 1711 to 1733: Ollard, *Fasti Wyndesorienses*, 69.

26. Ibid., 95. The twelfth stall was held by John Sumner between 1751 and 1772 (Headmaster of Eton, 1745-54), and John Foster between 1772 and 1773 (Headmaster, 1765-73).

27. J.C.D. Clark, *English Society 1660-1832. Religion, ideology and politics during the ancien regime* (Cambridge, 2000), 560. The reference is to Edmund Gibson, Bishop of London, Sir Robert Walpole's key ally in ecclesiastical affairs for over a decade.

28. Ollard, *Fasti Wyndesorienses*, 62.

29. Ibid., 114.

30. Ibid., 63-9.

31. He was also dean of Rochester, 1706-23: ibid., 88-9.

32. James Boswell heard Duvall preach there on 4 Aug. 1793 and 'saw a genteel congregation': *Boswell. The Great Biographer 1789-1796,* ed. M.K. Danzinger and F. Brady (London, 1989), 223.

33. William Arnald, (canon, 1779-1802), sub-preceptor to the Prince of Wales and Prince Frederick, 1776-81, was another.

34. Ibid., 89, 142.

35. Ibid., 28.

36. Ollard, *Fasti Wyndesorienses*, 49.

37. E.H. Fellowes, *The Vicars or Minor Canons of His Majesty's Free Chapel of St George in Windsor Castle* (Windsor, 1945), 23, 41. Minor canons often held livings in plurality.

38. C. Knight, *Passages of a Working Life during half a Century; with a Prelude of Early Reminiscences* (3 vols., London, 1864), i, 48. However, he spoke elsewhere of . '...

the unapproachable dignity of Canons of Windsor and Fellows of Eton': ibid., i, 84.

39. Hedley, 'Court and Chapel, 1760 to 1873', 20-6. There is an unauthenticated story of George III accompanying the time of the music at St George's with the printed form of the service rolled up into a baton: C. Hibbert, *The Court at Windsor. A Domestic History* (London, 1964), 114.

40. Brooke, *George III*, 286.

41. Ollard, *Fasti Wyndesorienses*, 71. R. Sweet, *Antiquaries. The discovery of the past in eighteenth-century Britain* (London, 2004) is the indispensable guide to this enhanced respect for the medieval inheritance post c.1750.

42. Full details given in P. Begent and H. Chesshyre, *The Most Noble Order of the Garter, 650 Years* (London, 1999), 210-11, 262-7. Knight, *Passages of a Working Life*, 64-5, offers a less respectful verdict on the ceremonies.

CHAPTER SEVENTEEN

1. The four great bronze candlesticks from around the tomb are now in St Bavon Cathedral, Ghent.

2. Wren's drawings for the proposed building are now in the Print Room at All Souls College, Oxford.

3. In all official publications this chamber is consistently referred to as the 'Royal Vault', using a capital 'V' for vault.

4. TNA, Works 4/7: Minutes of Meeting of Board of Works of 23 November 1737.

5. TNA, Works 4/7: Minutes of Meeting of Board of Works of 29 November 1737.

6. Until then he had resided at Buckingham House (later Buckingham Palace) which he had purchased in 1762.

7. S.M. Bond, *The Monuments of St George's Chapel, Windsor*, (Windsor, 1958), xxii-xxvii. The space was usually referred to as the 'Tomb House' in the eighteenth century.

8. Infant son of George III, translated from the Hanoverian vault in Westminster Abbey.

9. Eldest daughter of George III.

10. Infant son of George III, translated from the Hanoverian vault in Westminster Abbey.

11. Eldest daughter of George IV.

12. Eldest daughter of George II.

13. Fourth son of George III.

14. Second son of George III.

15. Alfred Nutt spent his entire career in the Office of Works at Windsor Castle, remaining as a draughtsman until 1901 when he was appointed Clerk of Works at Windsor Castle with overall control of the Office of Works there, a job which altered in title to Assistant Architect and Surveyor in 1902.

16. Kelly and Brown erroneously depicted only one mortuary table.

17. Husband of Princess Mary, third daughter of George III.

18. Fourth daughter of George III.

19. Fifth daughter of George III.

20. Youngest son of George III.

21. Third daughter of George III.

22. However, the *Weekly Dispatch*, 8 July 1837, 336, differs regarding the upholstery of George IV's coffin, recording that 'the colour of the covering of the coffin of George IV being of crimson velvet, while that of our late Sovereign (William IV) is purple'. The coffin of the unidentified infant was probably that of a stillborn child of the king of Hanover, originally deposited in the Hanoverian vault at Westminster Abbey and translated to Windsor on the night of William IV's funeral in 1837.

23. A.P. Stanley, *Memorials of Westminster Abbey* (5th ed., London, 1878), 169-171.

24. TNA, WORKS 34. There is an additional copy in the Royal Archives and a photographic copy in the Royal Borough Collection.

25. N. Oxley, *Alfred Young Nutt*, (Windsor, 1996), 18.

26. Ibid., pl. 3.

27. *Illustrated London News,* vol. 220, no. 5888, 23 February 1952, 346-347.

CHAPTER EIGHTEEN

1. In general, for Windsor and the Great Park in the reign of George III see J. Brooke, *King George III* (London, 1972); O. Hedley, *Queen Charlotte* (London, 1975); J. Roberts, *Views of Windsor. Watercolours by Thomas and Paul Sandby from the Collection of Her Majesty Queen Elizabeth II* (London, 1995); J. Roberts, *Royal Landscape. The Gardens and Parks of Windsor* (New Haven and London, 1997); *George III and Queen Charlotte. Patronage, Collecting and Court Taste*, ed. J. Roberts (Exhibition Catalogue: London, 2004); D. Watkin, *George III: Architect King* (London, 2004).

2. W.H. Pyne, *History of the Royal Residences* (London, 1819).

CHAPTER NINETEEN

1. William Whyte, 'Restoration and Recrimination: The Temple Church in the nineteenth century' in *The Temple Church* ed. R. Griffith-Jones and D. Park (Boydell & Brewer, forthcoming 2010).

2. *The Ecclesiologist*, 3 (1844), 99.

3. SGC, VI.B.10, 17 May & 22-23 June 1841.

4. SGC, M.166/1.

5. Ibid.

6. S. Brown, 'So Perfectly Satisfactory: The Stained Glass of Thomas Willement', in *A History of the Stained Glass of St George's Chapel, Windsor Castle* ed. S. Brown (Windsor, 2005), 123-124.

7. SGC, VI.B.10, 22-23 June 1841.

8. SGC, RBK W.284. The report was favourably reviewed in *The Ecclesiologist*, 3 (1844), 152.

9. SGC, VI.B.10, 23 April 1843.

10. SGC, RBK W.284, pp. 13-14.

11. SGC, M.166/14. His close supervision of the project was approved by *The Ecclesiologist*, 3 (1844), 152.

12. SGC, M.166/14.

13. SGC, RBK W.284, 19-20.

14. Brown, 'So Perfectly Satisfactory', 111.

15. SGC, RBK W.284, 14-16.

16. SGC, XIV/1848/16,32,43; XVII.17.18; XVII.61.26 .

17. SGC, XVII 61.21/9.

18. SGC, RBK W.284, 15,17.

19. Ibid. pp.12-13, 15, 20-22.

20. SGC, XIV Chapter bills *passim*. Other builders and craftsmen included Samuel Cundy, stonemason, Henry Ingalton, bricklayer, Thomas Adams, carpenter, Thomas George, builder and plasterer, and William Berridge, ironworker.

21. SGC, XVII 61.21/1.

22. Brown, 'So Perfectly Satisfactory', 111.

23. SGC, XVII 61.18 (b), XVII 61.37*, XIV/1841/33, XIV/1842/92, XIV/1843/27.

24. M. Harrison, 'Clayton & Bell and the Stained Glass of St George's Chapel, Windsor', *A History of the Stained Glass of St George's Chapel, Windsor Castle* ed. S Brown (Windsor 2005), 149. In addition to overseeing the replacement of the east window in the Chapel, George Gilbert Scott designed the alabaster reredos installed behind the High Altar in 1863 in memory of Prince Albert, and was responsible for transforming Henry III's Chapel into the Albert Memorial Chapel from 1863 to 1873. Scott also designed the Chapel's west steps, which were constructed under his direction in 1872. Clayton and Bell went on to design and install four additional windows within St George's Chapel – in the north and south aisles and the Rutland Chapel – as well accepting the commission to design stained glass for the Albert Memorial Chapel.

CHAPTER TWENTY

1. Administrative records relating to Brakspear's restoration of the Chapel held in St George's Chapel Archives and Chapter Library include Brakspear's reports to Chapter, 1918-1930 (SGC, IV.B.52); Chapter's correspondence with Brakspear (SGC, XVII.59.2); and plans submitted to Chapter (SGC, P. passim). These are supplemented by a number of Brakspear's own papers on the restoration of St George's Chapel (SGC, M.114) and his copies of the relevant architectural plans (SGC, P.200), which have also been deposited in the Chapel Archives. In addition, a substantial collection of photographs taken by Robert B. Robertson, Chapter surveyor and clerk of works to the restoration project,

provide a detailed photographic record of the work. The Robertson collection comprises photographic prints (SGC, PH R.1-93); glass plate negatives (SGC, GPN R.A-Z) and 2 presentation photograph albums.

2. Sir Harold Brakspear's obituary in the *Wiltshire Archaeological and Natural History Magazine*, 1935, 123-127

3. SGC, M.114/1

4. SGC, M.114/3/2. Sir Christopher Wren's survey of 1682 is held in the Chapel Archives (SGC, XVII.61.4)

5. SGC, M.114/3/1

CHAPTER TWENTY-ONE

1. R. Bowers, 'The Music and Musical Establishment of St George's Chapel in the Fifteenth Century', in *St George's Chapel, Windsor, in the Late Middle Ages*, ed. C. Richmond and E. Scarff (Windsor, 2001), 171-214 at 211.

2. SGC, VI.B.2, fos. 25b/26a.

3. When I began my research into the history of the organs in Windsor Castle, both in St George's Chapel and in the State Apartments, in 1999, I was aware that there were periods of that history which were either not chronicled or which were very imperfectly documented; and nothing that has happened since has brought about a substantial change in that situation. One period which has been a source both of interest and frustration to me is that of the seventeenth and eighteenth centuries: hence the concentration on that period here.

4. SGC, VI.B.2, fo.136a/b.

5. It was presumably destroyed – otherwise the new organ installed in 1660 would have cost much less than it did.

6. SGC VI.B.3,fo. 2.

7. R. Pennington, *A Descriptive Catalogue of the Etched Work of Wenceslas Hollar, 1607-77* (Cambridge, 1982).

8. Oxford, Bodleian Library, MS Ashmole 1131.

9. British Museum, MS Pennington 1084 i.

10. Worcester Cathedral Archive, A7/xvi, fo. 25.

11. A comprehensive history of the organs both in St George's Chapel and in the State Apartments of Windsor Castle is in the process of being prepared by Roger Judd for publication at a later date.

CHAPTER TWENTY-TWO

1. List of benefactors in 'The Commemoration' – The September Obit service sheet, 27 September 2009.

2. William Shawcross, *Queen Elizabeth The Queen Mother – The Official Biography* (Macmillan, 2009), p. 772 & n.

3. The late Mrs Robin Woods to Hugo Vickers, in conversation, 1968.

4. 5th Marquess of Salisbury to HRH Prince Paul of Yugoslavia, 2 December 1968 (Prince Paul papers, Bakhmeteff Archive, Rare Book and Manuscript Library, Columbia University, New York).

5. Service sheet for the Dedication of the King George VI Memorial Chapel, 31 March 1969.

6. The King George VI Memorial Chapel – accompanying the service sheet for the Dedication, 31 March 1969.

7. Queen Elizabeth The Queen Mother to 5th Marquess of Salisbury, 16 October 1969, quote in Shawcross, *Queen Elizabeth The Queen Mother*, 772.

CHAPTER TWENTY-THREE

1. S. Bond, 'The Return of the Church Commissioners' Documents to Windsor', *Report of the Society of the Friends of St George*, iv, 4 (1963), 138-45 and pls. VI-VII.

2. Thomas Delafield, *Notitia Haseleiana or Some Memorials of the Antiquities of the parish of Haseley in the County of Oxford*: Bodleian Library, Oxford, Gough Adds. Oxon. c.247

3. William Ravenhill, 'Joel Gascoyne: a pioneer of large-scale county mapping', *Imago Mundi*, 26 (1972), 60-70.

4. William Ravenhill, 'An Early Eighteenth-Century Cartographic Record of an Oxfordshire Manor', *Oxoniensia*, 39 (1973), 85-91, pl. VIIIA. The map [was in 1974] in private hands, but there is a copy in the Bodleian Library: (E) C17:49 (58), and the Oxfordshire Record Office, 08/1/m/1.

5. Now in Oxfordshire Record Office.

6. In Oxfordshire Record Office in classes DV/IV, IX and XII; the original 1910 material is in the National Archives (TNA, IR).

7. SGC, XV.31.35.

CHAPTER TWENTY-FOUR

1. The original Statutes do not survive, however later copies do exist in the Chapel Archives and in the British Museum.

2. SGC, XV.34.14.

3. SGC, XI.D.21, article 9.

4. SGC, XV.34.70.

5. SGC, XI.D.7, article 24.

6. Hope, *Windsor Castle*, ii, 505-6.

7. Printed in M.F. Bond, *The Inventories of St George's Chapel*, 1384-1667 (Windsor, 1947), 211-14.

8. SGC, VI.B.2, 2 March 1612/3.

9. SGC, VI.B.2.

10. SGC, VI.B.3, 8 July 1663.

11. SGC, VI.B.5, 20 November 1714.

12. SGC, VI.B.3, 21 January 1666/7.

13. SGC, VI.B.3, 22 May 1672.

14. SGC, XI.D.45.

15. SGC, VI.B.8.

16. SGC, VI.B.9, 9 January 1822.

17. SGC, VI.B.10, 361.

18. SGC, VI.B.10, 11 May 1861.

19. SGC, VI.B.11, 1 August 1867. The schedule survives as SGC, XIX.27.

20. SGC, VI.B.11, 21 April 1891.

21. SGC, VI.B.11, 15 & 16 November 1894.

22. SGC, VI.B.12, 3 November 1908.

23. SGC, VI.B.13, 25 March 1933.

24. SGC, VI.B.13, 6 April 1940.

25. SGC, VI.B.16, 6 November 1954. Described as 'archive-archaeology room'.

26. *Annual Report of the Friends of St George's*, iv, 8 (1966-7), 335

27. SGC, AT/1/2/2/56

28. Injunctions of 26 October 1550.

29. SGC, VI.B.18, 10 November 1975.

30. SGC, VI.B.18, 10-12 December 1975.

31. SGC, VI.B.19, 9 February 1977; VI.B.20, 7 February 1989.

32. SGC, VI.B.20, 4 July 1989.

33. SGC, VI.B.20, October 1990.

CHAPTER TWENTY-FIVE

1. *Guide to the location of collections described in the Reports and Calendars Series* (1982); *Records of British business and industry 1760-1914: Textiles and leather* (1990), and the early groundwork for the guide to *Principal family and estate collections*.

2. I have described these in greater detail in *Archive buildings in the United Kingdom 1993-2005* (2007), pp.114-5.

3. Keen and Scarff (2002, but arising from a conference in 1998); *St George's Chapel Windsor in the late Middle Ages*, ed. C. Richmond and E. Scarff (*Windsor*, 2001).

4. This appreciation could not have been written without the help of numerous friends and colleagues who have supplied information and answered many questions. They will understand how much more could have been said in these few pages, and I am most grateful to all of them. I should like to thank: Sonia Anderson, Enid Davies, Sheila de Bellaigue, Roger Bettridge, George MacKenzie, Patrick Mitchell, Richard Olney, Stephen Roberts, Anthony Smith, Brian Smith, Janet Stevenson, Tim Tatton-Brown and John White.

INDEX